The
NEW MODEL ME

The
NEW MODEL ME

Second Edition

John R. Rowe

Educational Consultant, Asheville, North Carolina

Marvin Pasch

Department of Teacher Education
Eastern Michigan University

William F. Hamilton

Educational Consultant

TEACHERS COLLEGE PRESS

Teachers College, Columbia University
New York and London

Published by Teachers College Press, 1234 Amsterdam Avenue, New York, N.Y. 10027

Grateful acknowledgment is made for permission to use the following material:

ARTWORK

Pages 81, 181, 182, 194, 226, 228–230, 279, 280, 284, Thomas Ertler
Pages 156–158, 277, 321, 325, 326, 352, 359, Duncan Greenlee
Pages 15, 257, Scott Johnson
Pages 300, 319, 335, 360, Greg Macek
Pages vii, viii, 3, 9, 16, 17, 19, 38, 82, 116, 120, 123, 132, 138, 162, 208, 212, 259, 263, 264, 269, Maria Stamoulis
Pages 7, 21, 23, 27, 49, 52, 68, 74, 110, 169, 170, 174, 261, 270, Charles Szabla
Cartoon on page 185 from *Phi Delta Kappan* (November 1980). Reprinted with permission by Otha J. Collins.
"Pepper . . . and Salt" cartoon on page 159 from *The Wall Street Journal*. Cartoon on page 176 from *Phi Delta Kappan* (December 1978). Cartoon on page 340 from *American Teacher* (November–December 1977). All three reprinted with permission by Clem Scalzitti.

PHOTOGRAPHS

Pages 118, 195, 207, Federation for Community Planning. Photographers: Father James F. Flood, Brenda Bock James, and Thomas Miller
Page 238, Joe Wright Griggs
Page 37, Sam Hooper
Page 93, Jewish Community Federation of Cleveland, Ohio
Page 361, Thomas Paine Associates
Pages 29, 33, 44, 47, 56, 59, 99, 102, 108, 129, 164, 201, 223, 248, 253, 255, 272, 273, 339, Terry Schordock

ISBN 0-8077-2732-6

Manufactured in the United States of America

88 87   3   4   5   6

Finding Your Way

Acknowledgments

We shall always be grateful to the Lakewood, Ohio, City Schools; The George Gund Foundation; and the Martha Holden Jennings Foundation. Their initial support provided the impetus that enabled us to realize our dream of writing a second edition of *The New Model Me*. Many individuals and several institutions provided valuable assistance and encouragement as we wrote this book. We thank them in the Preface of the Teacher's Manual.

—John R. Rowe
Marvin Pasch
William F. Hamilton

THE NEW MODEL ME

A Guided Journey to Understanding Yourself and Others

Why do you think some people appear to be so confident and secure?

Why do you think others seem to be constantly "out of step"?

Why are some folks·popular, while others drift in and out of crowded rooms without being noticed either when they arrive or when they leave?

There are also folks who are noticed—but for all the wrong reasons. They dress for some other time or place. Their personal cleanliness or hygiene leaves something to be desired, or they bully their way through life doing physical and emotional damage to the people they touch.

The New Model Me is a high school course that will help you to understand why people do what they do. Since you are an "important person," the curriculum should also be a resource for self-understanding. We call the course "A Guided Journey," and this title represents our wish that the curriculum will contribute to your movement toward a *sharper, more confident, more resourceful, more satisfied*

YOU!

The journey is not uncharted. It consists of ideas and activities contained in five units.

In Unit I, "Human Behavior," you will be introduced to the BEHAVIOR EQUATION, a useful way to understand and explain human behavior. As the journey continues, the BEHAVIOR EQUATION will be the primary guide through the ideas and activities you meet.

In Unit II, "Self-Identity," the important ideas are RESOURCES and VALUES. The emphasis is on recognizing and increasing your personal resources—the abilities, knowledge, attitudes, and energy that support your values. Your expanding resources and values make up your self-identity.

The topic in Unit III, "Controls," brings you into contact with the forces that limit and shape your actions. Controls can be inside you (your inner voices), or they can come from the outside world. Some controls help you grow as a person, while others prevent you from being all that you might be.

As the journey reaches Unit IV, "Decision Making," thoughts and feelings are brought into action as you consider a range of responses for any difficult problem you may face. Then the BEHAVIOR EQUATION is used to screen out unwise and self-destructive responses and to determine which of the remaining responses are most consistent with your resources and values.

The fifth unit, "Change: The New Model Me," is your ultimate destination. The activities will help you to review and evaluate the changes that have occurred in your needs, resources, and values as a result of your study of this curriculum. The activities will also help you to chart your future. If your self-identity has been brought into sharper focus and your confidence strengthened, the journey to THE NEW MODEL ME will have been successful.

THE NEW MODEL ME

is

YOU with

a sharper image!

more confidence!

more resources!

more satisfaction!

UNIT I

HUMAN BEHAVIOR

CONTENTS

Looking Ahead

WHY STUDY HUMAN BEHAVIOR?

Two brief news articles appeared on the same page of a big city newspaper on October 21, 1980.

> "Christiaan Barnard, the surgeon who pioneered the heart-transplant operation that has prolonged so many lives, says he believes that suicide may be the best form of treatment for some terminally ill patients."

> "The members of a condominium association added a section to the house rules to cover 'visiting dogs.' A non-resident dog may visit, but the dog must be small. Larger dogs may visit only once every three months and may not stay longer than 72 hours."

What do these articles have in common? In both cases, the subject is human behavior—the serious and the silly, the important and the trivial things we think about and do. Human behavior can be healthy, adding to the dignity and worth of each of us. Human behavior may also be dangerous and destructive, producing a loss of dignity and worth. Whatever the outcome of our behavior, the most important fact about each of us is that we are all human beings. As human beings we have the same basic needs—for food, shelter, love, and a sense of belonging. Yet, facing the same needs, we behave in unique ways. One purpose of this unit is to discover how the BEHAVIOR EQUA-TION can help you to understand the patterns of behavior that make you unique.

A second purpose of the unit is to learn how behaviors that are foolish or destructive can be replaced by others that are wise and healthy. Sounds impossible? Not really! Behavior is the result of the *needs* we try to satisfy, combined with our personal *resources*. If we understand our needs or increase our resources, we can behave differ-ently. Changing our *immediate surroundings* can also make a differ-ence in the ways we behave.

Always remember that only we, as human beings, have the power of reason, the ability to plan a series of moves and to predict the conse-quences of behavior, both for ourselves and for others. We can use our powers of reason to live more effectively as individuals and as mem-bers of the human community.

OBJECTIVES

When this unit is completed, we are confident that you will be able to:

1. Use the BEHAVIOR EQUATION to explain why a given person may act the way he or she does.
2. Recommend alternative behaviors by changing one or more of the elements of the BEHAVIOR EQUATION.
3. Match a given action to the kind of needs being satisfied, using the five levels of Maslow's "Hierarchy of Needs."
4. Write a personal objective for yourself, one that promises to strengthen a constructive behavior, develop a new construc-tive behavior, or discard an unwise or destructive behavior.

5. Understand the words and phrases listed in the following section. Every unit will have such a list. You may know some of these words and phrases already, but some may be unfamiliar to you. Each of them represents an idea that you must understand if your journey through *The New Model Me* is to be successful. Be certain that you can:
   - Tell what each WORD or PHRASE means.
   - Use the WORD or PHRASE correctly in a sentence.

WORDS AND PHRASES

Behavior

Behavior Equation

Constructive

Destructive

Causal Approach

Needs

Resources

Immediate Physical or Psychological Setting

Interacting

Consequences (Immediate and Remote)

Wants

Hierarchy

Frustration

Values

Value Dilemma

ACTIVITY 1

What Is Behavior?

DEFINITION

BEHAVIOR is anything and everything we do. Behavior is *eating, sleeping, loving, fighting, thinking, writing, stealing, shopping, running, daydreaming, fishing*—the list is endless. Behavior may be planned in advance. For example, Jimmy spends most of his free time for a week planning his strategy to ask Brenda to be his date next Saturday night. Behavior may be totally unplanned. For example, Johnny drives into a rut so deep that his teeth rattle, or his stomach rumbles because he skipped lunch.

Behavior may be CONSTRUCTIVE. Constructive behaviors are actions that are helpful to you and those around you. Behavior may be DESTRUCTIVE. Destructive behaviors are actions that are harmful to you and those around you. Destructive behaviors may be directed at persons or at property. They may be directed toward particular individuals or the general community.

Which of the behaviors italicized in the first paragraph are normally constructive? Which are normally destructive?

BEHAVIOR EQUATION

Behavior doesn't just happen; it has to be caused. That is, the behavior can be traced back to its source, the reason or reasons why it occurred. Only if we are aware of why we behave the way we do can we hope to predict and control our future behavior.

There are many explanations that attempt to shed light on human behavior. The one we are going to use as a guide in the journey toward THE NEW MODEL ME is called "The CAUSAL APPROACH to Human Behavior." It was developed by the late Dr. Ralph H. Ojemann (b. 1901–d. 1975) when he was a professor at the University of Iowa and the director of the Psychology Department of the Educational

6

Research Council of America. For 30 years Dr. Ojemann and his staff helped teachers and students to understand their own behavior and the behavior of persons with whom they came into frequent contact. Dr. Ojemann called his explanation the "causal approach" because it emphasizes the causes or reasons why a person acts in a particular way.

To explain the causal approach to behavior, Dr. Ojemann developed a BEHAVIOR EQUATION:

NEEDS (the forces that motivate us) + RESOURCES +
IMMEDIATE PHYSICAL/PSYCHOLOGICAL SETTING
= BEHAVIOR.

The equation may be abbreviated:

N + R + IPS = BEHAVIOR.

The plus sign in the equation is *not* an additive signal, as in arithmetic. Instead it means INTERACTING with (working together), just as hydrogen and oxygen interact to produce water.

As a human being tries to satisfy his NEEDS (N), the needs interact

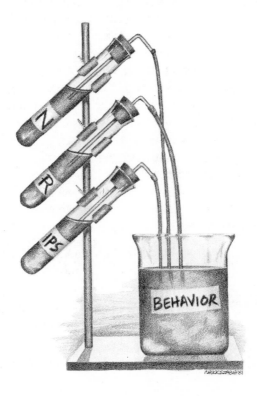

with his RESOURCES (R) and the IMMEDIATE PHYSICAL/
PSYCHOLOGICAL SETTING (IPS) to produce BEHAVIOR. This
behavior produces consequences (effects). Some of these effects
appear soon after the behavior. We label these IMMEDIATE CONSE-
QUENCES. Other consequences are REMOTE: that is, they appear
long after the behavior that produced them.

Let's provide some additional detail about each element in the
equation. The next few activities will look at needs.

NEEDS

> NEEDS
> are forces
> that motivate us
> to behave.

As we define them, NEEDS are things a human being *requires* to be
healthy and to grow in *body*, *mind*, and *spirit*. Needs may be physical,
such as a need for food. Needs may be psychological, such as a need
for acceptance by other human beings. Although lower-order animals
also experience needs, human needs are special because people have
the ability to reason and communicate ideas as well as emotions.

NEEDS should not be confused with WANTS. Needs are vital to
physical and/or emotional survival. Wants, although they come from
needs, are things we desire. For instance, food is a need; a favorite
spicy or rich food is a want. Shelter is a need; a four-bedroom home
with a mountain view is a want. Human beings cannot live normal
lives unless their needs are satisfied, but satisfaction of all our wants is
impossible. You may recall, as we do, encounters with parents over
being denied ice cream or a special bike or the privilege of staying up
late. In such cases, our desires (wants) get confused with our needs.
Note the following statements:

- Anything good is either illegal, immoral, or fattening.
- The three faithful things in life are money, a dog, and an old
  woman.
- Don't care if you're rich or not, as long as you can live
  comfortably and have everything you want.

It's fascinating to realize that an ancient Egyptian stone mason,
shaping the ornamentation of a burial monument to record the death of

a ruler, would have had the same needs that you and your friends have. Among all races and cultures, regardless of the historical period, human beings have sought to satisfy identical needs. These needs have been studied and classified by many psychologists. Though many of the studies have led to complex explanations (theories) that attempt to predict human behavior, the one developed by Abraham H. Maslow (b. 1908–d. 1970) seems most helpful to us. Maslow was a psychologist who studied healthy human beings to learn why we do what we do. He hoped to use his findings to improve mankind. He wanted people to satisfy their needs, to feel good about themselves, and to move upward to greater mental health.

Maslow's theory is based on his "HIERARCHY of Needs." One common definition of a hierarchy is "a group of persons organized according to their rank or grade." A hierarchy of military personnel, for example, looks like this:

General
Colonel
Major
Captain
Lieutenant

Hierarchies are typically organized from the *lowest* level at the *bottom* of the grouping to the *highest* level at the *top*.

Ideas, as well as people, can be grouped in a hierarchy, from simple to complex, or from least important to most important. In Maslow's hierarchy, needs are organized with the most basic needs at the bottom and higher-level needs in successive levels upward.

ACTIVITY 2

Hierarchy of Needs

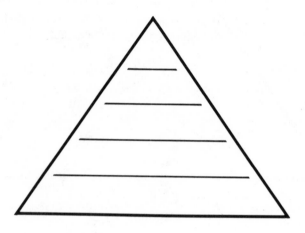

Imagine a pyramid with the basic human needs at the base and the higher-level needs moving upward to the highest need at the apex (or top) of the pyramid. Organize the following examples of needs into a pyramid, working from the most basic to the most complex.

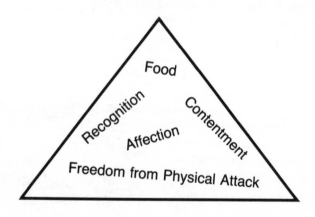

The examples fit Maslow's categories of needs. Organized hierarchically, they are as follows:

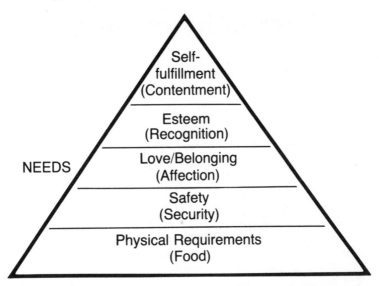

Physical requirements are the most basic and obvious needs. They include food, water, shelter, sex, sleep, and oxygen.

Safety (security) needs come next, after the basic physical needs are satisfied. For people to achieve higher levels of satisfaction, they must have some degree of freedom from personal attack, both physical and psychological.

Love/belonging needs tend to become important at the next level of the hierarchy. Human beings are social creatures. When their physical and safety needs are satisfied, people seek friendship, acceptance, and love.

Esteem needs refer to ideas such as confidence, achievement, independence, and reputation—being considered an important person by those who know of you.

Self-fulfillment is reaching your potential, being "all that you can be." It is quite probable that few, if any, of us achieve "self-fulfillment." If we did, there might not be any challenge left for us to overcome. Possibly we reach self-fulfillment for a short time as a result of achieving a goal that at one time was thought to be unreachable. Soon new goals emerge, and we are off in pursuit again!

ACTIVITY 3

A Letter to the Coach

This activity is designed to help you become more aware of how needs affect behavior.

Dear Coach Adams:

Remembering our discussion of your football men who are having trouble in English, I have decided to ask you, in turn, for help.

We feel that Paul Spindles, one of our most prominent students, has a chance for an academic scholarship, which would be a great thing for him and for our high school. Paul has the academic record for this award, but the candidate is also required to have other achievements and ideally should have a good record in athletics. Paul is weak physically. He tries hard, but he has trouble in athletics.

We propose that you give some special consideration to Paul as a varsity player, putting him, if possible, in the backfield of the football team. In this way, he can obtain the college scholarship. We realize that Paul will be a problem on the field, but—as you have often said—cooperation between our department and yours is highly desirable, and we do expect Paul to try hard, of course.

During his intervals of study we shall coach him as much as we can. His work in the English Club and on the debate team will force him to miss many practices, but we intend to see that he carries an old football around to bounce (or whatever one does with a football) during intervals in his work. We expect Paul to show spirited interest in his work for you, and though he will not be able to begin football practice until late in the season, he will finish the season with good attendance.

Sincerely yours,

Wilfong Pearson
Department Head
English Department

P.S. We are delaying a decision on your request to this department regarding a passing grade for your fullback, Butch Johnson, until we receive your favorable reply.

QUESTIONS FOR DISCUSSION

1. On which level of Maslow's "Hierarchy of Needs" would you place Mr. Wilfong Pearson? Paul Spindles? Coach Adams?
2. What are some alternative ways in which the needs of each of the individuals might be satisfied?
3. What might be some of the immediate and remote consequences of the various alternatives?

FRUSTRATION

When needs remain unsatisfied (not fulfilled), an individual experiences FRUSTRATION. Frustration is a part of life. In every period of life, we encounter frustration. Whether we are four years old and the frustration is our inability to tie a shoe, or 64 and the frustration is our inability to convince the boss that retirement is not for us, the feelings of anger and helplessness are the same.

The feelings cause stress. In healthy persons, frustrations and stress appear and disappear in a steady stream. Some frustrations we overcome; others we accept as temporary setbacks because we know we can bounce back later. Such disappointments can serve as a spur to move us forward. With still other frustrations, we accept failure and turn in other directions for a better chance at success.

For people who regularly experience frustration and the stress that comes along with it, movement up through the needs hierarchy may be blocked. Consequently the feelings of anger and powerlessness may produce aggressive, destructive behaviors. Other persons may choose the equally destructive path of withdrawal and isolation. People who are under severe stress may be restless, easily provoked into quarrels, or overly critical of others. They may be reckless and careless. Sometimes they may misuse alcohol, tobacco, and drugs.

A diagram of Maslow's "Hierarchy of Needs" appears again on page 14. The double line represents a frustration block. People who never are able to secure enough food and always fear for their safety may not be able to meet most of their higher needs for love, esteem, and self-fulfillment to any level of satisfaction. Because their needs are blocked, they end up experiencing extreme frustration and often resort to destructive behavior.

In any event, frustration is a key idea to understand in your journey.

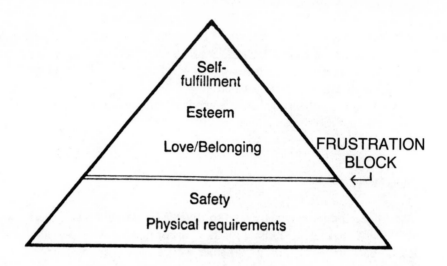

Being frustrated is disagreeable, but the real disasters in life begin when you get what you want.

—*Irving Kristol*[1]

[1]Quoted in George F. Will's column, "Pharaoh in the Promised Land," *Newsweek*, November 28, 1977.

ACTIVITY 4

Frustration Is . . .

The frustrations that we experience occur because we attempt to satisfy a need and fail.

This activity is intended to help you discuss some of your frustrations. Here are two examples of frustration:

Physical needs. Frustration is looking into the refrigerator and discovering nothing to put inside the bread to make a sandwich.
Esteem needs. Frustration is getting a C on the math test while my friends get As.

Close your eyes for a moment and think of a need you had that went unsatisfied, so that you were frustrated. Then:

- Identify the need.
- Complete a sentence beginning with "Frustration is . . . ."
- Or, as an alternative, draw a picture of a recent frustration.

ACTIVITY 5

Broken Squares

Have you ever experienced frustration as a member of a group? The purpose of this activity is to place you in a situation where you will.

The class will be divided into groups of six students each. Five students will participate in solving the group's task. One will observe.

INSTRUCTIONS TO EACH GROUP

Your teacher will give each group five envelopes that contain pieces of cardboard. The task is to form *five squares* of equal size, using only the pieces of cardboard in the envelopes. Your teacher will provide further instructions. Do not begin until your teacher gives you the signal.

ACTIVITY 6

A Typical Day

This is an activity that allows you to compare how frustration affects you and how it affects others.

NEVER A MOMENT OF FRUSTRATION FOR SALLY

I awaken before the alarm clock rings, refreshed and immediately alert. As I stand by my bed and stretch, I realize that every organ,

blood vessel, muscle, tendon—in fact everything inside of me—is humming along in perfect harmony, not an ache or an itch or a tremor.

As my legs slide smoothly into my jeans and I glance at the mirror, it is comforting to see that the jeans fit perfectly, without a wrinkle or an unsightly fold. Glancing at the mirror reveals a face with perfect features, without a blemish. I know without looking that every hair on my head is in beauty pageant order, as it was when my head hit the pillow and I fell asleep the night before.

Closing the door to the bedroom, and heading downstairs to break-fast, I can count on more raisins than flakes in my cereal; a smiling, thoughtful mother who cares only for my happiness; friends who compete for the privilege of driving me to school; and teachers who say things like:

> "You must really enjoy English because your work is so outstanding."
> "I appreciate your help."
> "Keep up the good work."
> "I bet your mom and dad would be proud."
> "Wow!"

TINA'S TYPICALLY TERRIBLE DAY

I do not complete my homework until 12:30 A.M. That guarantees me a miserable night of tossing and turning. At 6:45 A.M. the alarm rings, and, in blindly reaching for it, I knock it off the table. Instead of falling onto the soft carpet, it lands on the cat, who responds with an angry and pained *screech*. Stumbling out of bed, I remember that my mom forgot to wash until late last night and my favorite jeans are in the dryer. I grope my way down to the basement, bruising my big toe on a half-hidden shoe, and discover that my jeans are still damp. With no choice, I force the &*@! jeans onto my tired and now painful body. The phone rings. I learn that my usual ride to school is not available, and I can look forward to a standing-room-only spot on the bus.

When I arrive at school my lock acts up, and I am late to homeroom. The kind teacher sends me to the office for a tardy slip. Later I get hit in the stomach with a soccer ball in gym by some idiot boy who thinks

he's at war. Because of the slow recovery, I am late to lunch. By the time I am served, all my friends have left. I eat alone.

My French teacher sums up my day as well as can be expected:

"Ma pauvre petite fille! Quelle catastrophe!"
("My poor little girl! What a catastrophe!")

QUESTIONS FOR DISCUSSION

1. What needs are represented in each of the two stories?
2. Imagine a line with our two stories at opposite ends:

2. Tina's   Never a Moment
Typically   of Frustration
Terrible Day_____for Sally

Put an X on the line where you would place your typical day. Would it be closer to Tina's day or Sally's day?
3. Complete the frustration flow chart on page 20 and save it for your JOURNAL NOTES (which you will begin in ACTIVITY 7).

FRUSTRATION FLOW CHART

1. What are some frustrations I have met recently?

_____

_____

_____

2. How did I feel when I encountered the frustrations?

_____

_____

_____

4. How did I handle those frustrations?

_____

_____

_____

3. What need do I think was blocked?

_____

_____

_____

5. Is there something else I wish I had done?

_____

_____

_____

6. What were the effects of what I did on myself and on someone else?

_____

_____

_____

CHOICES

When frustration occurs, we are faced with choices. Let's assume your goal is to

Buy a pair of jeans

The pair you need to make you feel that you belong costs $37.00. That's $7.00 more than you have available. What are your choices?

- *Increase your resources*—in this case, earn, beg, or borrow more money.
- *Change the physical setting*—go to a different store, maybe one holding a sale.
- *Select an alternative behavior*—settle for a less expensive pair of jeans that may still satisfy your need to belong.

RESOURCES

Let's examine the idea of RESOURCES further. Resources are such things as:

- Knowledge
- Appearance
- Abilities
    Physical strength
    Intelligence
    Emotions
- Energy
- Experiences

- Spirit
    Courage
    Commitment
    Perseverance
- Other human beings
- Anything else that we can harness to help us reach our goals

The next two activities will involve you with two different kinds of resources.

ACTIVITY 7

Journal Notes

A journal is a useful RESOURCE on your journey to THE NEW MODEL ME. We refer to it as a journal rather than a diary because a diary demands that you write in it every day. We think *what* you write down is more important than *when* you write it down.

Use a small spiral notebook (5 by 7 inches):

> On page one, write your name, the date, and the words "Journal Notes."
>
> Write down the Behavior Equation: N + R + IPS = BEHAVIOR. Refer back to this formula when you wish to examine past behaviors, or when you have an important decision to make.
>
> Comment on class activities and things that happen out of class.
>
> Record your personal objective—an objective that commits you to strengthen a constructive behavior or develop a new constructive behavior or discard an unwise or destructive behavior.

From time to time, we will suggest that you use your JOURNAL NOTES as a resource. Your written thoughts and observations will give evidence of your growth in resources and confidence as you progress toward THE NEW MODEL ME.

ACTIVITY 8

Straw Tower

"Straw Tower" is a group activity. Often you will be asked to participate as a member of a group. A group can be a RESOURCE to each member, or it can be a drag that reduces the individual performance of one or more members of the group. Whether the group becomes a resource for constructive behavior or a force for destructive behavior can be explained by the BEHAVIOR EQUATION.

To discover how this is done:

Each group will build a straw tower at least five feet high, using plastic straws and cellophane or masking tape.

The group will have 15 minutes to complete the task.

Members of the group may communicate with each other, but *without speaking.*

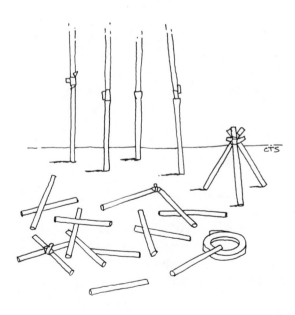

Each tower will be judged on the following standards:

- beauty
- originality
- application of engineering principles—can it stand by itself?
- durability and portability.

IMMEDIATE PHYSICAL/PSYCHOLOGICAL SETTING

N   +   R   +   IPS

NEEDS + RESOURCES +   IMMEDIATE PHYSICAL/
                           PSYCHOLOGICAL SETTING

What exactly is an IPS? IMMEDIATE PHYSICAL/
PSYCHOLOGICAL SETTING is an imposing phrase that can be
explained simply:

- *immediate*—right now, at the moment
- *physical setting*—room, chairs, tables, people, temperature, lighting, etc.
- *psychological setting*—how you feel and react in this physical surrounding.

As human beings, we react in different ways to different physical and psychological settings. We become sluggish and sleepy in rooms that are much too warm. Employers have found that workers will produce more with less waste in some physical settings than in others.

Waiting in line to view a favorite musical group or film is more pleasant than waiting to have our teeth drilled and filled by the dentist!

Often a simple change of physical setting can affect behavior. An observer looking only at behavior can tell whether students are in a physical education class or a science class. You probably behave differently in social studies from year to year, depending on the teacher. (Teachers are part of your IPS.)

As we grow older, our psychological setting becomes an increasingly powerful force that envelops us wherever we go. Consequently, a change in physical surroundings may not result in a change in behavior. The next activity should convince you of this.

ACTIVITY 9

Cipher in the Snow[2]

It started with tragedy on a biting cold February morning. I was driving behind the Milford Corners bus, as I did most snowy mornings on my way to school. It veered and stopped short at the hotel, which it had no business doing, and I was annoyed as I had to come to an unexpected stop. A boy lurched out of the bus, reeled, stumbled, and collapsed on the snowbank at the curb. The bus driver and I reached him at the same moment. His thin, hollow face was white even against the snow.

"He's dead," the driver whispered.

It didn't register for a minute. I glanced quickly at the scared young faces staring down at us from the school bus. "A doctor! Quick! I'll phone from the hotel . . ."

"No use, I tell you he's dead." The driver looked down at the boy's still form. "He never even said he felt bad," he muttered, "just tapped me on the shoulder and said real quiet, 'I'm sorry. I have to get off at the hotel.' That's all. Polite and apologizing like."

At school, the giggling, shuffling morning noise quieted as the news went down the halls. I passed a huddle of girls. "Who was it? Who dropped dead on the way to school?" I heard one of them half-whisper.

"Don't know his name, some kid from Milford Corners," was the reply.

It was like that in the faculty room and the principal's office. "I'd appreciate your going out to tell the parents," the principal told me. "They haven't a phone and, anyway, somebody from school should go there in person. I'll cover your classes."

"Why me?" I asked. "Wouldn't it be better if you did it?"

"I didn't know the boy," the principal admitted. "And in last year's sophomore personalities column I note that you were listed as his favorite teacher."

I drove through the snow and cold down the bad canyon road to the

[2]Jean Mizer Todhunter, "Cipher in the Snow," *Today's Education* (November 1964). Reprinted with permission by the author and *Today's Education*.

Evans place and thought about the boy, Cliff Evans. "His favorite teacher!" I thought. "He hasn't spoken two words to me in two years!" I could see him in my afternoon literature class. He came into the room by himself and left by himself. "Cliff Evans," I muttered to myself, "a boy who never talked." I thought a minute. "A boy who never smiled. I never saw him smile once."

The big ranch kitchen was clean and warm. I blurted out my news somehow. Mrs. Evans reached blindly toward a chair. "He never said anything about being ailing."

His stepfather snorted, "He ain't said nothin' about anything since I moved in here."

Mrs. Evans pushed a pan to the back of the stove and began to untie her apron. "Now hold on," her husband snapped, "I got to have breakfast before I go to town. Nothin' we can do now anyway. If Cliff hadn't been so dumb, he'd have told us he didn't feel good."

After school I sat in the office and stared bleakly at the records spread out before me. I was to close the file and write the obituary for the school paper. The almost bare sheets mocked the effort. Cliff Evans, white, never legally adopted by his stepfather, five young half-brothers and sisters. These meager strands of information and the list of D grades were all the records had to offer.

Cliff Evans had silently come in the school door in the morning and gone out the school door in the evening, and that was all. He had never belonged to a club. He had never played on a team. He had never held an office. As far as I could tell, he had never done one happy, noisy kid thing. He had never been anybody at all.

How do you go about making a boy into a zero? The grade school records showed me. The first- and second-grade teachers' comments read, "Sweet, shy child, timid but eager." Then the third-grade note had opened the attack. Some teacher had written in a good, firm hand, "Cliff won't talk. Uncooperative. Slow learner." The other academic sheep had followed with "dull"; "slow-witted"; "low I.Q." They became correct. The boy's I.Q. score in the ninth grade was listed as 83. But his I.Q. in the third grade had been 106. The score didn't go under 100 until the seventh grade. Even shy, timid, sweet children have resilience. It takes time to break them.

I stomped to the typewriter and wrote a savage report pointing out what education had done to Cliff Evans. I slapped a copy on the principal's desk and another in the sad, dog-eared file. I banged the typewriter and slammed the file and crashed the door shut, but I didn't feel much better. A little boy kept walking after me, a little boy with a peaked, pale face, a skinny body in faded jeans, and big eyes that had looked and searched for a long time and then had become veiled.

I could guess how many times he'd been chosen last to play sides in a game, how many whispered child conversations had excluded him, how many times he hadn't been asked. I could see and hear the faces and voices that said over and over, "You're dumb. You're dumb. You're a nothing, Cliff Evans."

A child is a believing creature. Cliff undoubtedly believed them. Suddenly it seemed clear to me: When finally there was nothing left at all for Cliff Evans, he collapsed on a snowbank and went away. The doctor might list "heart failure" as the cause of death, but that wouldn't change my mind.

We couldn't find ten students in the school who had known Cliff well enough to attend the funeral as his friends. So the student body officers and a committee from the junior class went as a group to the church, being politely sad. I attended the service with them and sat through it with a lump of cold lead in my chest and a big resolve growing through me.

I've never forgotten Cliff Evans or that resolve. He has been my challenge year after year, class after class. I look up and down the rows carefully each September at the unfamiliar faces. I look for veiled eyes or bodies forced down into a seat in an alien world.

"Look, kids," I say silently, "I may not do anything else for you this year, but not one of you is going to come out of here a nobody. I'll work or fight to the bitter end doing battle with society and the school board, but I won't have one of you coming out of here thinking himself into a zero."

Most of the time—not always, but most of the time—I've succeeded.

—*Jean Mizer Todhunter*

The story is true, but the names of the characters and the location have been changed.

QUESTIONS FOR DISCUSSION

1. What do you think is the meaning of the title "Cipher in the Snow"?
2. How would you describe Cliff's Immediate Psychological Setting in the years before he died?
3. Did Cliff change his behavior as he moved from one physical setting (home) to another (school)? Explain.
4. Without meaning to do so, Cliff's family, teachers, and classmates reduced his resources. What resources were reduced, and how was this done?
5. What do you think you could have done to increase Cliff's resources if you had been:
   • One of Cliff's classmates?
   • His favorite teacher?
   • His brother or sister?

RESOURCES AND VALUES

The next activity demonstrates the close relationship between our RESOURCES and our VALUES. Each resource we possess or might possess is weighed and judged by our values. Values are things that people see as being worthy, good, and important.

Resource	*Value*
Knowledge of chemistry	To become a doctor of medicine
Money	To own an automobile
Listening ability	To be a more helpful friend

Values can be traced back to the satisfaction of needs; however, the process is made more difficult by the fact that human beings often are motivated by a combination of needs, and a need may have many values associated with it. Quite often in our complicated world we must choose among competing values. In such cases, we may be forced to select what we think is the most worthy, good, or important value and, for a time, discard the others. In the next activity, "A Renewed Chance for Life," you will be placed in a situation where your values will be in competition.

PHYSICAL RESOURCES

ACTIVITY 10

A Renewed Chance for Life

Prospero is a dying planet! The culprit is a layer of ozone, harmless in small quantities, but deadly in larger concentrations. As it accumulates in the atmosphere, ozone robs the land of the warming rays of the sun. Even now the annual yield of food crops has fallen from year to year as the green plants struggle to produce the required amount of oxygen to nurture and sustain life.

As the average temperatures around the world have dropped, the delicate balance of forces that control natural events has changed. Consequently natural disasters—earthquakes, hurricanes, droughts, blizzards—have increased in number and intensity. No scientist has been able to explain why the ozone has accumulated to the present life-threatening level; no one offers any hope that anything can be done to prevent the slow but certain destruction of civilized life on Prospero within the span of a hundred years.

In your role as a government minister, you take your assigned chair in the council room. The prime minister begins to speak.

"Fellow ministers, our time is short! We must select the first voyagers to the new planet, where we hope our people will have a renewed chance for life. As you know, the remote-controlled space-ship has room for only eight persons and very limited provisions. Our scientists tell me that the new planet has a breathable atmosphere, edible plants, and animals. No relief or new personnel can be expected to arrive for another three years. Thus the eight persons who are finally chosen must become self-sufficient until then.

"Now you are to complete a biographical sketch of two persons you wish to nominate. When that task is completed, my chief of staff will inform you about the next steps." (See the bio-sketch on page 31.)

BIO-SKETCH

Check one: Male ☐   Female ☐

Check one: Married ☐   Single ☐

Name of Nominee ⎯⎯⎯⎯⎯⎯⎯⎯⎯⎯⎯⎯⎯⎯⎯⎯

Age ⎯⎯⎯⎯⎯⎯⎯⎯⎯

Present Role
or Occupation ⎯⎯⎯⎯⎯⎯⎯⎯⎯⎯⎯⎯⎯⎯⎯⎯⎯

My nominee should be selected because ⎯⎯⎯⎯⎯⎯⎯

⎯⎯⎯⎯⎯⎯⎯⎯⎯⎯⎯⎯⎯⎯⎯⎯⎯⎯⎯⎯⎯⎯⎯⎯⎯⎯

⎯⎯⎯⎯⎯⎯⎯⎯⎯⎯⎯⎯⎯⎯⎯⎯⎯⎯⎯⎯⎯⎯⎯⎯⎯⎯

⎯⎯⎯⎯⎯⎯⎯⎯⎯⎯⎯⎯⎯⎯⎯⎯⎯⎯⎯⎯⎯⎯⎯⎯⎯⎯

⎯⎯⎯⎯⎯⎯⎯⎯⎯⎯⎯⎯⎯⎯⎯⎯⎯⎯⎯⎯⎯⎯⎯⎯⎯⎯

(Be sure to describe any knowledge, talents, experiences, or
other RESOURCE that you think might influence the decision.)

The problem faced by the leaders of Prospero is often referred to as a VALUE DILEMMA. A value dilemma is a situation in which values that we support appear to be in competition, and we must choose which value is worthiest, best, or most important. We shall explore many different kinds of dilemmas in Unit II, but the dilemma faced by the Prospero ministers deserves some discussion here.

What dilemma do they face? As leaders of society they wish to:

Protect all human beings

At the same time they are required to select eight persons who will have "A Renewed Chance for Life." Whom shall they select? They are faced with a second value that conflicts with the first one:

> Select human beings who are best able to survive

OTHER VALUE DILEMMAS

This same dilemma can take many different forms, but regardless of its form, the basic dilemma has been with us since man first stepped upon the earth. Firemen trying to rescue victims trapped in a hotel fire face the dilemma. A physician in an emergency room trying to cope with the victims of a terrible automobile crash may face it.

During recent years, new medical and surgical procedures have brought the promise of life and health to many seriously ill patients. Unfortunately these new procedures are scarce and costly. Often decisions have to be made about who receives the help and who does not.

One of the most difficult dilemmas facing medical people today involves the transplanting of body organs. These organs are taken from patients whose death cannot be prevented and are surgically given to patients whose lives or normal functions can be restored through the use of the new organs. The dilemma is created because the supply of organs will probably never catch up to the demand for them. Somebody must decide how the limited supply of organs is to be distributed. A real dilemma, to be sure!

ACTIVITY 11

Medical Board

Assume that you are a member of a board whose responsibility is to decide which patients are to receive one of the very limited supply of donated kidneys. For those who are chosen, there is the possibility of immediate restoration of vitality and a promise of a normal life. Those who are rejected must remain on a kidney machine with its limitations—inconvenience, opportunity for injury and disease, and reduced chances for a normal life span.

The following have been proposed as possible means or criteria (standards) for determining who is to receive a donated kidney:

- past contributions to society
- estimate about future contributions

33

- age
- health, if kidney function is restored
- family situations (single, married, divorced, married with children)
- likelihood of a successful transplant

As a member of the medical board:

Rank order the criteria. That is, determine which has most importance, which is second, third, etc. In addition, consider as an alternative to these personal criteria the use of a lottery.

Prepare a written argument that defends the use of one or more of the criteria and rejects one or more of the others.

Be ready to defend your argument in discussion with other members of the board.

YOUR PROGRESS SO FAR

The final two activities in Unit I make it possible for you to see how far you have moved along toward THE NEW MODEL ME. Keep your BEHAVIOR EQUATION handy for easy reference.

ACTIVITY 12

Putting the Behavior
Equation to Music

Quite often human needs are expressed most clearly in artistic state-ments—art, music, and literature. These expressions of joy, sorrow, hope, and despair provide us with an opportunity to apply the BEHAVIOR EQUATION to what we do.

Read some verses from the following popular song of the mid-1970s. Even better, if you have the record, bring it to class.

Cat's in the Cradle[3]

My child arrived just the other day.
He came to the world in the usual way.
But there were planes to catch and bills to pay.
He learned to walk while I was away.
And he was talkin' 'fore I knew it, and as he grew
He'd say, "I'm gonna be like you, dad,
You know I'm gonna be like you."

My son turned ten just the other day.
He said, "Thanks for the ball, dad, come on let's play.
Can you teach me to throw?" I said, "Not today
I got a lot to do." He said, "That's O.K."
And he walked away, but his smile never dimmed,
And said, "I'm gonna be like him, yeah,
You know I'm gonna be like him."

I've long since retired. My son's moved away.
I called him up just the other day.
I said, "I'd like to see you if you don't mind."
He said, "I'd love to, dad, if I can find the time.
You see my new job's a hassle and the kids have the flu

[3]Lyrics by Harry and Sandy Chapin. © Story Songs Ltd. 1974. Reprinted with permission.

35

But it's sure nice talking to you, dad.
It's been sure nice talking to you.''

And as I hung up the phone it occurred to me—
He'd grown up just like me.
My boy was just like me.   —*Harry and Sandy Chapin*

QUESTIONS FOR DISCUSSION

1. What NEEDS are described in the song?
2. What FRUSTRATIONS are mentioned?
3. What RESOURCES were available to satisfy the needs of both father and son?
4. How does the IMMEDIATE PSYCHOLOGICAL SETTING affect the father with the young son? The father with the grown son?
5. What was the IMMEDIATE CONSEQUENCE of the father's behavior when his son was a child? What was the REMOTE CONSEQUENCE of his behavior?

Play two or three other songs that your class feels have significance for high school students today. The activity will be most successful if each person has a copy of the lyrics. Listen carefully to the lyrics.

ACTIVITY 13

Chris

Role playing is useful in applying the BEHAVIOR EQUATION in a realistic setting. Assume that it is the second week of a new school year in your high school. There are four characters in our role play:

- *Chris*—An eleventh grader who has not experienced much success in school and is thinking of dropping out and getting a job. Chris's grades are mostly Cs with a sprinkling of Ds and Bs and an A only in art. Selected teacher comments about Chris: "Chris is not attentive or interested." "Ability is greater than schoolwork would suggest."
- *Pat*—A close friend who has concern but has not had much influence on Chris's decisions in the past.
- *Chris's only parent*—A hard worker who has not had a high school education and wishes that Chris could have the maximum opportunities and advantages.
- *Art teacher*—One person in the high school whom Chris respects and who respects Chris's artistic abilities.

The role play involves encounters between and among the four characters. When all characters have been heard, discuss the following:

- the NEEDS of the characters in each situation
- the RESOURCES the characters possess or desire to possess
- the effect of the IMMEDIATE PHYSICAL/PSYCHOLOGI-CAL SETTING on the behavior of each character
- the alternative BEHAVIORS available to Chris
- the probable IMMEDIATE and REMOTE consequences of each behavior.

A Review of the Objectives

Now that you have completed the activities in Unit I, can you:

1. Use the Behavior Equation to explain human behavior?
2. Recommend alternative behaviors by changing one or more of the elements of the Behavior Equation?
3. Recall the five levels of Maslow's "Hierarchy of Needs"?
4. Write a personal objective for yourself in your JOURNAL NOTES? The objective might be a promise to develop or strengthen a constructive behavior or to discard an unwise or destructive behavior.
5. Tell what each WORD or PHRASE means?
6. Use the WORD or PHRASE correctly in a sentence?

UNIT II

SELF-IDENTITY

CONTENTS

Looking Ahead

WHY STUDY SELF-IDENTITY?

"There's just one person in the world like you, and people can like you just the way you are."[1]

The public television program *Mister Rogers' Neighborhood* has been delighting its young audience for many years. Its creator and central character, Fred Rogers, closes each show by emphasizing the individuality and self-worth of each child. He was introduced to the concept of self-identity as an eight-year-old child when, after a particularly exciting day, his grandfather said: "You made this a special day, just by being yourself. Always remember, there's just one person in this world like you—and I like you just the way you are."[2]

Fred Rogers' anecdote is an appropriate introduction to your journey through a unit on SELF-IDENTITY. Every human being is more than a walking, talking, breathing body with a name. Each individual has needs and wants, resources and values that are just as much a part of him or her as a name. There are as many combinations of characteristics as there are people. Each of us is unique.

The purpose of this unit is to examine your self-identity—to take stock of your present RESOURCES and make plans for the addition of new resources to enable you to reach goals that you VALUE, goals that you think are good, worthy, and important.

---

[1]Fred Rogers, "I Like You Just the Way You Are," *Guideposts* (September 1980). Reprinted by permission from GUIDEPOSTS MAGAZINE. Copyright © 1980 by Guidance Associates, Inc., Carmel, NY 10512.
[2]Ibid.

OBJECTIVES

When this unit is completed, we are confident that you will be able to:

1. Explain the relationship between RESOURCES and VALUES as part of an individual's SELF-IDENTITY.
2. Use resources such as friends, reading, listening, and negotiating skills to strengthen your self-identity.
3. Write a paragraph in your JOURNAL NOTES describing what combination of resources and values makes up your self-identity.
4. Explain how (a) labels, (b) killer statements, (c) stereotypes, (d) prejudice, (e) unemployment, and (f) dependency diminish a person's resources.
5. Become clear about your personal values and your position on community (group) value issues by (a) watching the way the issue is phrased, (b) identifying value dilemmas, (c) selecting a value standard, (d) separating factual statements and value statements, and (e) determining the logic of arguments and the weight of evidence.
6. Tell what each WORD or PHRASE means.
7. Use the WORD or PHRASE correctly in a sentence.

WORDS AND PHRASES

Self-Identity

Self-Esteem

PARS Study-Reading System

Assertive/Non-Assertive

Label

Attribute

Killer Statement

Stereotype

Prejudice

Independence/Dependence

Values for Concrete Things

Values for Abstract Ideas

Traditional Values

Dignity and Worth of Human Beings

Personal Values

Community Values

Public Policy Issue

Value Standard

Factual Statement

Value Statement

Logic

Weight of Evidence

WHO AM I?

In his book *Why Am I Afraid to Tell You Who I Am?* John Powell writes: "There is no fixed, true, and real person inside of you or me, precisely because *being a person* necessarily implies *becoming a person, being in process.* If I am anything as a person, it is what I think, judge, feel, value, honor, esteem, love, hate, fear, desire, hope for, believe in, and am committed to."[3]

What is there about each of us that can accurately identify our uniqueness? The first group of activities in this unit will provide you with an opportunity to look carefully at yourself—to study your SELF-IDENTITY. You may be surprised to learn that you possess more resources than you imagined.

[3]Reprinted from *Why Am I Afraid to Tell You Who I Am?* by John Powell, S.J., © 1969, Argus Communications, Niles, Ill. Used with permission.

ACTIVITY 1

Who Am I?

Use your JOURNAL NOTES to record your responses to the questions asked in this activity. In answering, consider your

- needs
- values
- resources
- behaviors

1. What kind of person am I?
2. How do others see me?
3. What kind of person do I wish to be?

ACTIVITY 2

Personal Inventory

Write a two- or three-paragraph personal inventory. A personal inventory is a description of you and your possessions, qualities, and interests. Choose from among the following:

- experiences you have had
- things you have done
- ideas you have acquired
- skills you possess
- talents
- people you like or admire
- values
- anything else of importance to you

Use your JOURNAL NOTES to record your inventory.

ACTIVITY 3

It's My Bag

Bring to class a bag containing something that makes you feel proud or that you think you do well. You may bring a specific item or something that represents what you feel good about.

Since you will have the opportunity to share what's in your bag with your classmates, bring something that you will feel comfortable telling others about.

This activity may sound a little like the "show and tell" activity that you did in kindergarten. There are some similarities. We believe, however, that it is a good way to let others know about your interests and to learn about the interests of others. The chances are your teacher will bring a bag and share what he or she does well or feels good about.

Form a circle. If the class has more than 12 or 15 people in it, you may want to form more than one circle.

Each person in your circle has the opportunity to tell others in the circle what's in his or her bag.

Respect each individual's right to remain silent if he or she prefers.

If there is more than one circle, you may want to share with other circles after your original circle has shared.

ACTIVITY 4

I Don't Mean to Brag, but . . .

This activity is designed to help you appreciate your unique resources. There have been times when you have been proud of something you did or had. You wanted to tell someone about it, but our society does not encourage people to share their feelings of pride. Someone else may mention the accomplishment, but otherwise it may go unrecognized and unshared.

Pride is related to how a person feels about himself or herself. Select an opening phrase for the following sentence from the suggested list, and then complete the sentence as it fits you. You may want to do several of these sentences in your JOURNAL NOTES.

_____ that makes me feel proud is . . .

- An occasion when I helped someone
- A habit I have
- A thing I've done for a member of my family
- An item I own
- A school project
- An achievement
- A thing I did for a friend

ACTIVITY 5

Art and Me

Think about the question, What makes me feel like a somebody? Make a collage out of symbols and pictures of work that represent your strengths. Find pictures of any object in magazines, cut them out, and randomly arrange them on poster board. Be sure to find the kinds of pictures that truly represent you when you are "feeling like a somebody."

ACTIVITY 6

Looking Back, Looking Forward

Write a brief personal story that discusses how you see yourself in the past and in the future.

Think back six years ago. How have your resources changed? Have you increased your resources? Explain.

What resources would you like to possess six years from now? Why are these resources important to you?

Use your JOURNAL NOTES to record the story.

ACTIVITY 7

A Eulogy Now: An Obituary Much Later

If I knew I was going to die tomorrow, whom would I choose to speak the eulogy to the assembled family members and friends? What would I like the person to say about me in the eulogy?

An obituary is an announcement of death in the news media, telling the essential details about the death itself, the memorial service, and the burial plans and providing an insight into the resources, values, and accomplishments of the deceased. When I die, what should the obituary say?

Use your JOURNAL NOTES to respond to the questions in this activity. Limit your eulogy and obituary to 100–200 words.

Death Notices	Death Notices	Death Notices	Death Notices	Death Notices	Death Notices
CLEAVELAND	DAVEY	EYMAN	KORMOS	MYSLIWIEC	REMBIELAK
COSTANZO	DEL VECCHIO	FLETCHER	KOZAK	NEELON	RICCHIUTO
CALABRESE	DEMING	FORTE	KRUCZEK	NEUREUTHER	RICHARDS
	DESMONE	FRAGOLA	LAZAR	O'CONNOR	RIGGS
	DEY	FURMAN		O'NEIL	

52

INCREASING
YOUR RESOURCES

Knowing that you are a unique
person and being satisfied with
yourself is SELF-ESTEEM.

How do I know when I have self-esteem? Do I

- respect myself?
- show that same respect for others?
- ask for responsibility? behave responsibly?
- accept defeat without lasting anger and envy?
- accept victory with generosity?

Am I

- authentic? neither stuck up nor ashamed, neither "overselling" myself nor "underselling"?
- comfortable as a leader and a follower?
- willing to accept the consequences of my own behavior?
- on a schedule to increase my resources?

To increase your confidence and thus your
self-esteem, try increasing your resources.

Others have done it successfully. Let's look at some examples.

Parachute to Disaster

Roger Reynolds, a member of the U.S. Army's parachute skill team, the Golden Knights, experienced a sudden loss of resources on April 24, 1974. He smashed to earth on his nine hundredth jump when his parachute failed to open properly. Every major bone in the left side of his body was broken. Although he survived, doctors believed that he would never walk again. Instead of accepting a diminished self-identity, he set out to recover through a painful program of self-conditioning. As of 1980, he has fully recovered. He runs marathon distances each day and studies to be an orthopedic (bone) surgeon.

The Bonnie Consolo Story

The popular television program *60 Minutes* interviewed an unusually gifted woman and mother in 1980. She is unusual because she was born without arms. She is gifted because her legs and feet have learned to do double duty. Rather than allow her disability to become a handicap (an explanation for reduced resources), she has taught her feet to perform tasks that we normally identify with hands. She uses her feet to wash dishes, to prepare food, to type, and to drive an automobile. During the *60 Minutes* interview, it was apparent to viewers that the usually tough Mike Wallace was overwhelmed by Bonnie's casual acceptance of her disability. Her children have also learned to view their mother not as a person without arms, but simply as "Mom." You may someday meet Mrs. Consolo, for she is a very popular after-dinner speaker at conferences and meetings.

Taking On a City

Did you ever hear the names Marva Collins and Renault Robinson? They both live in Chicago. Marva Collins was a teacher in the city schools, and Renault Robinson was a patrolman. Both were disheartened by what they believed was racism toward blacks. Mrs. Collins became so upset at the low expectations that teachers had about the learning potential of black children that she quit her job in the Chicago school system and founded her own school, the Westside Preparatory School. In 1980 the school expanded into new and spacious quarters. If you were to visit the Westside Preparatory School, you might see inner-city black children from low-income backgrounds discussing Plato's *Republic* or practicing creative writing.

Renault Robinson was frequently criticized by his superiors for publicly complaining about police treatment of black citizens and the fact that blacks were hardly visible in the ranks of Chicago's "Finest." In 1970 he sued the department for racial discrimination in personnel hiring and promotions. After a six-year court battle he won his case, although he was forced to resign from the police force. Lately Robinson has turned his attention to other city services. He has urged that incompetent and dishonest public housing officials be fired. He is proud to note that Chicago has a few hundred more minority police today than it had in 1970.

Roger Reynolds, Bonnie Consolo, Marva Collins, and Renault Robinson have increased their resources, and so can you.

In this section of Unit II, we will present four kinds of resources that you should explore and expand. They can make a difference in your self-identity. They are:

- friends
- reading
- listening
- negotiating skills

ACTIVITY 8

Advertising for a Friend

THE FRIENDS YOU MAKE

One of the best resources we have is *friends*. Friends are inexpensive to find and keep. They may last for a lifetime and demand little more than an occasional "helping hand" or "ear" when times get tough. Some friendships are based on shared interests and activities. For example, people who attend the same school or work in the same office often become friends. Usually the friendship lasts as long as the shared interests and activities bring the friends together.

A personal friendship runs deeper than common interests and activities. It results when two people share their thoughts, feelings, hopes, and fears. Personal friendships are difficult to establish, but once established they may last a lifetime. Over a lifetime, a person is fortunate to have four or five close personal friends. You may have watched a phone company commercial intended to encourage long-

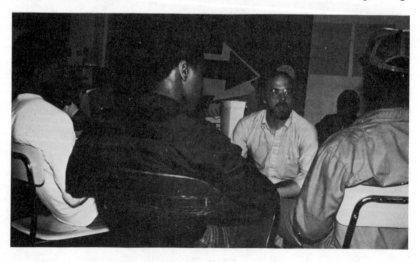

distance calling. Notice how the commercial message emphasizes the closeness and love between personal friends who may live far apart but who are very near in thoughts and feelings.

It may surprise you to learn that the reasons friendships begin are different for different people. Some teenage friendships begin because one or more of the friends sees the friendship as a way to gain approval or to impress other people. Interestingly, these friendships often turn out to be very meaningful. The wrong reasons can lead us to the right persons!

If they turn out to be "right," then the friends' personalities will "fit" or "mesh" together. If this occurs, trust and loyalty will grow and strengthen the relationship.

At 16, 17, or 18, a person's friendships change a great deal. Friends seem to trust each other more than before. They choose each other because they have common interests and ideas. Friendships become deeper and last longer. Often these are the beginnings of relationships that last a lifetime.

NEWSPAPER AND MAGAZINE WANT ADS

Have you ever read the "Personals" columns in a newspaper or magazine? Here are some examples:

"Man (mid-50s) enjoys the theater, dining out, travel, seeks honest, dependable widow for companionship."

"Beautiful, sincere female (29) would like to meet good-looking success-oriented gentleman who is interested in sharing an active, loving, respectable, complete life."

"Warm, gentle, intelligent man (45–55) needed by same variety woman as sailing crew."

What do these personals have in common? Each states something about the individual and states a preference for particular resources in the friends he or she wishes to make.

Using your JOURNAL NOTES, advertise for a friend, either male or female.

List the resources and values you think you possess that might be attractive to others, and list the requirements you wish to find in a friend.

How many of your present friends would respond to the ad? Would you select all of your present friends if they responded to the ad? Why or why not?

Be prepared to discuss your ad with other class members.

FRIENDSHIP CHECKLISTS

How to Lose Friends[4]
- Be undependable.
- Be grumpy.
- Exaggerate often.
- Be bossy.
- Be sarcastic.
- Criticize often.
- Be dominating.
- Act superior.

Ways to Nourish Friendship[5]
- Permit your friends to be themselves.
- Give each other space.
- Be ready to give and to receive.
- Make your advice constructive.
- Be loyal.
- Give praise and encouragement.
- Be honest.
- Treat friends as equals.
- Trust your friends.
- Be willing to risk.

[4]"How to Lose Friends," *News Notes*, No. 240. Reprinted with permission of The Christophers, 12 E. 48th St., New York, NY 10017.

[5]"Ways to Nourish Friendship," *News Notes*, No. 240. Reprinted with permission of The Christophers, 12 E. 48th St., New York, NY 10017.

ACTIVITY 9

Reading Is Fundamental: The PARS Study-Reading System[6]

Have you ever read a page in a textbook several times before you realized that you couldn't remember anything you read? If so, you

[6]Written especially for *The New Model Me* by Frederick R. Smith, Professor of Social Studies Education, Indiana University.

have a reason for wanting to increase your ability to understand what you read. You know that words do not appear only in schoolbooks. They appear also in newspapers and magazines, on street signs and safety information, and on products we buy and sell.

Fortunately help is on the way! We will be using the PARS STUDY-READING SYSTEM as a resource to help you read. PARS has helped many people to get more out of their reading.

PARS consists of four steps to success in reading any assignment:

1. Purpose
2. Ask
3. Read
4. Summarize

Let's look at each step.

1. *Purpose.* Quickly skim through what is to be read, paying special attention to headings and words in bold print. Look at the pictures, charts, and graphs. From this quick skimming, make guesses about the meaning of what you will read. For example:

"I am going to learn about something called the Behavior Equation, which explains why people behave as they do."

"I am going to learn how I can improve my resources."

After you have developed a purpose, write it down or discuss it with a friend.

2. *Ask.* Think of questions you will want to have answered. One question deals with the author's "point of view" (the resources and values that guide the author). Will you agree or disagree with it? Other questions get at the major points in the reading. Try changing headings and sub-headings into questions:

Heading: "Reading Is Fundamental"

Question: "Why is reading fundamental? Can't I get along without it?"

You may write out your questions, or you may just keep them in mind as you read.

3. *Read.* Setting purposes and asking questions made up a warm-up exercise. They helped you scout the assignment and plan your attack. Now follow your plan and read. Don't forget your purpose and questions. They will help you to complete the final step.

4. *Summarize.* After reading, you should be able to restate the essay or story in your own words. Some people like to organize a summary around the questions they have asked. Others prefer to organize it around main ideas and supporting arguments or evidence. How you do it is not as important as doing it. After you write your summary don't file it away and forget it. Review it before a test, and compare it with summaries written by classmates.

Remember that reading skill is a precious resource that can be improved. With use and practice, PARS can assist you to be a more confident and successful reader. Let's get on with the job!

—Frederick R. Smith

USING THE PARS SYSTEM

As we continue on our journey through the units in *The New Model Me*, you will be asked to use the PARS Study-Reading System to read essays and stories about some ideas that we think are valuable. To aid you in following each of the four steps, you will be given a PARS Worksheet each time you are to use the system. (See the sample worksheet on page 62.)

The first essay is in ACTIVITY 10 that follows next. Many of the essays were gathered from the "My Turn" editorials in the introductory pages of *Newsweek* magazine. The PARS System will increase your ability to read and gain meaning from what you read. Whether the assignment is a "My Turn" essay or a carefully selected story, we hope that you will find that the completed task was worth the effort. When you find success, don't stop there! Use the PARS System to make all of your reading more efficient and valuable as a resource to meet your needs.

PARS WORKSHEET (Number _____)

Essay title_____

Author_____ Text page nos. _____

Purpose.   Quickly skim the essay. What do you think you will learn from it?

Ask.   What is the author's "point of view"? (What are the resources and values that guide the author?)

Read.   Keep your purpose and questions in mind.

Summarize.   Concentrate on the main idea and points made by the author as you write a paragraph summarizing the essay in your own words.

ACTIVITY 10

A Cult of Ignorance[7]

AUTHOR
ISAAC ASIMOV

Let's use the PARS System to read "A Cult of Ignorance" by the noted scientist and science fiction author Isaac Asimov. As an aid, we have prepared a sample PARS Worksheet (number I) to use with the article.

It's hard to quarrel with that ancient justification of the free press: "America's right to know." It seems almost cruel to ask, ingenuously, "America's right to know what, please? Science? Mathematics? Economics? Foreign languages?"

None of those things, of course. In fact, one might well suppose that the popular feeling is that Americans are a lot better off without any of that tripe.

There is a cult of ignorance in the United States, and there always has been. The strain of anti-intellectualism has been a constant thread winding its way through our political and cultural life, nurtured by the false notion that democracy means that "my ignorance is just as good as your knowledge."

Politicians have routinely striven to speak the language of Shakespeare and Milton as ungrammatically as possible in order to avoid offending their audiences by appearing to have gone to school. Thus, Adlai Stevenson, who incautiously allowed intelligence and learning and wit to peep out of his speeches, found the American people flocking to a Presidential candidate who invented a version of the English language that was all his own and that has been the despair of satirists ever since.

George Wallace, in his speeches, had, as one of his prime targets, the "pointy-headed professor," and with what a roar of approval that phrase was always greeted by his pointy-headed audience.

Buzzwords

Now we have a new slogan on the part of the obscurantists: "Don't trust the experts!" Ten years ago, it was found that the inevitable alchemy of the calendar converted them to the untrustworthiness of the over-30, and, apparently, they determined never to make that mistake again. "Don't trust the experts!" is absolutely safe. Nothing, neither the passing of time nor exposure to information, will convert these shouters to experts in any subject that might conceivably be useful.

We have a new buzzword, too, for anyone who admires competence, knowledge, learning, and skill, and who wishes to spread it around. People like that are called "elitists." That's the funniest buzzword ever invented because people who are not members of the intellectual elite don't know what an "elitist" is, or how to pronounce the word. As soon as someone shouts "elitist" it becomes clear that he or she is a closet elitist who is feeling guilty about having gone to school.

All right, then, forget my ingenuous question. America's right to know does not include knowledge of elitist subjects. America's right to know involves something we might express vaguely as "what's going on." America has the right to know "what's going on" in the courts, in Congress, in the White House, in industrial councils, in the regulatory agencies, in labor unions—in the seats of the mighty, generally.

Very good, I'm for that, too. But how are you going to let people know all that?

Grant us a free press, and a corps of independent and fearless investigative reporters, comes the cry, and we can be sure that the people will know.

Yes, provided they can read!

As it happens, reading is one of those elitist subjects I have been talking about, and the American public, by and large, in their distrust of experts and in their contempt for pointy-headed professors, can't read and don't read.

To be sure, the average American can sign his name more or less legibly, and can make out the sports headlines—but how many non-elitist Americans can, without undue difficulty, read as many as a thousand consecutive words of small print, some of which may be trisyllabic?

Moreover, the situation is growing worse. Reading scores in the schools decline steadily. The highway signs, which used to represent elementary misreading lessons ("Go Slo," "Xroad") are steadily being replaced by little pictures to make them internationally legible and incidentally to help those who know how to drive a car but, not being pointy-headed professors, can't read.

Again, in television commercials, there are frequent printed messages. Well, keep your eyes on them and you'll find out that no advertiser ever believes that anyone but an occasional elitist can read that print. To ensure that more than this mandarin minority gets the message, every word of it is spoken out loud by the announcer.

Honest Effort

If that is so, then how have Americans got the right to know? Grant that there are certain publications that make an honest effort to tell the public what they should know, but ask yourselves how many actually read them.

There are 200 million Americans who have inhabited schoolrooms at some time in their lives and who will admit that they know how to read (provided you promise not to use their names and shame them before their neighbors), but most decent periodicals believe they are doing amazingly well if they have circulations of half a million. It may be that only 1 percent—or less—of Americans make a stab at exercising their right to know. And if they try to do anything on that basis they are quite likely to be accused of being elitists.

I contend that the slogan "America's right to know" is a meaningless one when we have an ignorant population, and that the function of a free press is virtually zero when hardly anyone can read.

What shall we do about it?

We might begin by asking ourselves whether ignorance is so wonderful after all, and whether it makes sense to denounce "elitism."

I believe that every human being with a physically normal brain can learn a great deal and can be surprisingly intellectual. I believe that what we badly need is social approval of learning and social rewards for learning.

We can all be members of the intellectual elite and then, and only then, will a phrase like "America's right to know" and, indeed, any true concept of democracy, have any meaning.

—*Isaac Asimov*

QUESTIONS FOR DISCUSSION

1. What needs are satisfied when a person is a successful reader? What frustrations might result for a person who is unable to read?
2. What is "A Cult of Ignorance"?
3. Do you agree or disagree with Isaac Asimov that "the slogan 'America's right to know' is a meaningless one when we have an ignorant population"? Why or why not?
4. Do you agree or disagree that "every human being with a physically normal brain can learn a great deal and can be surprisingly intellectual"? Explain.

ACTIVITY 11

Johnny Lingo and the Eight-Cow Wife[8]

The second essay, by Patricia McGerr, appeared originally in Wom-an's Day *in the sixties. Since then it has become part of our folk literature. Use the PARS System (Worksheet II) as you read it.*

On my three-week leave between assignments in Japan, I went by boat to the island of Kiniwata. Among all the notes I made, only one sentence still interests me: Johnny Lingo gave eight cows to Sarita's father. I'm reminded of it every time I see a woman belittling her husband or a wife withering under her husband's scorn. I want to say to them, "You should know why Johnny Lingo paid eight cows for his wife." But, of course, I don't say anything. I only think about it.

I learned about Johnny Lingo and the eight cows from Shenkin, the fat manager of the guest house at Kiniwata. He and many other people mentioned Johnny in many connections. If I wanted to spend a few days on the island of Narabundi, a day's sail away, Johnny Lingo could put me up, they told me, since he had built (unheard-of-luxury!) a five-room house. If I wanted to fish, he could show me when the biting was best. If I wanted fresh vegetables, his garden was the greenest. If it was pearls I sought, his middlemanship would bring me the best buys. Yet when people spoke they smiled, and the smiles were slightly mocking.

"What goes on?" I demanded. "Why do people smile when John-ny's name is mentioned? What's the joke?"

"There's no joke," said Shenkin. "When we tell you to see Johnny it's good advice."

"Then why all the winking and snickering?"

"They like to laugh. And Johnny's the brightest, the quickest, the strongest young man in all this group of islands. And, for his age, the richest. So they like best to laugh at him."

"But what is there to laugh about?"

"Only one thing. Five months ago, at fall festival time, Johnny came

to Kiniwata and found himself a wife. He paid her father eight cows!"

I knew enough about island customs to be thoroughly impressed. Two or three cows would buy a fair-to-middling wife, four or five a highly satisfactory one.

"Good Heavens!" I said. "Eight cows! She must have beauty that takes your breath away."

"She's not ugly," he conceded. "But the kindest could only call Sarita plain. She was three months past marriage age when Johnny came, and no one had offered for her. Old Sam Karoo, her father, was beginning to be afraid she'd be left on his hands."

"But then he got eight cows for her? Isn't that an extraordinary number?"

"Never been paid before on Kiniwata or any neighboring island. Did you notice the girl who brought the fruit this morning?"

"The tall one?" I asked.

"The tall one," he agreed.

"She's magnificient," I said. "Is she Johnny's———?"

"Oh, no. Sarita's on Narabundi. She's not been back since she married. I only mention the girl of the fruit because she's the most beautiful woman on the island. She brought her father seven cows with four men bidding."

"Yet Johnny paid eight, and you call his wife plain?"

"I said it would be kindness to call her plain. She was little and skinny with no—ah—endowments. She walked with her shoulders hunched and her head ducked, as if she was trying to hide herself. Her cheeks had no color, her eyes never opened beyond a slit; and her hair was a tangled mop half over her face. She was afraid to speak up or laugh in public. She never romped with the girls, so how could she attract the boys?"

"But she attracted Johnny?"

"Yes, he sat beside her on the first night of the festival and walked home with her, the long way. And on the seventh day he met her father to make a marriage contract. The village has been open-mouthed ever since."

"It's queer," I admitted, "but not impossible. Those shy timid girls quite often appeal to strong men. There's just no accounting for love."

"That's true enough," said the fat man. "So we accepted Johnny's falling in love with Sarita. But when he paid her father eight cows . . . "

"Oh, yes. And that's why the villagers grin when they talk about

Johnny. They get a special satisfaction from the fact that Johnny was bested by dull old Sam Karoo.''

"But there must have been something special about the girl. Has she an inheritance or . . . ''

"She'll inherit Sam's eight cows, if he still owns them when he dies. Nothing more.''

"Then why?''

"That's what no one knows, and everyone wonders. The cousins who went with him to the marriage meeting tell the same story he does.''

"What is the story?''

"All the way to the Council tent the cousins were urging Sam to ask for three cows, and hold out for two until he was sure Johnny would only pay one. But Sam was so afraid there'd be some slip in this marriage chance for Sarita that they knew he wouldn't hold out for anything. Then Johnny came into the tent and, without waiting for a word from any of them, went straight up to Sam Karoo, grasped his hand and said, 'Father of Sarita, I offer eight cows for your daughter.' Sam thought he was making game of him and tried to pull away. But Johnny held on till the father and the cousins were all convinced that he'd gone mad and they'd better seal the contract before he came to his senses.''

"And he delivered the cows?''

"At once; they were waiting outside the tent, all eight of them. The wedding was that same evening and, as soon as it was over, Johnny took Sarita to the island of Cho for the first week of marriage. Then they went home to Narabundi, and we haven't seen them since. Except at festival time, there's not much travel between the islands.''

"Eight cows," I said unbelievingly. "And that girl with the fruit was only worth seven. I'd like to meet Johnny Lingo.''

"That's what we've all been telling you.''

So the next afternoon I beached my boat at Narabundi. I asked directions to the five-room house of Johnny Lingo. The mention of his name brought no sly smile to the lips nor even a twinkle to the eyes of his fellow Narabundians. And when I met the slim, serious young man, I was glad that from his own people he had respect unmingled with mockery.

We sat on softly plaited bamboo chairs in the main room of his house, and he agreed to guide me to good fishing, to sell me vegetables, to bargain for pearls. And then he said, "You come here from Kiniwata?"

And I said, yes, that was where I'd been told to look him up.

"They speak much of me on the island?"

"Yes," I said. "They say there's almost nothing I might want that you can't help me get."

He smiled gently, "My wife is from Kiniwata."

"Yes, I know."

"They speak much of her?"

"A little."

"What do they say?"

"They told me her name and who her father was and that you were married at fall festival time."

"Nothing more?"

"They also say the marriage settlement was eight cows. They wonder why."

"They say that?" His eyes lighted with pleasure. "Everyone in Kiniwata knows about the eight cows?"

I nodded.

"And in Narabundi everyone knows it, too." His chest expanded with satisfaction. "Always and forever, when they speak of marriage settlements, it will be remembered that Johnny Lingo paid eight cows for Sarita."

So that's the answer, I thought with disappointment. He had to make himself famous for his way of buying a wife.

And then I saw her. I watched her enter the adjoining room to place a bowl of blossoms on the dining table. And she was the most beautiful woman I have ever seen. The dew-fresh flowers with which she'd pinned back her lustrous black hair accented the glow of her cheeks. The lift of her shoulders, the tilt of her chin, the sparkle of her eyes, all spelled a pride to which no one could deny her the right. And, as she turned to leave, she moved with a lithe grace that made her look like a queen.

When she was out of sight, I turned back to Johnny Lingo and found him looking at me with eyes that reflected his pride in the girl.

"You admire her?" he murmured.

"She—she's glorious. Who is she?"

"My wife."

"But she's not the Sarita from Kiniwata," I said.

"There's only one Sarita. Perhaps you wish to say she does not look the way they say she looked in Kiniwata."

"She doesn't. I heard she was homely, or at least nondescript. They all made fun of you because you let yourself be cheated by Sam Karoo."

"You think he cheated me? You think eight cows were too many?" A slow smile slid over his lips as I shook my head. "Soon it will be spring festival and I will take my Sarita back to Kiniwata. She wishes to see her father and her friends again. And they can see her. Do you think anyone will make fun of me then?"

"Not likely. But I don't understand. How can she be so different from the way she was described?"

"She has been five months away from Kiniwata. Much has happened to change her. Much in particular happened the day she went away."

"You mean she married you?"

"That, yes. But most of all, I mean the arrangements for the marriage.

"Do you ever think," he asked reflectively, "what it must mean to a woman to know that her husband has met with her father to settle the lowest price for which she can be bought? And then later when all the women talk, as women do, they boast of what their husbands paid for them. One says four cows, another maybe six. How does she feel, the woman who was sold for one or two? This could not happen to my Sarita."

"Then you paid that unprecedented number of cows just to make your wife happy?"

"Happy? I wanted Sarita to be happy, yes. I wanted more than that. You say she's different from the way they remember her in Kiniwata. This is true. Many things can change a woman. Things that happen inside, things that happen outside. But the thing that matters most is what she thinks about herself. In Kiniwata, Sarita believed she was worth nothing. Now she knows she's worth more than any other woman on the island."

"Then you wanted . . ."

"I wanted to marry Sarita. I loved her and no other woman."

"But . . ." I was close to understanding.

"But," he finished softly, "I wanted an eight-cow wife."

—*Patricia McGerr*

QUESTIONS FOR DISCUSSION

1. How does this story involve the expansion of resources?
2. Do you think it is possible to make a "one-cow" person into an "eight-cow" person through the strategy used by Johnny Lingo? Why or why not?
3. Assume that the story can be renamed "Juanita Lingo and the Eight-Cow Husband." What characteristics would a woman wish to see in an "eight-cow husband"?
4. In the United States, do you think there is too much emphasis on the importance of the physical attractiveness of both men and women? Explain.
5. This story has been criticized by some people because it gives the impression that marriage is the most desirable career for women to pursue. Do you agree with this criticism? Why or why not? Do you think in the United States today there is too much emphasis on marriage for women and too little emphasis on other careers? Explain.

LISTENING HELPS YOU HEAR

Listening effectively, so that you really hear what is being said to you, requires *work*. Too often listening is confused with hearing. We may hear voices, music, and other sounds, but we do not record the information in our minds. Listening, as opposed to merely hearing, forces you to concentrate and open up all channels to receive and record the information. Effective listening is actually a *skill* that can be developed over a period of time. In the activities that follow, you will have an opportunity to enhance your listening skills, thereby adding to your personal resources.

ACTIVITY 12

The Classic Telephone

What happens when a message is communicated from one person to the next? What happens when the message is repeated by many people?

Form a large circle.

Your teacher or a classmate has prepared a written message of four or five sentences. It includes details about well-known people, places, and events.

The message is whispered to one student, who will then whisper it to a neighbor, and so on around the circle.

The last person who receives the message repeats it to the entire group.

QUESTIONS FOR DISCUSSION

1. How did the message as repeated by the last person differ from the original version?
2. How might this same thing happen in real life situations?
3. What problems might arise when a message gets scrambled?
4. Can you think of personal examples of scrambled messages?

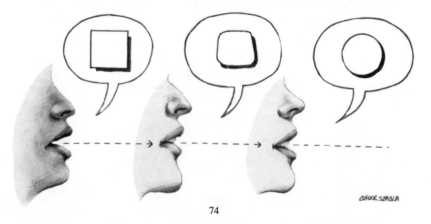

CHUCK SZABLA

ACTIVITY 13

Improving Listening Skills: Non-Verbal Behavior

One way to improve listening skills is to pay attention to non-verbal behavior. Non-verbal behavior includes such things as posture, eye, head, hand, and other kinds of movements, physical distance, silence, and gestures. Anything except words that communicates ideas and feelings to another person can be considered a form of non-verbal communication.

List in JOURNAL NOTES non-verbal actions that would suggest that someone is listening to you.

Do the same for non-verbal actions that suggest that someone is not listening.

Compile the examples of both kinds of behavior suggested by the class. Display both lists on newsprint.

After the lists are compiled, form into groups of four.

One person will talk about something: a problem, an idea, a dream, or an interest.

Listener A will stare at the speaker, using no head movements or any other gestures. If asked a question by the speaker, Listener A will answer with as few words as possible.

Listener B will nod his or her head at appropriate times, lean forward, and use other supportive non-verbal gestures from the "listening" list.

One person will observe.

QUESTIONS FOR DISCUSSION

1. How did the speaker feel while talking to Listener A? Listener B?

2. How did the listeners feel when the speaker was trying to communicate to them?

3. What did the observer observe?

75

ACTIVITY 14

Improving Listening Skills: Verbal Behavior

Here are ways to tell someone in words that you are listening.

- Repeat what is said.
    Speaker: "My parents are always griping about the mess in my room."
    Listener: "Your parents are always griping about the mess in your room."
- Summarize what is said.
    Speaker: "My parents are always griping about the mess in my room."
    Listener: "Your parents always gripe about your messy room."
- Ask questions.
    Speaker: "My boss is about to fire me!"
    Listener: "Why is she unhappy with your work?"
    "How do you know you are about to be fired?"
- Comment, react, give opinions. Postpone your response until you are sure you understand the message.
    Speaker: "My boss is about to fire me!"
    Listener: "I never liked your boss anyway!"
    "Good! Now we can see more of each other!"
    "Not again!"

Working with a partner, practice using these four methods of telling someone in words that you are listening. Try each of the four methods as you respond to the following comments.

1. "I just don't know what to do. I really need a part-time job so that I can get a new winter coat. But I have so much homework I don't have the time. I'm barely passing now!"
2. "I want to break up with Barbara/Bill but I don't want to hurt her/his feelings. It's just that there are other girls/boys I want to attract."

3. "One of my teachers is so boring that he's paralyzing me and everyone else. I don't think he is even aware of our reactions!"

ADDITIONAL LISTENING TIPS

- Silence can be golden.

    You can't listen and talk at the same time.

    Don't rush to respond after a speaker pauses. Often a speaker wishes to continue.

    Don't be threatened by a moment or two of silence. Silence permits thought and may stimulate new ideas.

- When you pick up an emotion, say:

    "You seem (angry, upset, sad, happy)."

    "You're feeling (happy, sad, hurt). Is that right?"

    "Your (voice, eyes, gestures) tell me that you feel (happy, sad, etc.)."

- When verbal and non-verbal messages are mixed, say:

    "You say (yes, no, maybe) but your (eyes, voice, nearness) tells me something else. I'm confused." Note: Remember the song lyric, "Your lips tell me no-no, but there's yes-yes in your eyes."

- When two speakers agree, say:

    "I see some clear agreement between what Ann and Bob are saying."

- When speakers disagree, say:

    "The essential differences between Ann's and Bob's positions are . . . ."

FIGHT OR NEGOTIATE

In any relationship with another person, conflict is possible. Among the common responses to conflict situations are (1) avoiding them; (2) giving in (surrendering) to the other person; (3) fighting (either with words or fists); and (4) negotiating.

Responses one and two are called NON-ASSERTIVE, since they do not maintain or defend one's rights. The others are ASSERTIVE, since they do defend one's rights. We do not recommend fighting as an appropriate response except in extreme situations. That leaves negotiation. How does one negotiate? The chart on the next page describes a sequence of five steps for negotiating conflict situations.

STEPS FOR NEGOTIATING CONFLICT SITUATIONS[9]

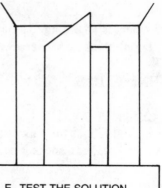

E. TEST THE SOLUTION.
Observe the plan as it is put into action. Revise it if necessary.

D. AGREE ON A SOLUTION.
Make oral agreements, or written ones if necessary.

C. SEEK ALTERNATIVES.
1. Find options that give all parties as much as possible of what they want.
2. Consider "trade-offs" (I'll go to the movie with you tonight if you'll go to the art fair with me Saturday).

B. FIND OUT WHAT EACH PERSON WANTS.
Everyone describes what he/she hopes to achieve if the conflict is removed.

A. IDENTIFY THE CONFLICT SITUATION.
1. Individuals involved describe how they see the conflict situation.
2. The parties then summarize the other person's description of it.
3. No judging or arguing is permitted.

[9]Written especially for *The New Model Me* by Beverly Lund, Guidance Counselor, Riverton Community Unit, School District #14, Riverton, Ill.

ACTIVITY 15

Negotiating Conflict Situations

The statements that follow reflect different conflict situations.

1. Someone of your own age with whom you are friendly appears to be very upset for some reason unknown to you.
2. Someone at school often picks on you, bullies you, or insults you.
3. You have reason to believe that someone at school has been telling an untrue story about you.
4. Your mother, who is tired or distracted, is not listening to something important that you are trying to tell her.
5. You think that your father is unreasonable when you argue with him.
6. You go shopping with your mother to buy some clothes for yourself, but she wants to make all the choices for you.
7. You are laughing at a movie that is supposed to be serious. An elderly man tells you to be quiet.
8. A neighbor complains of the noise you make late at night with your motorcycle or transistor radio.
9. A man pushes past you in line at the supermarket, and the cashier insists on serving him first.
10. The teacher gives the whole class a detention because one student broke a rule.

Form groups of three people, two to role-play, the third to act as observer/reporter. Group members choose three of the above situations or develop their own and take turns role-playing.

As you negotiate, try to follow the negotiation steps:

A. Identify the conflict situation.
B. Find out what each person wants.
C. Seek alternatives.
D. Agree on a solution.
E. Test the solution.

Discuss each role play after it is completed.

ACTIVITY 16

Making Plans for Improving My Resources

The chart below describes skill clusters that you may wish to work to improve. Think carefully about each skill cluster area as you complete the questions in the chart. Answer by giving each area a number from 1 to 10: 1 = very low; 5 = OK; 10 = very high.

Skill Cluster Areas	How Important Is This to Me? (1–10)	How Able Am I Now? (1–10)	What Would I Like My Ability to Be? (1–10)
SPIRITUAL • Religious observance • Morals • Optimism • Concern for others			
HANDIWORK • Building • Repairing • Shaping • Designing			
SOCIAL • Making friends • Entertaining • Making conversation			
INTELLECTUAL • Knowing • Thinking			
ARTISTIC • Musical • Dramatic • Painting/sculpture • Literary			
PHYSICAL • Speed • Strength • Dexterity • Endurance			

DIMINISHING RESOURCES

Resources can also be diminished. Ask yourself:

- How are resources diminished?
- When resources are diminished, what happens to us?
- How can loss of resources be prevented?

> Diminished resources mean lower self-esteem.

There are a number of ways to lose resources. People can slowly or quickly diminish their own resources, or other people can do the job for them.

ACTIVITY 17

How Resources Are Diminished

An individual can lose resources by his own actions or by the actions of others. List some of the ways you think resources can be lost.

THREATS TO SELF-ESTEEM

We will consider some of the ways in which human beings respond to a loss of resources. Let's first look at some losses that do not involve precious resources such as sight, hearing, grasping, or mobility. Remember Cliff Evans in "Cipher in the Snow" in Unit I. He was the victim of a common threat to self-esteem.

LABELS

LABELS can negatively affect a person's self-esteem. An individual who is labeled becomes known by that label. Usually the label

Hi, Beautiful!

What's new, Rocky?

is an ATTRIBUTE (characteristic) that the person supposedly possesses. In the case of Cliff Evans, his label was "dumb." It doesn't appear to make any difference whether the label is justified or accurate. Often the label sticks with an individual into adulthood, possibly in the form of a nickname.

Labels are not always meant to hurt or ridicule. Sometimes the giver intends to have fun or even to compliment the receiver.

It may surprise you to learn that a label may be resented even if it is based on a desirable attribute. Have you ever heard a friend announce that she really hates a nickname that she has carried since childhood? It happens very often!

To experience the response to labeling we have developed the next activity.

ACTIVITY 18

The Labels on Us

This activity requires the cooperation of six volunteers. Each volunteer will be given a sign that will identify him or her by a label, which may be complimentary or uncomplimentary. Each volunteer will wear the sign on his or her back and will not know what is written on it.

If you are a sign-wearer, try to discover your label by observing the behavior of the group toward you.

If you are a member of the group, move around to each sign wearer and behave toward him or her in ways consistent with his or her label. Try *not* to be so obvious that the sign-wearer will instantly recognize the label.

QUESTIONS FOR DISCUSSION

To be answered by sign-wearers:

1. Did you discover what your label was?
2. What clues in the group's behavior helped you to identify how you were labeled?
3. How did you feel about your label?

To be answered by non-sign-wearers:

1. Why did you choose to act as you did?
2. How did it make you feel to act this way?
3. How did your actions make the labeled people react?

Labels
lead ▷ to
killer statements.

KILLER STATEMENTS

KILLER STATEMENTS (also known as put-downs) are destructive statements or gestures directed at someone. They often result in lowered self-esteem. Killer statements can be intentional or unintentional. The recipient judges whether what is said or done is a killer statement, since he or she is the one affected by it.

For Better or For Worse   by Lynn Johnston

ACTIVITY 19

Killer Statements Versus Put-Ups

Use your JOURNAL NOTES to list examples of the killer statements exchanged between any or all of the following groups:

By	Directed To
Males	Females
Females	Males
Sibling (Brothers, Sisters)	Sibling
Parent	Teenager
Teenager	Parent
Teacher	Teacher
Student	Student
Teacher	Student
Student	Teacher
Principal	Teacher
Teacher	Principal

As a contrast, write a second list of statements that *increase* self-esteem. Call these statements "strokes" or "put-ups." Use the same groups, or select from others on the list.

QUESTIONS FOR DISCUSSION

1. Look at the list of put-downs. How would you feel if you were fed a steady diet of them?
2. Now look at the put-ups. How would you feel if your steady diet included nothing but put-ups?
3. How can you and the other members of the class help to decrease put-downs and increase put-ups?

STEREOTYPES

Labels and killer statements can be directed toward groups. A group label is known as a STEREOTYPE.

The word "stereotype" originally referred to a printing plate that, once formed, produces an identical copy over and over and over. When we transfer that meaning to a group of human beings, it means that each member of the group is treated as if he or she had the same attributes as every other member of the group. Since a stereotype is usually a negative label, it can result in a drastic loss of self-esteem.

ACTIVITY 20

Shape Up, Kiddies[10]

AUTHOR
KATHARINE BARRY

Using the PARS Worksheet (number III), read the essay that follows. The author, Katharine Barry, is most upset about the stereotypes she faces every day.

I am a senior citizen and I appreciate to the full the dispensations this inoffensive title authorizes. But . . .

I deeply resent being treated like what I can only describe as an "old baby." As an instance, at a church supper recently, a young woman welcomed me effusively. "Hi, there! What's your name, dear? Nell Gwyn?" (Yes, that's the name I supplied, with instant malice.) "Well, Nellie, I'm sure you're going to enjoy your supper. You look very sweet. Oh, Janie, doesn't Nellie here look sweet? Look at that cute little face. Now, here's a good seat, Nellie. Just stay put, dear. We don't want you getting lost, do we? And don't get too hungry; din-din won't be ready for a few minutes. Well, then, see you later, Nellie. Be good!"

Do you believe that? Yet it happened, it happened. For the record, din-din was anemic chicken casserole and tasted like the first one I ever made as an exuberant bride—rotten.

That's another thing: open a newspaper or a magazine and you're hit with "senior citizens must be taught to cook properly and should also learn which foods are the most wholesome, etc." I try to grin and forget it, but end by grinding my teeth, unwisely. What's wrong with these people that they fail to realize that we are the experienced cooks, the experienced shoppers, and the experienced housekeepers? Haven't we endured years of the blasted routine? Have we never heard of protein or served nourishing meals? Do they suppose we have forgotten? I personally find it embarrassing and humiliating to read that if I go to this or that meeting, Ms. Newcomer will demonstrate the best way to break an egg. These college gals with their newly won master's degrees and swollen egos—how they patronize us hapless "babies." Furthermore, when such a one addresses me by my given name, I cringe. It is not seemly and it is in execrable taste—and I wonder if she really enjoys hearing her own parents called Gladys and Harry by her enthusiastic peers.

Ill-Mannered

The present junior-high generation seems especially ill-mannered. Young women and young men often relinquish their seats to us old ones, but not the younger kids. Stand too near one and more than likely you'll be the recipient of a kick in the shins—by accident, of course. On an escalator not long ago, one small lad in a group behind me suddenly tapped me gently on the head. I frowned mightily, turned around, and asked, "Who did that?" "Who did what? Nobody did nothing, lady." I regret that prudence forbade me to reciprocate.

I find we seniors are pointedly courteous to one another. We seem to be sympathetically aware of hardships endured, and now our hope is for peace, lovely peace. "Old and crotchety?" No, sir and madam, not so: a canard pure and simple, and I'd dearly enjoy venting a little crotchetiness on the benighted nincompoop who first used that expression. Obviously, he (I'm sure it was a he) was old and crotchety and judged others to be the same. I heard that phrase quite recently, and it did bad things to my blood pressure. I like "old and full of wisdom." Or maybe "boldly old," you think?

There are those of gentle heart who continually extend a helping hand to us seniors—and may fortune always smile on them. But, although it's one thing to present a strong right arm to a visibly frail elder at a street crossing, it's a pig in a different poke to grab the elbow of a still-spry and bouncy lad or lassie in his or her 70s or even 80s. A few of our lively ones resent it, and are not happy to appear in need of help, however kindly meant. Ungrateful? Not at all. Just jealous of the ability to function efficiently.

There are a few misguided souls who take advantage of us. I've been sold newspapers folded to conceal torn and wrinkled sections. Later, I imagine the dealer chortling, "An old lady like her just reads the TV section anyway." It doesn't occur to the dear man that I will never—but never—buy another paper from him. Think I'm nit-picking? Not so. The daily newspaper is very important to me, in its entirety. You, sir, would you enjoy an unreadable or missing sports page? And you, Ms., would you like your recipes shredded before you've had a whack at them?

Unflattering
Then there are the big department stores. Employees stand at strate-gic places and courteously ask passing customers, "Do you have a charge account with us?" I have passed and passed again, and not one has ever questioned me. I can only assume they've been told to recognize brown, blond, or streaked hair, but not gray or white. This is not flattering. Nor is it flattering to be ignored by saleswomen offering sample squirts of the latest perfume. I'm no clotheshorse, but neither am I Tugboat Annie. I like to smell nice, too.

Last week at the shopping center there were several pretty girls distributing free cigarette samples. There was also a chap thrusting a leaflet into the hand of each passerby. Smoking is not limited to any specific type, yet I was not offered samples. Nor was I given a leaflet. Angrily amused, I asked for and received both items, startled expres-sions notwithstanding. I gave the cigarettes to a news dealer and understood why I had not been given the leaflet after reading its introduction—"Learn What the Future Has in Store for You." No doubt the clever young fellow snidely assumed my future was practi-cally nonexistent. And maybe it is, but I'll be alive until my last breath, won't I? He looked askance at me as I settled beside him and openly read the entire leaflet, then folded it carefully and tucked it into my pocketbook. I was avenged.

These slights distress me. To belittle the old is destructive and demeaning to us all, whatever age we happen to be. For the years have equipped us senior citizens with a lot of strength, and the sense to tell life's little problems to go climb a tree. We have much to give to the younger generations. Some of us have become less spry, but most of us try our best to stay in the swim. Could more be asked?

I affectionately salute my fellow aged.

—*Katharine Barry*

QUESTIONS FOR DISCUSSION

1. Which of Maslow's needs do you think the author is attempting to satisfy by writing this essay?
2. Name five examples of stereotyping of senior citizens mentioned by the author.
3. Is the author justified in her anger? Why or why not?
4. Are teenagers the victims of stereotypes? Can you list five examples of stereotyping you or friends have experienced?
5. In what ways do you think the author may be guilty of using stereotypes?

ACTIVITY 21

The Enslavement of Masculine and Feminine

How different are men and women? Are stereotypes about each accepted by both groups? Are these stereotypes helpful or harmful?

To examine these questions, complete the following exercise. Be sure to turn it in with your responses. Do not sign it, but do indicate whether you are male or female.

SEX ROLE SURVEY

Check whether you are male or female: ☐ Female ☐ Male

Do you agree or disagree with the following general statements? Indicate your choice by placing a check in the appropriate box to the left of the statement. (If you are not to write in your book, number a sheet of paper from 1 to 8 and write "agree" or "disagree" next to each number. Be sure to indicate your sex at the top of the page.)

Agree   *Disagree*

☐ ☐ 1. Women have a natural desire to give birth to children.

☐ ☐ 2. Men are less emotional than women.

☐ ☐ 3. Turning a quarrel into a violent confrontation is natural for men.

☐ ☐ 4. If the United States and the Soviet Union were led by women, there would be less likelihood of war.

☐ ☐ 5. Women are more tender and loving than men.

☐ ☐ 6. It makes for a better marriage if the husband has a higher income than the wife.

☐ ☐ 7. Women should run the household even if they also work outside the home.

☐ ☐ 8. Men would be better off if they learned to express emotion and even cried occasionally.

QUESTIONS FOR DISCUSSION

1. When the surveys were tabulated, were any male/female differences seen? If so, what accounts for these differences?
2. Are these eight general statements accurate or useful? Or would it be better if we never heard them again?
3. How could a person get into difficulty by applying any of these general statements in a relationship with a particular man or woman?

STEREOTYPING, PREJUDICE, AND OTHER THREATS TO RESOURCES

The most extreme example of suffering because of actions related to stereotyping is found in recent world history. Adolph Hitler, dictator of Nazi Germany from 1933 to 1945, believed that all Jews possessed identical characteristics. To Hitler, Jews were shrewd, crafty, driven by lust for money, and inferior to other German citizens. As a visual

reminder of their status, Jews were required to wear a Star of David sewn onto their clothes. Hitler became so vicious and mentally unbalanced in his behavior toward Jews and other groups he despised that his final solution was to try to rid Europe of them through mass murder. Stereotypes result in PREJUDICE, an opinion arrived at before a thorough examination of the facts of a particular case.

Until now we have been concentrating on direct threats to people's emotional or spiritual resources. Labels, killer statements, stereotypes, and prejudice are obviously threats, and those who use them usually aim to injure individuals or groups. You should be aware of another threat to resources: *unemployment*. Unemployment has become a serious concern for Americans, especially young Americans, blacks and Hispanics, and those Americans who are relatively unskilled. For example, the percentage of young people (18–21 years) who are unemployed is always many times as large as the adult percentage. For black and Hispanic youths, the unemployment rate is often as high as 30 or 40 percent of those actively seeking work. A Congressional report published in 1980 suggests that unemployment will be a continual concern in the 1980s. There will be 15 million new workers competing for available jobs during the 1980s, while available unskilled jobs in manufacturing will actually decline. Some of the 15 million new workers, as well as some of the present workers, will experience a short or long period of unemployment.

ACTIVITY 22

How It Feels to Be
Out of Work[11]

**AUTHOR
JAN HALVORSEN**

In this essay, Jan Halvorsen shares her feelings about the loss of self-esteem, the fear of the future, and the stress and depression that accompany unemployment. Use the PARS System (Worksheet IV) as you read the article.

Layoffs, unemployment, and recession have always affected Walter Cronkite's tone of voice and the editorial page. And maybe they affected a neighborhood business or a friend's uncle. But these terms have always been just words, affecting someone else's world, like a passing ambulance. At least they were until a few weeks ago, when the ambulance came for me.

Even as I sat staring blankly at my supervisor, hearing, "I've got bad news: we're going to have to let you go," it all still seemed no more applicable to my daily life than a "60 Minutes" exposé. I kept

[11]*Newsweek* (September 22, 1980). Copyright 1980 by Newsweek, Inc. All rights reserved. Article and photo reprinted by permission. Since Jan Halvorsen wrote this during four months of unemployment, she has become assistant editor of the *Twin Cities Courier* in St. Paul, Minnesota.

waiting for the alternative—"but you can come back after a couple of months," or "you could take a salary cut, a different position," or even "April fool." But none of these came. This was final. There was no mistake and no alternative.

You find yourself going back over it in your idle moments. There wasn't so much as a "Thank you" for the long nights working alone, the "Sure, no problem, I'll have it tomorrow," the "Let me know if I can help," the "I just went ahead and did it this weekend" and, especially, for the "You forgot to tell me it changed? Oh, that's all right, I'll just do it over. No big deal."

No big deal. How it all echoes through your evenings and awakens you in the morning. The mornings are probably the worst—waking up with the habitual jar, for the first two weeks, thinking, "I'm late!" Late for what? The dull ache in your lower stomach reminds you: late for nothing.

Depression

Again, you face the terms. "Loss of self-esteem and security, fear of the future, stress, depression." You wonder dully if eating a dozen chocolate-chip cookies, wearing a bathrobe until 4, combing your hair at 5, cleaning behind the stove (twice), and crying in an employment-agency parking lot qualify as symptoms of stress or maybe loss of self-esteem. Fighting with your spouse/boyfriend? Aha—tension in personal relationships.

The loss of a job is rejection, resulting in the same hurt feelings as if a friend had told you to "bug off." Only this "friend" filled up 40 to 60 (or more) hours of your week. Constant references to the staff as "family" only accentuate the feeling of desertion and deception. You picture yourself going home to your parents or spouse and being informed, "Your services as our daughter/my wife are no longer required. Pick up your baby pictures as you leave."

Each new affirmation of unemployment renews the pain: the first trip to the employment agency, the first friend you tell, the first interview, and, most dreaded of all, the first trip to the unemployment office.

Standing in line at the unemployment office makes you feel very much the same as you did the first time you ever flunked a class or a test—as if you had a big red "F" for "Failure" printed across your forehead. I fantasize myself standing at the end of the line in a crisp and efficient blue suit, chin up, neat and straight as a corporate executive. As I move down the line I start to come unglued, and a half-hour later, when I finally reach the desk clerk, I am slouching and sallow in torn jeans, tennis shoes, and a jacket from the Salvation Army, carrying my worldly belongings in a shopping bag and unable to speak.

You do eventually become accustomed to being unemployed, in the way you might accept a bad limp. And you gradually quit beating yourself for not having been somehow indispensable—or for not having become an accountant. You tire of straining your memory for possible infractions. You recover some of the confidence that always told you how good you were at your job and accept what the supervisor said: "This doesn't reflect on your job performance; sales are down 30 percent this month."

But each time you recover the hallowed self-esteem, you renew a fight to maintain it. Each time you go to a job interview and give them your best and they hire someone else, you go another round with yourself and your self-esteem. Your unemployment seems to drag on beyond all justification. You start to glimpse a stranger in your rear-view mirror. The stranger suddenly looks like a bum. You look at her with clinical curiosity. Hmmm. Obviously into the chronic stages. Definitely not employable.

We unemployed share a social stigma similar to that of the rape victim. Whether consciously or subconsciously, much of the work-ethic-driven public feels that you've somehow "asked for it," secretly wanted to lose your job and "flirted" with unemployment through your attitude—probably dressed in a way to invite it (left the vest unbuttoned on your three-piece suit).

Satisfaction

But the worst of it isn't society's work-ethic morality; it's your own, which you never knew you had. You find out how much self-satisfaction was gained from even the most simple work-related task: a well-worded letter, a well-handled phone call—even a clean file. Being useful to yourself isn't enough.

But then almost everyone has heard about the need to be a useful member of society. What you didn't know about was the loneliness. You've spent your life almost constantly surrounded by people, in classes, in dorms, and at work. To suddenly find yourself with only your cat to talk to all day distorts your sense of reality. You begin to worry that flights of fancy might become one-way.

But you always were, and still are, stronger than that. You maintain balance and perspective, mainly through resorting frequently to sarcasm and irreverence. Although something going wrong in any aspect of your life now seems to push you into temporary despair much more easily than before, you have some very important things to hang on to—people who care, your sense of humor, your talents, your cat, and your hopes.

And beyond that, you've gained something—a little more knowledge and a lot more compassion. You've learned the value of the routine you scorned and the importance of the job you took for granted. But most of all, you've learned what a "7.6 percent unemployment rate" really means.

—Jan Halvorsen

QUESTIONS FOR DISCUSSION

1. In what ways does the author relate the loss of a job to the loss of self-esteem?
2. Which of the author's resources appeared to help her recover?

SELF-ESTEEM AND PHYSICAL RESOURCES

Self-esteem can be lowered through the loss of physical resources.

The gift of sight is taken for granted unless it is slowly or quickly taken away from us. Sighted people depend on their eyes to gather information about the world around them. This biological miracle is denied to people who have lost the sense of sight.

- What do you think it would be like to be blind?
- How might your other senses assume some of the burdens formerly assumed by your eyes?
- How do you think you would react to the need to depend on others because of blindness?

ACTIVITY 23

The Blind Walk

The purpose of this activity is to experience a world without sight.

Volunteers are needed to work in groups of two.

One person is to walk with eyes closed; the second person is to act as guide during the walk. The person who is "blind" places a hand on the guide's shoulder as they walk.

The guide's responsibility is to assist when needed. Whoever assumes the role of the blind person is to concentrate on his or her emotions—feelings and fears. When the signal is given, the two persons will reverse their roles so that both experience the blind walk.

QUESTIONS FOR DISCUSSION

For "blind" person:

1. What were your reactions as you walked with your eyes closed?
2. What resources other than sight did you use to identify objects and locations?
3. What were your feelings toward your guide? Did you develop a sense of trust? Did you feel comfortable or upset when you became dependent on someone else?

For guide:

1. What were your feelings toward the person who was "blind"?
2. How did you feel about helping a person who was dependent on you?

ACTIVITY 24

A Conversation
with Two Friends

Mitchell Darling is an insurance man who is very active in civic affairs. He is married and has a married daughter and two grandchildren. William Kemmett is a high school mathematics teacher. He is married and has two small children.

Mr. Darling has been blind since he was eight years old, and Mr. Kemmett has been blind since he was three months old.

We talked with them about a number of subjects. The first was their thoughts on being blind.

I. ON BEING BLIND[12]

Interviewer: "What do you recall as your immediate response when you realized that you were blind?"

Mr. Darling: "I don't recall any response except that I could not return to school at the time.

"Youngsters seem to make an easier adjustment to their physical disabilities than their parents do. Parents may say, 'My God! What am I going to do with the problems that I'm going to face in life? What's my son or daughter going to do?' The child, of course, knows nothing about the problems in the years ahead. So he or she takes it day by day."

Mr. Kemmett: "I had a final operation when I was around five. All I could see before that was shadows, and that doesn't put a whole lot in front of you except a light or dark object, and you can't see the object.

---

[12]From interview with Mitchell Darling and William Kemmett, December 17, 1980, Lakewood, Ohio. Used by permission.

"I remember being in the hospital and recall the operation. I remember having a great time in the hospital, but I don't recall having any big traumatic experience of losing sight."

Interviewer: "What would you say has been your response to your blindness over the passage of time?"

Mr. Darling: "I do not recall regretting being blind or ever being depressed by not being able to see. I knew I wasn't going to be able to see, so I decided to do the best I could with what I had."

Mr. Kemmett: "Oh, sometimes I regret not being able to see. I regret that I can't see my children and regret not being able to see my wife.

"Every once in a while I get a fleeting regret and I'll think, 'Oh, gee, if only I could—oh well, I can't. Tough, oh well, I'll just keep going!' I think this is just normal, and probably any blind person gets those feelings every once in a while."

Questions for Discussion

1. What seems to be the attitude of the two men toward their blindness?

2. How do you feel about Mr. Darling's statement that children make an easier adjustment to their physical handicaps than their parents do?

3. Which of Maslow's needs come to your mind as you read "On Being Blind"?

The loss of physical resources creates a condition of dependency. Remember Maslow's "Hierarchy of Needs," discussed in Unit I?

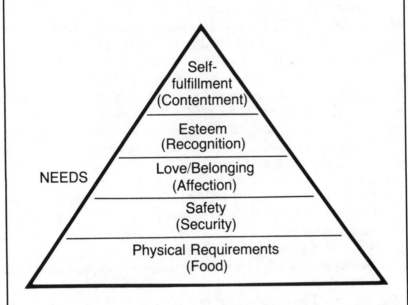

A substantial disability—loss of sight, mobility, or intellectual functioning—could cause a temporary or permanent uncertainty about the satisfaction of physical and safety needs. After all, loss of the use of one or both legs would require substantial changes in life style. Satisfying the need to move about would require extraordinary effort.

A danger in the process of recovery is to become overly dependent—permitting others to do for us what we can accomplish for ourselves. Yet loss of physical resources has to make us somewhat more dependent on others. The dilemma is to satisfy our need for love/belonging without blocking further progress toward self-esteem.

Our two friends, Mr. Darling and Mr. Kemmett, continue their conversation with the interviewer. They discuss their attitudes toward dependency and everyone's need for self-esteem.

II. ON DEPENDENCY[13]

Interviewer: "I'm interested in your attitude toward dependence. Are you comfortable with it, or do you resist being dependent? Or maybe you don't feel dependent!"

Mr. Kemmett: "Well, I'm not real pleased when 'dependent' is used strictly to mean that I'm blind and I need to depend on someone. Every one of us at some time or another has to depend on somebody. If we don't, then we're not human. I depend on people sometimes. For example, I depend on my wife to drive us if we go somewhere in the car."

Mr. Darling: "Of course all of us depend on someone. The only particular dependency I have as far as going somewhere is for someone to drive the automobile."

Mr. Kemmett: "I don't like to have to depend on people to do things for me. I try to do them myself if I can. If I can't do them, I won't hesitate to ask for help. Everyone ought to ask for help—if they need it. One of the big problems I find in teaching is that kids won't ask for help. They are afraid people are going to think they are stupid. If we can all get over that, the world will be a much better place."

Mr. Darling: "I think this matter of dependency is pretty much due to a person's attitude. Somebody asked me some time ago if I would rather be referred to as blind or as sightless. I said, 'Frankly it doesn't make any difference because I can't see either way.'"

Interviewer: "Do you think your attitudes about dependency may have changed over the years?"

Mr. Kemmett: "No! My mother, God rest her soul, was a lady who came down on you if you didn't do it. She'd say that there's nobody else who is going to do it for you. Consequently, I've done things for myself from when I was a young child to now. I've not expected somebody else to do it for me."

Mr. Darling: "Bill was fortunate in having a mother with that attitude. My mother and father had the same attitude."

Mr. Kemmett: "There are a lot of blind people around who use their parents to shelter them. Some blind people almost have a chip on their shoulder and feel like the world owes them. The world owes them nothing."

[13]Ibid. Used by permission.

Mr. Darling: "Blindness is a tragedy, but a worse tragedy can be the poor attitude of the parents toward the blind youngster. That is where the disability becomes a handicap."

Mr. Kemmett: "Blindness isn't the chief disability. It's the attitude."

Mr. Darling: "I think that's true with other disabled people—physically handicapped, mentally retarded, otherwise. The attitude of their parents toward them is so significant!"

Questions for Discussion

1. What resources do you think Mr. Darling and Mr. Kemmett use to substitute for their lack of sight?
2. Why do you think the need is so strong for Mr. Kemmett, Mr. Darling, and all the rest of us to be independent of others?
3. What do you think of this statement by Mr. Kemmett: "Every one of us at some time or another has to depend on somebody. If we don't, then we're not human."
4. How do you feel about asking for help when you need it?
5. What can be done to help parents and others develop more positive attitudes toward persons with disabilities?

III. ON SELF-ESTEEM[14]

Interviewer: "What ideas about self-esteem would you want to share with high school students?"

Mr. Darling: "You're talking about our self-image, which changes over many, many years. When I did something well as a high school student many years ago, my self-esteem increased. Our estimate of our own worth can be too high, or it can be too low. Sometimes we need to take ourselves by the collar. I meet people without sight who are way out in front in doing this. But they didn't have all the opportunities that I had. Meeting these people helps me find myself."

Mr. Kemmett: "You should feel good about yourself. Your self should be important to you. If it's not important to you, it's not going to be important to anyone else. If you don't feel good about yourself, there are some people around who will try to help you feel

[14]Ibid. Used by permission.

good about yourself. I can tell when my students don't feel good about themselves.''

Interviewer: "How do you sense when students don't feel good about themselves? I'm interested in that.''

Mr. Kemmett: "Again, it's all in attitude. These people seem to have a sour type of attitude toward life.''

Interviewer: "What kinds of things do you do as a teacher that you think help students' self-esteem grow?''

Mr. Kemmett: "Being available and able to talk with them when they need help. To be more than willing to take a day out of mathematics to talk about life. To show them that just because I'm blind doesn't mean that I'm not human. It takes them a couple of days, but they all of a sudden understand that . . . usually quicker than their parents do.''

Interviewer: "How do you feel about today's youth?''

Mr. Kemmett: "Students are great. Today's youth are really OK. If you're fair with someone, they're going to be fair back to you. I stress that with my students. If they ever think I'm not fair with them, they tell me and we work it out. Consequently, they are fair with me. They don't try to get away with a lot of stuff just because I can't see them. It's just really nice how things work out when people treat each other as human beings.''

Mr. Darling: "I think that Bill is saying that he looks at his students as unique people with individual talents and skills. He gives a part of himself to those students to make those talents and skills a little better.''

Questions for Discussion

1. What unique self-esteem problems might a blind person have?
2. Why do you think Mr. Kemmett's students don't take advantage of him and try to get away with things?
3. What do you think Mr. Darling means by our need to "take ourselves by the collar'' every once in a while?
4. Now that you have heard these two men, which of their characteristics do you sense have especially contributed to their success in life?

DEPENDENCE VERSUS INDEPENDENCE

It's a fact of human existence that the dilemma of INDEPEN-DENCE/DEPENDENCE never leaves us. At birth, infants are almost totally dependent on their mothers; within months the growing child begins the journey toward independence. As teenagers, you are in the midst of a struggle for independence. No doubt you are irritated when adults remind you that they are responsible for your behavior and that until you become independent you must obey them. Have you ever been told:

> Don't forget your coat!
> Clean up your room! It's a pigsty!
> Don't you dare come home after 12:00!

Bear in mind as you slowly rise to anger that much of your present teenage dependence will disappear as you reach adulthood. If you doubt this, remember how the father's and son's needs were reversed in the "Cat's Cradle" lyrics in Unit I! Signs of a turn toward more independence are:

- assuming responsibility for important tasks at home
- being responsible for valuable property—stereo, jewelry, automobile
- holding a part-time or full-time job
- living away from home
- dating, engagement, marriage, motherhood/fatherhood

When the milestones in your life are achieved, the kind of dependence that goes with growing will disappear. It will, that is, unless you join the small group of youths who remain dependent until it becomes unhealthy. Warning signs of this condition are:

- permitting your resources to remain low
- having nothing you value
- making no plans for tomorrow, next year, the rest of your life
- fearing to make even the most trivial of decisions
- frequent episodes of blaming others when you are at fault
- often feeling powerless and inadequate
- using drugs, alcohol, or tobacco to excess

THE PRAYER OF THE STUDENT[15]
Lord,
with your guidance
and with the guidance of parents, teachers,
    counselors, friends, and books
I have learned to guide myself.

How much more important I am
than calculus, chemistry, and phys. ed.
I have learned much of these,
and I have enjoyed discoveries in these areas—
    they have helped to make me what I am.
But how much more wonderful it is
    to begin to discover myself.

I can learn by studying,
    but I can also learn by living.
Lord, thank you for life.
I will always be a student.

—Kyle Koehler

[15]From *Prayers from the Classroom*, collected by Charles R. Keller, edited by Evelyn M. Copeland. Written during the senior year at Moorestown High School, New Jersey. Reprinted with permission.

ACTIVITY 25

Diminishing Resources, Dependence, and Death

Thinking about dying is not one of our most pleasant daydreams. Yet death will someday claim those closest to us, and eventually we, too, will die. As we age, our bodies age as well. After reaching the age of 40, an individual wages a constant battle to maintain health. After 70 the loss of physical and mental skills accelerates. If we live on to a ripe old age, we will experience dependency again. For some of us, this dependency may take us back to the days of our childhood.

A few years ago, a family recorded through photographs and journal notes the three-year deterioration of their grandfather, which ended in his death at 81. Prior to death, "Gramp" Tugend experienced a severe case of senility (old age deterioration). The symptoms of senility, which grew worse at the very end, included:

- loss of memory
- inability to recognize family members
- inability to shave, dress, or eat without assistance
- strange behavior and dress
- sleeping during the day, tearing up his room at night
- loss of desire to maintain personal hygiene
- loss of control of bodily functions

As you would guess, Gramp required care around the clock by family members. Friends and neighbors, embarrassed by the sights, sounds, and smells at the Tugends', chose to stay away. Facing all of these difficulties, the family nevertheless decided that Gramp would remain at home rather than be placed in a nursing home.

When Gramp died, the moment was recorded by one of the grandchildren:

"Gramp finally lapsed into a very deep sleep. For nine or ten hours he didn't move. I was sitting in the room with him, lost in my own thoughts, when suddenly he became very animated. His arms began moving and he emitted a low moan. I went out into the kitchen and said to Nan [Gramp's wife], 'I am positive that I witnessed the spirit or life force, or whatever, leaving Gramp's body.'"[16]

Gramp's obituary appeared in the *Scranton Tribune* on March 5, 1974.

Frank C. Tugend

Frank C. Tugend, Glenburn, Clark's Summit RD 2, died Monday night at home after a long illness. He was the husband of the former Anna M. Schmidt.

Born in Scranton, a son of the late John and Elizabeth Barth Tugend, he had retired after 54 years as hoisting engineer for the Glen Alden and Moffat Coal Cos. Mr. Tugend was a member of Dalton United Methodist Church and the United Mine Workers of America.

Other survivors are two daughters, Miss Florence Tugend, at home, and Mrs. Anna Jury, New Haven, Ind.; a brother, Albert Tugend, Taylor, Pa.; two sisters, Mrs. Joseph Fontinell, and Miss Ann Tugend, Berlin, N.J., and four grandchildren and four great-grandchildren and several nieces and nephews.

The funeral will be conducted Friday at 2 p.m. from the George Ondrick Funeral Home, 108 N. Abington Road, Clark's Green. The Rev. Earle Cowden, Dalton United Methodist Church, will officiate. Interment, Fairlawn Cemetery, Dalton. Viewing, Thursday, 7 to 9 p.m.

—The Scranton Tribune
March 5, 1974

[16]Mark and Dan Jury, *Gramp* (New York: Grossman, 1976). Copyright © 1975, 1976 by Mark and Daniel Jury. All rights reserved. Reprinted with permission.

QUESTIONS FOR DISCUSSION

1. What needs would be satisfied if Gramp remained at home until he died?
2. What needs would be satisfied if Gramp were placed in a nursing home until he died?
3. What do you think of the family's decision to have Gramp at home until he died?
4. How do you think Gramp felt as he lost his physical and mental resources? How do you think he felt as he became increasingly dependent?
5. Have you experienced the death of a family pet, or worse, the loss of a family member? If so, how did you feel when it occurred?
6. Someone has said that the "death of a person is not as terrible for the deceased as it is for the loved ones who have to live on alone." Do you agree or disagree? Why or why not?

MOVING ON TO VALUES

Resources can be increased or diminished. Now on to values.

> **Resources support values.**

Human beings use resources to support values. Values are things human beings think are worthy, good, and important. CONCRETE things—things that can be seen and touched—can be valued. We can value

- family
- friends
- automobiles
- stereo systems
- antiques

Ideas can also be valued. We call ideas ABSTRACT because they are created in our minds and explain things in our world that we cannot touch or see. We can value

- God
- freedom
- love
- quality
- justice

ACTIVITY 26

What Do I Value? Where Did the Values Come From?

Excluding people, list five concrete things that you value. Indicate their source (where or from whom you learned to value the object). Then list five ideas that you value. As before, indicate the source of each value. Be prepared to share your chart with others.

	VALUE	SOURCE
Concrete things:	1.	1.
	2.	2.
	3.	3.
	4.	4.
	5.	5.
Ideas:	1.	1.
	2.	2.
	3.	3.
	4.	4.
	5.	5.

QUESTIONS FOR DISCUSSION

1. How do your values compare with others' values?
2. How do the sources of your values compare with others' sources?

WHERE DO WE GET OUR VALUES?

Although each of us has unique attributes, we discover our values as we come into increasing contact with other human beings. No doubt the family, even in our complex world, remains the single most important source of values. As children we observe and listen to our parents, grandparents, and older brothers and sisters, and we absorb what they believe is good, worthy, and important.

If we attend church regularly, religious teaching becomes a source of values. When we begin school, we learn from teachers and schoolbooks. Furthermore, our friends and acquaintances (peer group) begin to have an influence on us and our values.

One of the facts of life today is that TRADITIONAL sources of values—family, church or synagogue, school—are now facing increasing competition for our attention and loyalty. Through television, newspapers, films, and records, we learn what celebrities believe is good, worthy, and important. We are constantly being introduced to new ideas about every aspect of our lives. In contrast to the ideas obtained in the family, the church, and the school, these new ideas often promise—although they rarely deliver—quick solutions to life's problems with little or no confusion or frustration.

At the same time competition is increasing, our traditional sources of values are under attack. The family unit, which a hundred years ago was both emotionally and geographically close, is changing. The number of Americans living in a traditional family—father working, mother a homemaker, children at home—amounts to a mere 15 percent of the population. The number of two-parent working families has been increasing at a phenomenal rate. There has been an increasing trend toward divorce and single-parent families. In the United States there are now 12 million or more children under the age of 18 whose parents are divorced. Psychologists who specialize in the troubles that stem from divorce suggest that only the death of a parent is more serious to the child than a divorce. The stress and confusion that result from divorce can have very serious effects on a child's satisfaction of needs. You may recall from "Cipher in the Snow" in Unit I that Cliff Evans's resources began to diminish after his parents were divorced.

As family influence has been reduced, so has the influence of organized religion. A Gallup political opinion poll in 1980 discovered that teenagers are clearly divided about the impact of religion on their lives. Fifty-seven percent of the teens questioned responded that religion can be an effective answer to today's problems. In contrast, 32 percent of the teens responded that they believe religion is outdated. A second Gallup survey, which investigated the influence of the Ten Commandments on U.S. teenagers, found that 79 percent of the young people questioned believe that the Commandments are still valid rules to guide one's life today. The problem is that only 35 percent of those surveyed could name five or more Commandments. Only three teens in 100 could name all of the Ten Commandments.

American schools have long been uncertain about their place in teaching values. Recently the issue has sparked a widespread and often angry debate. Some people believe that schools have no business teaching young people what is good, worthy, and important. They argue that schools have enough to do to teach students to read and write effectively and to compute well enough to perform everyday tasks. Others believe that schools should teach values, but only those that are supported by most parents in the local community. Yet a third group suggests that the school should be a forum where young people clarify their own values by studying issues, looking at alternatives and consequences, and, finally, making decisons.

Where does THE NEW MODEL ME stand? We think the school is an important agent for values education. Whether openly or without notice, schools do teach values. Although each school has its own blend, all schools teach the value of learning, delayed rewards, maturity, decision making, obedience, punctuality, responsibility, and respect. These values become standards by which behavior is judged.

We also believe that schools should teach that all values are *not* equal. Negotiation and compromise are more consistent with American ideals than violence. Behavior reached through use of the BEHAVIOR EQUATION—

$$\text{Needs} + \text{Resources} + \begin{array}{c} \text{Immediate} \\ \text{Physical} \\ \text{Setting} \end{array} = \begin{array}{l} \text{Behavior (with} \\ \text{immediate} \\ \text{and remote} \\ \text{consequences)} \end{array}$$

—is preferable to behavior based upon emotions or impulse or whim.

Decisions should also be examined in schools. Decisions reached

- through debate
- by majority rule
- with respect for the rights of the minority

are preferable to decisions made by the privileged few.

VALUES AND BEHAVIOR

Behavior must also pass a test in school classrooms:

> Our behavior should promote the
> **DIGNITY AND WORTH OF HUMAN BEINGS.**

Behavior that takes advantage of others for personal gain does not pass the test. Behavior that attempts to divide society into competing camps and increases hate and prejudice is destructive of dignity. Behavior that diminishes an individual's or group's resources does not promote dignity. On the other hand, behavior that enhances self-esteem, that improves resources, that enlarges the rights of others, and that promotes cooperation also promotes the dignity and worth of human beings.

How do people get to practice such behavior? Urie Bronfenbrenner points out that

>"In the United States it is now possible for a person eighteen years of age, female as well as male, to graduate from high school, college, or university without ever having cared for, or even held, a baby; without ever having looked after someone who was old, ill, or lonely; or without ever having comforted or assisted another human being who really needed help. The psychological consequences of such a deprivation of human experience are as yet unknown. But the possible social implications are obvious, for—sooner or later, and usually sooner—all of us suffer illness, loneliness, and the need for help, comfort, or companionship. No society can long sustain itself unless its members have learned the sensitivities, motivations, and skills involved in assisting and caring for other human beings."[17]

[17]Urie Bronfenbrenner, *The Ecology of Human Development* (Cambridge, Ma.: Harvard University Press, 1979).

ACTIVITY 27
Caring for Others

How are you doing in caring for others? In the spaces provided, give the name of the person you cared for and write a brief description of what you did and why you did it.

	Who?	What Did You Do?	Why Did You Do It?
Baby			
Elderly person			
Ill person			
Someone who needed help			

PERSONAL VALUES

Next you will get to examine your PERSONAL VALUES—the values that you believe are good, worthy, and important.

ACTIVITY 28

Identity Auction

You have just won $5,000 in a state lottery! So has everyone in your class. Since you have unlimited wants and limited resources, an auction is planned.

Use your JOURNAL NOTES to list five things you would like to do or to be in the next few years. You may wish to vacation in the South of France, own a small farm, be a ballet star, or build automobiles. Give the list to your teacher.

Your teacher will give you back a list of everything the members of the class have said they want to do or be. Look over the list carefully and select some things you would like to do or be. All items will be put up for auction. You may use all, part, or none of the $5,000 to bid for these items, with the high bid receiving each item. Plan your purchases with care. Ask yourself, "Which thing do I value the most? How much will I be willing to bid to get it?" If your money is exhausted, you cannot bid any more. At the end of the auction, make a list of everything you purchased.

QUESTIONS FOR DISCUSSION

1. Did you pay more for something than you had planned?
2. Did you *not* buy something that you had listed for purchase? Did you buy something that was not on your original list?
3. Are you pleased with your purchases?
4. Given your selected purchases, what can we say about what you think is worthy, good, and important?

ACTIVITY 29

Fifteen Things I Like to Do

The directions for completing this chart are on page 122. Use your JOURNAL NOTES to record your responses.

Things I Would Enjoy Doing	I	II	III	IV	V
1.					
2.					
3.			ⱻ		
4.					
5.					
6.					
7.					
8.					
9.					
10.					
11.					
12.					
13.					
14.					
15.					
16.					
17.					
18.					
19.					
20.					

Under "Things I Would Enjoy Doing," first list 15 things that you *have done* and enjoy; then list 5 things (from 16–20) that you have *not yet done* but think you would enjoy.

In Column I, put an *x* next to activities that your mom or dad would have on their lists.

In Column II, put an *x* next to activities that you have learned to value in the past five years.

In Column III, place a date to tell the last time you did the activity. If you have never done the activity, list the date when you might reasonably expect to do it.

In Column IV, put an *A* beside each activity that you would do alone, and a *P* beside each activity that you would do with other people.

In Column V, rank-order your five most enjoyable activities. Place a *1* next to the most enjoyable, and so on.

QUESTIONS FOR DISCUSSION

1. What do your activities tell you about your values?
2. How do your valued activities differ from those of your parents? How are they similar?
3. Have your activities changed over the last five years? Are there any changes between five years ago and now in your activities or in those activities you have not done but would enjoy?
4. How many of your activities require money? How will you accumulate resources to enable you to do what you enjoy?

COMMUNITY VALUES

PERSONAL VALUES are important, but so are COMMUNITY VALUES. The term "community" is meant to include a group of human beings in a geographical region who share common goals, interests, and values. The term can be used to describe a school community or a political, economic, or social community, from a town to a large city, state, or nation. Obviously the larger the community,

the more difficult it is to determine what it believes is worthy, good, and important.

HOW COMMUNITY VALUES ARE DETERMINED

Learning what the community values is a difficult process. In the United States we vote for public officials and for public issues. Public opinion polling is another vehicle to gather information from community members. A third method is a public debate, such as the one between former President Carter and Ronald Reagan during the presidential election campaign of 1980. These are more formal methods. Less formal methods include listening to discussions in hair styling shops and to radio talk shows, and reading the "Letters to the Editor" section in newspapers and magazines.

ACTIVITY 30

Interpreting
Community Values

Gathering information about community values is easy; making sense of the information (interpreting it) is more difficult. To aid you as you listen to or read about community values, we will present five strategies to improve your ability to interpret the information you get. This activity will acquaint you with the five strategies; the next three activities will give you a chance to apply them.

We will assume that the information relates to a PUBLIC POLICY ISSUE. A public policy is a plan of action to allocate (distribute) community resources to support a value. Regardless of whether the information is presented through formal or informal means, these strategies can be helpful as you attempt to interpret it.

1. WATCH THE PHRASING

Strategy #1 is: *Watch the way the public policy issue is phrased.* The way a policy issue is phrased colors the way it is received by the audience. To illustrate this, consider the following alternative phrasings of a policy issue—the drafting of women into the armed forces.

1. Should women be required to serve their country in the armed forces?
2. Should women be required to serve (alongside men) in the armed forces?

The second phrasing opens up the possibility that women might serve as combat personnel. When "alongside men" is inserted, the issue becomes more controversial and thereby less likely to gain approval from the public. Actually both debaters may view the issue in the same way, but the phrasing of the policy question can affect the public's opinion on the issues.

Here is a second example involving a different issue:

1. Should children be bussed across town to provide more racial balance in the schools?
2. Should children be bussed across town to remedy past discrimination by school officials?

Again, reactions to the issue are affected by the way it is phrased. The second example is more likely to gain approval from the public than the first.

2. IDENTIFY THE VALUE DILEMMAS

Strategy #2 is: *Identify the value dilemmas within the public policy issue.* You may recall the activities "A Renewed Chance for Life" and "Medical Board" in Unit I. Both involved public policy issues. Both imply the same value dilemma. Recall that a dilemma is a situation in which two or more of your values are in competition. In supporting one value, you are forced to reject others. For example:

Issue	*Value Dilemma*
Who should be given an opportunity to survive and lead a normal life?	Equal opportunity for all *versus* selection of the people who are the most worthy candidates
Issue	*Value Dilemma*
Should women be drafted into the armed forces?	All Americans should sacrifice *versus* women have been and should be protected by men
Issue	*Value Dilemma*
Should bussing be used to improve the racial balance in our schools?	Integration of races, social classes, and ethnic groups is desirable in a democratic society *versus* children ought not to suffer to remedy past discrimination by adults

3. SELECT YOUR VALUE STANDARD

Strategy #3 is: *Select your VALUE STANDARD*. A standard is a rule or test to use in determining whether you are willing to support a policy decision. Standards can be highly specific and relate to only one kind of dilemma. For example, if you are against abortion except in cases of rape, you have a standard to use in judging abortion policy. Or, if you support government-sponsored health insurance provided the patient can select the doctor and the hospital, you have a standard to judge one issue in the health field.

Obviously it would be impractical to list all the possible standards in every public policy field. Yet two standards are so general that they can apply to every public policy issue.

Standard A: Protect the community	Standard B: Protect the individual
The highest concern is the welfare of the community.	The highest concern is the welfare of the individual.

- Every person is one, and no one is more than one.
- The right decision is the one that will produce the greatest benefit to the members of the community.
- In the unhappy case where one must choose between alternatives both of which are largely harmful, the choice is the one that promises the least harm as compared to the benefits.
- Immediate and certain consequences are to be given greater weight than those that are remote and uncertain.

- Each individual has certain rights that cannot be taken away even for the welfare of the community.
- Individuals should not be sacrificed in pursuit of what is best for the community.
- When uncertain, select the decision whose *worst* possible outcome is better than the worst possible outcome of the alternative.
- Even supporters of the "protect the community" standard will reject it when they are called upon to sacrifice to protect the community.

Questions for Discussion

1. Think of a public policy issue. Is your support of one side or the other consistent with protection of the community or protection of the individual?
2. Can you think of a public policy issue in the United States or elsewhere that has been defended by a community protection position? Can you think of a public policy decision that has been defended by an individual protection standard?

4. SEPARATE FACTS FROM VALUES

Strategy #4 is: *Separate FACTUAL STATEMENTS from VALUE STATEMENTS*. Can you distinguish between factual statements and value statements? Often in a debate there is confusion about whether a statement is a fact or something the speaker wishes or desires because he or she believes it is worthy, good, and important. Most factual statements can be checked for accuracy. They can be verified as true or false, or right or wrong. Here are examples of factual statements about public policy issues:

- Capital punishment reduces violent crime.
- The United States has permitted its armed forces to decline in strength in the last 10 years.
- The federal budget for education has increased more than 100 percent in the last 20 years.
- Prolonged smoking of marijuana increases health risks.
- In the United States over the last 10 years, health costs have increased at a greater rate than costs for housing, education, and food.

Bear in mind that all statements claimed as facts may not necessarily be facts. But we know we can find out if they are true through commonly accepted methods: experimentation, questioning witnesses, examination of documents, and so on.

Value statements, on the other hand, cannot be verified as true or false. Value statements imply that something is good, worthy, and important. We may agree or disagree with the worth of a value, but it is inappropriate to argue about whether a value is true or untrue. The following statements imply a preference for a value:

- Capital punishment should be opposed because it is wrong to take a human life.
- The United States should be the most powerful nation on earth.
- The federal budget for education should be increased.
- Smoking marijuana is immoral.

5. WEIGH THE LOGIC AND EVIDENCE

Strategy #5 is: *Determine the LOGIC of the arguments and the WEIGHT OF THE EVIDENCE.* After we have identified the value dilemmas involved in a debate and distinguished between factual and value statements, we are ready to score the debate. We will not consider here the ability of each debater to communicate with the audience. Instead we will emphasize the importance of the arguments the speaker or writer makes. An argument is a statement that a speaker makes to prove a point. An argument consists of evidence and its relationship to the point under consideration. To illustrate an argument, let's turn to an article on drug abuse that makes the following assertions:

> The use of drugs among youngsters is frightening (a point the speaker wishes to make).
> It can reduce sperm counts in men, and it can cause irregularity in menstrual cycles in women. It has caused structural changes in animal brains, and it has been shown to impair memory and physical coordination (evidence).

Is the point that the use of drugs is frightening clearly and closely related to the evidence? If so, then the author's LOGIC (the reasoning of the argument) is effective and should be so judged. Is the WEIGHT (the amount) OF EVIDENCE sufficient to convince you (recognizing that only one side has been heard from) that the use of drugs is frightening?

People who judge an argument must be careful listeners or readers if they are to determine the logic of the argument and the weight of evidence that supports it. Imagine yourself as a juror in a highly emotional murder trial. Do you think you could assess the conflicting arguments and evidence being introduced by the prosecution and the defense?

What really matters is the name you succeed in imposing on the facts—not the facts themselves.[18]
—*Professor Jerome Cohen, Harvard Law School*

Let's apply the strategies to some controversial public policy issues.
As you investigate the issues in the next three activities:

1. Watch the way the public policy issue is phrased.
2. Identify the value dilemmas within the public policy issue.
3. Select your value standard.
4. Separate factual statements from value statements.
5. Determine the logic of the arguments and the weight of the
   evidence.

[18]Quoted in *Time*, June 7, 1971.

ACTIVITY 31

Identifying Value Statements and Factual Statements

Examine the following information taken from an article, "Parents Must Fight Child Drug Abuse," by Craig Hitchcock, which appeared in the *Cleveland Press* on October 16, 1980. In the space next to each statement, indicate whether it is a factual (F) or a value (V) statement. (If you are not to write in your book, use a separate sheet of paper for your answers. Number your paper 1 through 5 and write your answers next to the numbers.)

_____ 1. One in every four youngsters over 15 smokes marijuana regularly; one in 10 smokes it daily; and the total number of daily users of marijuana has doubled since 1975.

_____ 2. Marijuana causes more damage to lungs than tobacco.

_____ 3. Parents must renew their efforts to work with schools, professional agencies, and local governments to combat drug abuse.

_____ 4. Parents and their children are not equal, and that is good!

_____ 5. Parents have to take positions and learn how to hold them against the dickering, the blackmail, and other tactics youngsters use to get their way.

Statements 1 and 2 are factual. Statement 1 can be checked through analysis of existing statistical information. Statement 2 can be verified through observation and experimentation.

Statements 3, 4, and 5 are value statements. A useful way of identifying value statements is to try to insert "should" or "ought" into the statement. If it doesn't substantially alter the meaning, then the expression probably is a value statement.

ACTIVITY 32

For and Against Capital Punishment

The death of a Utah prisoner before a firing squad on January 17, 1977, marked the first criminal execution in the United States by a governmental unit in almost 10 years.

In June 1972 the Supreme Court of the United States ruled that the death penalty laws in many states were arbitrary (not uniformly applied; that is, some judges gave it, others did not) and, therefore, often resulted in "cruel and unusual punishment" in violation of the Eighth Amendment to the U.S. Constitution. The court stated that judges and juries had too much discretion in deciding who should be permitted to live and who should die.

But the court also said that capital punishment itself was not cruel and unusual punishment. It thereby left the door open for states to rewrite their capital punishment laws. As the various states have rewritten their laws, the Supreme Court has made individual rulings as to whether it is now permissible for a state to enforce the death penalty.

Whether or not the United States should allow the death penalty is a major community value dilemma for society to resolve. Arguments for and against the death penalty are listed below.

For Capital Punishment

1. Punishment should fit the crime.
2. Statistics do not show that a higher percentage of persons in minority groups who are convicted are also executed.
3. The writers of the Constitution did not mean to exclude the death penalty, which certainly was usual in their day.
4. Many capital crimes are committed by irrational persons. No penalty can deter the irrational. But penalties do influence those who are rational enough to be influenced.

5. There are repeated references in the Bible to the use of the death penalty as an approved form of justice.
6. There is no evidence that the majority of Americans now regard the death penalty as cruel.

Against Capital Punishment

1. Capital punishment does not prevent crime.
2. The purpose of the death penalty cannot be achieved when it is so rarely and unpredictably used.
3. The worst and most dangerous criminals are rarely the ones executed.
4. Reverence for life applies not just to innocent persons but also to the guiltiest.
5. The death penalty deprives a person of his right to forgiveness and excuses society from its responsibility to rehabilitate.
6. The death penalty is representative of everything that is brutal and futile in our present system of criminal justice.

Keeping all these arguments in mind, imagine that a relative of one of your classmates has just taken office as a state senator. In his or her

first term, the issue of capital punishment is certain to be debated. In fact, a bill has already been prepared. It reads:

"Death is the penalty for any of the following crimes committed in this state:

1. murder of a police officer, a corrections officer, or a fireman on duty
2. murder by a hired killer
3. murder by the malicious use of a bomb
4. murder by a person previously convicted of murder
5. murder by any person imprisoned for life
6. murder committed during a rape
7. murder resulting from the hijacking of any public vehicle
8. multiple slayings
9. murder of a public official"[19]

Apply the strategies to the issue.

1. Watch the way the issue is phrased.
2. Identify the value dilemmas within the issue.
3. Select your value standard.
4. Separate value statements from factual statements.
5. Determine the logic of the arguments and the weight of the evidence.

In your JOURNAL NOTES write a letter to the new senator, expressing your views on the capital punishment bill.

[19]From Paul Harvey, "The Death Penalty Should Be Restored," *Human Events* (July 28, 1973). Reprinted with permission.

ACTIVITY 33

Guns Versus Butter

Six hundred billion dollars! ($600,000,000,000.) That was the yearly income of the national government in fiscal year 1980–81. (The fiscal year ran from October 1, 1980 to September 30, 1981.) Most of this income comes from the taxes we pay. How that income is spent by the government is the major problem that elected officials and their staffs confront in their daily tasks.

The decisions about how the federal income is to be spent reflect the needs, resources, and values of the people who represent us in government. There is often disagreement. One of the key points of this disagreement has been whether more should be spent on military and related programs or on programs that directly help people in their daily lives. This is usually called the "guns versus butter" debate.

This activity will involve you in a public policy debate about guns versus butter. It will allow you to examine what one does with an enormous amount of money. It will help you to understand how your values compare with the values of the community.

Listed on the accompanying chart are categories of federal programs. One of these categories, defense, obviously belongs in the guns group. Defense includes programs for the Army, Navy, Marines, and Air Force, their personnel, weapons, equipment, and facility costs. Veterans' benefits, also in the guns group, include insurance, health, and education for military personnel after they leave the service. Two other programs have both guns and butter characteristics: international affairs, economic and military aid and science, space, and technology. The remaining seven categories are in the butter group. Next to each category are the billions of dollars that were designated for each of the programs in the 1980–81 national budget. In 1980–81, these 11 categories of programs were given a total of $500 billion, which is about five-sixths of the total budget.

Assume that, as the President's budget director, you must prepare next year's budget to present to the President for his approval before it is submitted to Congress. He has asked you to rank the budget categories according to how the programs qualify as good, worthy, and important ("1" is most important; "11" is least important). Fill in this ranking in the appropriate column in the chart. Then indicate in the last column (next year's budget column) how much of the $500 billion you would give to each category.

Budget Categories	Guns or Butter	Amount in 1980–81 Budget (in billions of dollars)	Your Rank Order	Amount You Will Allot in 198__–198__ Budget (in billions of dollars)
Defense: military needs, Army, Navy, Marines, Air Force	Guns	136		
Veterans' benefits	Guns	22		
International affairs, economic and military aid	Guns and Butter	9		
Science, space, and technology	Guns and Butter	6		
Medicare, other health programs	Butter	58		
Aid to agriculture (e.g., price-support program, research, future farmers)	Butter	4		
Public assistance, food stamps, and other aid	Butter	55		
Education, manpower, social service programs	Butter	31		
Aid to transportation, business	Butter	20		
Energy and environment	Butter	21		
Social security benefits (e.g., aid to elderly, widows, and orphans and disability insurance)	Butter	138		
Total		500		500

QUESTIONS FOR DISCUSSION

1. Given your decisions about next year's budget, where would you place yourself on the following continuum line? Be prepared to explain and defend your judgment.

Guns_____Butter

2. Assume you are a member of Congress. Suppose that a new President recommends that Congress increase the defense budget by $30 billion. His public policy position is as follows:

   "Since the Soviet Union during the last 15 years has increased its spending on defense needs to a greater extent than the United States has, a dangerous situation has developed. The United States must now catch up. I propose that we spend an additional $30 billion in the next year on our defense needs. No new revenue can be expected; therefore you will have to decide which areas of the budget to reduce in order not to increase the total budget."

   Defend or attack the President's position in writing. Be sure to recognize value statements and factual statements. Be aware of the logic of your arguments and the weight of evidence.

ACTIVITY 34

Let's Plan a Wedding

This last activity will enable you to apply the ideas of RESOURCES and VALUES in a realistic problem of SELF-IDENTITY.

An event that most of you will experience in the next several years is your wedding. There are few events that so clearly reveal the particular values of the couple being married and those of their parents.

Weddings can be very simple affairs that cost less than $500, or they can be extravagant social events that cost $10,000 or more. In a simple wedding, there would be hand-written invitations, no special gowns for the bridal party, and a modest reception at the church following the ceremony. Cake and punch would be served. The extravagant wedding would include an elaborate wedding gown, a large wedding party in formal dress, special floral arrangements, and a reception for 300 guests at a country club or hotel. This would be followed by a sitdown dinner, open bar, and a band for dancing.

The particular type of wedding that you will experience may be well established because of family or ethnic traditions. Although more and more young people are having non-traditional weddings, the great majority still follow the long-standing rules of proper etiquette.

As you plan your wedding, you may refer to one of the many wedding manuals, or you may wish to make an appointment with a wedding consultant. Consultants have all the latest information on how to plan tension-free weddings. They are happy to share their knowledge and create the perfect wedding.

Imagine that you are employed by Wedding Consulting Services, Inc. You have been asked to handle all the details of the forthcoming wedding of Sally Jones and Jim Brown. Sally is one of three children, and her father's income is in the $20–25,000 range. The family lives in a middle-class neighborhood and has approximately $10,000 in savings and investments.

Having been a bridesmaid in several large weddings, Sally has

Wedding Consulting Services, Inc.

123 Main Street
Anytown, U.S.A.
666-1900

decided she would like an elaborate wedding. Sally's father, not wishing to exhaust his entire savings on a wedding, would like something modest. Jim is an interested participant-observer who is willing to go along with whatever is decided.

Sally, her father, and Jim make an appointment to see you about wedding plans. You give them time to study the schedule of wedding costs that follows. After they read the schedule, you must be prepared to guide them to the right choice. What questions will you ask? Jim, who is eager to arrive at some decision, asks for your recommendation. What recommendation will you make about the kind of wedding that is perfect for Sally and Jim?

WEDDING CONSULTING SERVICES, INC.

Comparative Schedule of Wedding Costs

	Simple (At home, 50 guests)	Modest (Community hall, 150 guests)	Elaborate (Country club or hotel, 300 guests)
Invitations	$ 25	$ 50	$ 150
Wedding gown	100	250	500
Bridal party dress	—	500	1,000
Flowers	25	150	450
Photographs	50	200	500
Reception			
Cake	50	150	300
Food*	175	1,500	4,600
Beverage	75	500	2,000
Band	—	200	500
Total	$500	$3,500	$10,000

*The food provided is as follows:
Simple: nuts, mints, small sandwiches
Modest: buffet table
Elaborate: sit-down dinner

QUESTIONS FOR DISCUSSION

1. How do your recommendations in this situation affect resources? Will your recommendations improve or diminish the resources of Sally? of her father? of Jim?
2. What values are involved in planning for a wedding? What value conflicts are present?
3. An individual's self-identity is a product of his or her resources and values. What did you learn about your self-identity as you participated in this activity?

A Review of the Objectives

Now that you have completed the activities in Unit II, can you:

1. Explain the relationship between resources and values as part of an individual's self-identity?
2. Use resources such as friends, reading, listening, and negotiating skills to strengthen your self-identity?
3. Write a paragraph in your JOURNAL NOTES describing what combination of resources and values makes up your self-identity?
4. Explain how (a) labels, (b) killer statements, (c) stereotypes, (d) prejudice, (e) unemployment, and (f) dependency diminish a person's resources?
5. Clarify your personal values and your position on community (group) value issues by (a) watching the way the issue is phrased? (b) identifying value dilemmas? (c) selecting a value standard? (d) separating factual statements and value statements? (e) determining the logic of arguments and the weight of evidence?
6. Tell what each WORD or PHRASE means?
7. Use the WORD or PHRASE correctly in a sentence?

CONTROLS

CONTENTS

Controls Through the Mass Media   223

Impact People: A Positive Control   237

Looking Ahead

WHY STUDY CONTROLS?

All traffic in this lane must stop before proceeding.

Stop only if other traffic is affected; so *look* and *give* *way* to *all* oncoming traffic.

What do these symbols and statements have in common? Each represents a CONTROL on human behavior. In Unit II we discovered that self-identity is the product of resources used in support of our values and that we can expand our self-identity by improving our resources. We also learned that resources can be diminished through the actions taken by others or by ourselves. The idea that resources can be enhanced, maintained, or diminished is an excellent introduction to your understanding of controls.

Controls are acts or powers that affect self-identity in three ways. Some controls *regulate* action (keep things running smoothly and effectively). Other controls *apply force* to promote or hinder actions. Still other controls *limit* the freedom of action people have in satisfying their needs.

Some controls come from within ourselves and are a natural outgrowth of our needs, resources, and values. These controls are collectively referred to as SELF-CONTROL.

Other controls are external. EXTERNAL CONTROLS are established by people, groups, or organizations in our Immediate Physical/

Psychological Setting (IPS). Some external controls influence behavior in a healthy sense. These can be called WISE CONTROLS. Wise controls make it possible for each individual to have maximum freedom of action while protecting the rights of the community. Other external controls unfairly or foolishly force or limit possible actions or alternatives. UNWISE CONTROLS injure the dignity and worth of individuals even as they attempt to protect the community.

The purpose of this unit is to help you to become more aware of how controls affect your behavior. The unit begins with an explanation of wise and unwise controls. The focus of attention then shifts to ROLE and STATUS. These are often significant controls on a growing self-identity. The next segment of the unit discusses family, school, peer, political, and economic controls. The following segment considers the MASS MEDIA both as ways we learn about controls and as controls in themselves. The final segment introduces the idea of IMPACT PEOPLE—people who help you make major decisions.

By the end of this unit you will have gained insights about both wise and unwise controls. We hope that these insights will enable you to respect and use wise controls that protect the dignity and worth of individuals. We also charge you to work through thoughtful and democratic means to change controls that are unwise.

Write down your reactions to and feelings about the ideas and activities of this unit in your JOURNAL NOTES.

OBJECTIVES

When this unit is completed, we are confident that you will be able to:

1. Describe the differences between self-control and external controls and between wise and unwise controls.
2. Explain how role and status can act as controls on self-identity.
3. Describe how controls are used in the family, school, peer group, and political and economic communities.
4. Explain how the mass media can be both ways we learn about controls and controls in themselves.
5. Recognize the impact people who guide and influence your decisions.
6. Tell what each WORD or PHRASE means.
7. Use the WORD or PHRASE correctly in a sentence.

WORDS AND PHRASES

Control
- Self-Control
- External Control
- Wise Control
- Unwise Control

Role

Conformist

Non-Conformist

Role Conflict

Status

Peer

Culture

Economic Security

Political Freedom

Market

Monopoly

Mass Media

Propaganda

Impact People

SELF-CONTROL AND EXTERNAL CONTROL: DEFINITIONS

A CONTROL is an act or power that regulates, applies force to, or limits our alternatives. Controls are part of our IPS. Recall the BEHAVIOR EQUATION:

$$N + R + IPS = \text{Behavior (with immediate and remote consequences)}$$

Each of us has natural controls, represented by our SELF-CONTROL or conscience. Self-control is a product of our self-identity—our needs, resources, and values. Many psychologists have studied self-control. Most express the thought that self-control, if wisely applied, is the most valuable control because it is not easily influenced by what others tell us to do. Thomas Huxley, the famous English biologist, once described self-control as the ability to make yourself do what you must do when it ought to be done, whether you like it or not.

ACTIVITY 1

External Control
Out of Control

In the early 1960s, a Yale University social psychologist, Stanley Milgram, conducted a series of experiments in which his co-workers played the role of learners. Unknowing subjects were told that the experiments were designed to see how electric shocks would affect learning. When the learners, who were in on the experiment, made mistakes on the learning tasks, the subjects were told to give the learners an electric shock. If the learners continued to make mistakes, the subjects were told to give them increasingly severe shocks until the learners did the task correctly. Actually, the shock machine was not connected to the learners, but the subjects did not know that. They thought they were really giving shocks since the learners jumped about and screamed as the "shocks" became more severe. The subjects knew what the minimum shock felt like because they had received one before the experiment.

What percentage of the subjects do you think gave learners the most severe shocks—shocks that appeared to be extremely painful for the learners? Did you guess 10 percent? 25 percent? 50 percent? Fully 65 percent of the subjects (people like you and me) gave out the most severe shocks.

QUESTIONS FOR DISCUSSION

1. What might you have done if you had been a subject?
2. How does this experiment relate to the idea of self-control?
3. What are the dangers to a community from an overemphasis on the use of self-control to protect the community? Think of examples of such overemphasis.
4. What are the dangers to a community from an overemphasis on the use of external controls to protect the community? Think of examples of such overemphasis.

ACTIVITY 2

Planning for Self-Control

This is your chance to refer back to the OBJECTIVES in Unit I. Recall objective 4:

"Write a personal objective for yourself, one that promises to strengthen a constructive behavior, develop a new constructive behavior, or discard an unwise or destructive behavior."

QUESTIONS FOR DISCUSSION

1. Have you reached your objective? Why or why not?
2. How difficult was it to exercise the self-control needed to reach the objective?
3. Now that you have traveled about half way toward THE NEW MODEL ME, can you think of a new personal objective to reach? What self-control will be necessary if you are to succeed?

EXTERNAL CONTROLS

In addition to our individual self-control, there are EXTERNAL CONTROLS that regulate, apply force to, or limit our behavior. External controls can be WISE or UNWISE.

A wise control is:

- effective
- protective of individual justice
- free from undesirable side effects

If the control is *effective*, then the community's objective is reached.

Objective: To eliminate voting more than once in an election.
Example of an effective control: Keep a record of all voters. Place an

x next to the voter's name when his or her vote is cast. Have the voter sign a registration book and show identification as a further control.

If the control is *protective of individual justice*, it should do no serious or permanent harm to an individual or individuals, even if the community benefits.

Objective: To reduce alcohol and drug abuse among high school students.

Example of a control protective of individual justice: The PTA asks all parents, if they wish, to sign an authorization giving school officials permission to contact them if they suspect that their son or daughter is under the influence of alcohol or drugs.

Finally, the control should be *free from undesirable side effects*.

Objective: To penalize students in gym class who are late.

Example of a control rejected for its undesirable side effects: The teacher decides *not* to assign laps to tardy students because she realizes that students might grow to hate running.

ACTIVITY 3

Brother, Can You Spare
a John?[1]

AUTHOR
ART BUCHWALD

In this essay columnist Art Buchwald expresses his anger at an external control. Use the PARS System (Worksheet V) as you read it.

Something is happening in America, and I think you should all know about it. There is a conspiracy underfoot to prevent a majority of people in this country from emptying their bladders. Don't go away— I'm dead serious.

The power elite in this country are locking their washrooms, putting "keep out" signs on their water closets, and warning people that only those favored by the management have bathroom privileges.

I know what I'm talking about. As a member of the Kidney Foundation, and a person who has to tinkle more often than the norm, I have discovered it is getting harder and harder to find public accommodations where the welcome mat is out.

While great strides have been made in this country to help the handicapped, the government has turned its back on people who must go to the john.

[1]*Newsweek* (February 4, 1980). Copyright 1980, by Newsweek, Inc. All rights reserved. Article and photo reprinted by permission. Buchwald writes a syndicated column that appears in 525 newspapers.

Get Lost

Any non-customer who asks a restaurant owner or gas-station atten-
dant if he can use the bathroom is told to get lost. Department stores,
catering to thousands of people a day, hide their washrooms in inac-
cessible corners of the building where only stock clerks can find them.
Sports arenas holding 16,000 people have men's and women's rooms
that will handle no more than five at a time. Offices lock their
washrooms tighter than they do their safes. Hotels have lavabos that
are reserved for the use of "registered" guests.

In a society where everyone is guaranteed equal rights, there is no
such thing as a free tinkle.

On a recent trip to New York, I discovered how difficult it was to go
to the bathroom.

I was walking down the Avenue of the Americas when I got the
urge. I looked around desperately for some place I could make a pit
stop. A large black building loomed up in front of me. I rushed in and
took the elevator to the fifth floor, where an attractive receptionist
smiled and asked if she could help me.

"Yes, you can," I told her. "Could I please have the key to the
washroom?"

Her expression immediately changed, and she said coldly, "I'm
very sorry. I'm not permitted to give the key to strangers."

"But this is an emergency," I begged. "I promise I won't even use
the paper towels."

"I don't have the authority to make exceptions," she said. "Why
don't you go to the subway?"

"I haven't time to make it to the subway."

She would not be moved. I took the elevator down, rushed out into
the street and looked around frantically. I saw a bookstore and went in.
"May I use your men's room?" I asked the man behind the counter.

"We don't have one," he snarled.

"Where do the employees go?" I cried.

"That's none of your damn business," he said.

I didn't have time to argue, so it was back on the sidewalk. There
was a class hotel on the corner. I went in looking as nonchalant as I
possibly could, under the circumstances. My eyes spotted a sign—
"Barber Shop." Experience has taught me that a hotel always places
the men's room next to the barber shop—presumably to attract shoe-
shine business. I pounded down the steps. There it was in all its tiled

splendor. I made a dash for it, but was stopped at the entrance by the house detective.

"May I help you, sir?"

"Not really. I'm on my way in there."

"Are you a guest of the hotel?" he wanted to know.

"No, but I have a friend staying here."

"That's what everyone says. Now get out of here before I nab you for trespassing."

I ran two blocks down the avenue until I found a bar advertising the "Happy Hour." I went in and said to the bartender, "Give me a drink."

"What kind of a drink?"

"Who cares?" I said. "Where's the men's room?"

"That will be three dollars," he said.

"Why do I have to pay now? Why can't I pay after I've finished my drink?"

"You're not the first guy who walked in here and wanted to use the men's room."

The incident I describe is not unusual, as anyone who works in New York City will testify.

But it's not just New York. The lockout is sweeping the country. The public washroom, as we have known it, is disappearing from the face of the land. It is now easier to get an artificial kidney than to use those you've got.

What's even more frightening is that architects, in order to save space, are cutting down on washroom facilities in everything they design.

It's even worse for women than it is for men. Anyone who has gone to a theater knows the agony and defeat of waiting in line for 20 minutes during intermission to get near a stall.

Crisis

The airlines are putting fewer bathrooms on planes so they'll have more room for passenger seats. The designers of concert halls, football stadiums, and movie houses couldn't care less about the physical needs of the people who go there.

The United States, which leads the world in modern plumbing, now heaps scorn and abuse on those who want to use it.

No President of the United States will take a stand on it. Editorial writers ignore it. Even Mike Wallace is afraid to investigate it.

Yet it affects every single person in the country.

The right to tinkle is a God-given one, so basic to every man, woman, and child that unless it is acknowledged as such, citizens will soon take the law into their own hands. A person who has to go in a hurry considers jail a small price to pay for civil disobedience.

The time has come for the people to raise their voices in protest. It is imperative to remember that each time a washroom door is slammed in anyone's face, something in all of us dies.

—*Art Buchwald*

QUESTIONS FOR DISCUSSION

1. Does Mr. Buchwald think he is confronting a wise or an unwise control?
2. Do you agree or disagree?
3. What is the objective of the control? Is it effective? Is it protective of individual justice? Is it free from undesirable side effects?

ACTIVITY 4

The Controls on You

Make a list of several external controls on your behavior in the chart that follows (or make your own chart on a separate sheet of paper if you are not to write in your book). In the column to the right of each control, indicate what you think is the objective of the control. Then judge whether the control is WISE or UNWISE, and state the reasons for your judgment. Remember, wise standards are effective, protect individual justice, and are free from undesirable side effects.

External Control	Objective	Wise/ Unwise?	Reasons

Be prepared to discuss the controls on you and your classmates.

QUESTIONS FOR DISCUSSION

1. What common controls can be found among the lists?
2. Are there disagreements about the wisdom of the listed controls?

ACTIVITY 5

My Life with No External Controls

Imagine life with no controls to safeguard life and property or to regulate traffic or to compel people to attend school.

What would my life be like without any external controls? Suppose a community had no external controls. In your JOURNAL NOTES write down some short-range and long-range consequences.

Think of positive consequences and negative consequences.

Would we as a community advance if no external controls existed, or would the quality of our lives be diminished?

In the same place in your JOURNAL NOTES, list the first three external controls on your actions and alternatives that you would eliminate if you had the power. Be specific about the purpose of each control. Explain why the controls are unwise.

CONTROLS AND ROLES

Examine the four cartoons that follow. Each one shows human beings in conversation. What do all the cartoons have in common?

If you concluded that each cartoon displays unexpected behavior, you are thinking the same way we did. Teenagers do not give traffic citations to policemen. Elementary school children do not have lounges. Teenage boys do not stay up to insure that parents return home before midnight. In our community, we would find it surprising for a construction worker to be a woman and for a man's legs to be objects of admiration.

We often have expectations about people because of who they are or what they do—because of their ROLE. Role expectations are an important external control on human behavior. Human beings in every community and in every period of human history face the challenge of behaving in ways consistent with their roles. We expect bankers to dress in conservative clothing, to be cautious in speech and non-verbal behavior, and, in general, to make us feel that our money is safe in their custody. We expect rock musicians to have a particular style and speak a language of their own.

CONFORMITY AND NON-CONFORMITY

When an individual acts in a way consistent with his or her role, we say that person is a CONFORMIST. People who conform (accept their role) encounter less resistance from the community than those who do not. Conformity is natural and right for people who are comfortable with their roles—mother, father, male, female, child, teacher, minister, automobile mechanic, and so on. For people who accept their roles, conformity becomes self-control. If I enjoy my work, and getting to the workplace on time is an expected behavior for my role, then I find ways to get to work on time. If I am comfortable with my role as child-rearer, then I accept the task of caring for my children when they are sick.

People who rebel against their roles are called NON-CONFORMISTS. Such people refuse to conform—to behave in the ways expected of them. Non-conformists believe that their self-identity is of more value to them than the criticism or ridicule they can expect from others. The father who chooses to remain home and rear the children is a non-conformist. Teenagers who choose to dress differently from most of their peers are non-conformists.

The decision to conform or not to conform should be based on a careful weighing of the benefits and the costs. As the BEHAVIOR EQUATION reminds us, behavior has both *immediate* and *remote* consequences.

A further complicating fact about role expectations is that we assume dozens of roles as we grow older. It is also common to assume many roles at the same time.

"You can march to the beat of whatever drummer you choose. Just remember that *I'm* the metronome."

ACTIVITY 6

Roles I Play in Life

Each person plays a great many roles throughout life. For example, a man may adopt the roles of husband, parent, wage earner, club member, big brother, and teacher. He may feel that, having so many roles, he cannot do any of them well.

You, too, may be expected to play a number of roles. This activity is designed to help you prove this.

Make a list of the various roles you think you are expected to play during a week's time.

Now form groups of four to six persons. Compare the roles you have listed with those listed by others.

QUESTIONS FOR DISCUSSION

1. What roles did everyone or almost everyone include?
2. What needs are being satisfied in any given role?
3. Which of the listed roles are the easiest for you to conform to? Which are the hardest?
4. How do you show that you are comfortable in conforming to role expectations? How do you show that you are a non-conformist?
5. In general, do you see yourself as a conformist or a non-conformist? Is this judgment the same for all your roles or for only one or two? Explain.

ROLE CONFLICT

Life would be simpler if all of us were comfortable in our many roles and if each role created the same expectations. But that is not the case. In our complex lives, the roles differ in expectations to such an extent that we sometimes experience ROLE CONFLICT. In the following activity, you will experience role conflict.

ACTIVITY 7

A Union Leader in Trouble

As president of one of the largest automobile union locals, you are responsible for the 13,500 members of the local. All of your members work for one of the largest American automobile companies. Recently times have turned bad for all American auto companies. High prices, a growing preference for foreign cars with higher gasoline mileage, and high inflation have combined to change past profits into present losses. Last year the company had one of the largest annual losses ever experienced by an American business. Nearly one-third (4,000) of the members of the local are on indefinite lay-off.

The company has informed you that conditions force it to ask for a re-opening of negotiations on its contract, which has two more years to run. The company wishes to freeze wages at their present levels and eliminate the cost-of-living increase protection clause. Acceptance of their terms will mean that each member of your union will earn less money next year and the following year. Refusal to re-negotiate may mean larger lay-offs of your workers and even a possible company bankruptcy.

You worked long and hard at negotiating the present contract. What recommendation do you make to your membership?

One of the greatest difficulties you will face as you try to develop a recommendation is the conflict among the many roles you play in life. We will not consider all the roles, although roles such as citizen, churchgoer, and neighbor may be in conflict. We have selected roles that are sure to conflict. These roles are described below.

THE CONFLICTS

Breadwinner

Your role as the breadwinner of your own family must be taken into consideration. The mortgage has to be paid; inflation is affecting you as well as others. You have four teenagers—two in college, two in

161

high school. If wages are frozen and the cost-of-living protection is eliminated, how will you meet the needs of your own family?

Negotiator

In your role of negotiator, you must be concerned that bowing to company pressure now may set a pattern for the future. Each time the company experiences a setback, it may threaten to close the plant unless wage, fringe, health, and safety demands are reduced.

Union President

The old timers in the union who hold your presidency in their hands have been divided about your performance. Since you speak your mind both to the national union leaders and to members of your local, you have made some enemies. There has even been open dissension within the local. On the issue of re-opening the contract, the old timers, who are protected from lay-offs by their years of service, expect you to offer resistance to the company. They do not wish to see their wages frozen and cost-of-living protection eliminated. They are not as concerned about the possibility of plant closing and bankruptcy as you are.

Labor Leader

The present lay-offs and promised future lay-offs if the contract negotiations are not re-opened threaten the future health of the union. No union can maintain its strength and vitality if membership declines. Younger workers, who are the future of the union, are most affected by lay-offs. Support for the union's goals and promises has understandably weakened among younger workers. On the issue of the wage freeze and other concessions, the younger workers support any actions that end the lay-offs and restore full workshifts in the plants.

QUESTIONS FOR DISCUSSION

1. Would you resist the re-negotiating of the contracts? If you agree to re-open negotiations, would you agree to a wage freeze and an end to the cost-of-living protection? Explain.
2. What conflicts exist among the roles you play in life? For example, might there be a conflict for a full-time student who is employed 30 hours a week?
3. How do you handle role conflict so that it does not paralyze you and prevent you from taking any action?

STATUS

For every role there is a STATUS position. Status is the relative standing or position a person has in the community. Some people have high status; others have low status. Some people achieve high status in a community because they are recognized as being best at a role they play. It is possible to achieve high status even though your work role generally has low status. It is even possible for a group of people with high self-esteem to move the community to shift a role to a higher status.

Yet it is important to recognize that the role a person chooses, especially in regard to occupation, is often a significant factor in determining the status he or she is given by the community. We may wish it were otherwise, but role and status together are substantial external controls on self-identity.

ACTIVITY 8

Occupational Social Standing

Most of you probably have given a fair amount of thought to what you want to do for a living when you are finished with your schooling. Perhaps you feel that you have complete freedom in making this choice. Among the controls that society places on us, however, are predetermined ideas about the social standing or status of various occupations. The degree to which you are concerned with society's acceptance of you may well determine what job you have in later years.

In 1947 two sociologists interviewed more than three thousand people, asking them to rate 90 occupations according to the prestige associated with them. The same study was done in 1963 with virtually the same results.

How would you rate the social standing of people who work at each of the occupations listed in the chart on the following page? Pick the adjective that describes the rating you would give each occupation and put a check in the corresponding box.

QUESTIONS FOR DISCUSSION

1. What are some of the needs you thought of as you rated these occupations?
2. What two or three needs seemed to be more important than others?
3. How do you think a career choice you have made would stand in these ratings? Is that why you chose it?
4. Can you think of any highly respected people whose occupation would rate rather low in social standing?
5. What things have you done this week primarily because they were the socially expected thing to do?

Occupation	SOCIAL STANDING				
	1 Poor	2 Below Average	3 Average	4 Good	5 Excellent
Artist					
Banker					
Bookkeeper					
Building contractor					
Carpenter					
Clergyman					
College professor					
Electrician					
Garage mechanic					
Gasoline station attendant					
Janitor					
Mayor of a large city					
Physician					
Plumber					
Public school teacher					
Reporter on a daily newspaper					
Shoeshine stand attendant					
Soda fountain clerk					
Taxicab driver					
U.S. Supreme Court Justice					

Note: From the Instructor's Guide for *Class and Race in the United States*, SRSS Episodes in Social Inquiry Series (Boston: Allyn and Bacon, 1972). Copyright © 1972 by the American Sociological Association. Reprinted with permission. Designed by Melvin Tumin of Princeton University, Edward Tumin of Weequahic High School, and Israel Tumin of South Side High School, both in Newark, N.J.

CONTROLS AND SELF-IDENTITY

The next segment of this unit is a study of external controls as they regulate and limit self-identity in five areas:

- family
- PEER group
- school
- political community
- economic community

As each group is studied, we will ask you to determine which controls you think are wise and unwise and how role and status affect the people in each group.

FAMILY CONTROLS

The family is the group most familiar to us. Every large community throughout history has adopted the family as its basic group. In the past, the family has been defined as a married couple and their children. The father was the breadwinner; the mother supervised the home.

As discussed in Unit II, the American family has been changing over the last 25 years. More women than ever before have chosen or have been forced to work full time. With the growth of the suburbs, one or both parents often travel long distances to and from work, reducing the time available to control family activities. In a growing number of families, divorce has forced one parent to perform the roles traditionally assumed by two parents.

Even with the changes in the family, however, it remains the group in which we develop many of our personal resources and learn the values we grow to believe in. As you participate in the activities on family controls, think about how your family has affected the resources and values that make up your self-identity.

ACTIVITY 9

Parent and Teenager Bill of Rights and Responsibilities

What are the proper role expectations for a parent? For a teenager? This activity will enable you to identify the rights and responsibilities that you think make up an ideal role for each.

On a separate sheet of paper complete both the parent's and the teenager's bills of rights and responsibilities. Be prepared to discuss them with other members of the class.

Then read the testament on the scroll on page 170. Would you feel comfortable completing it? You may want to copy it on a separate sheet of paper. (Do not write in your book.)

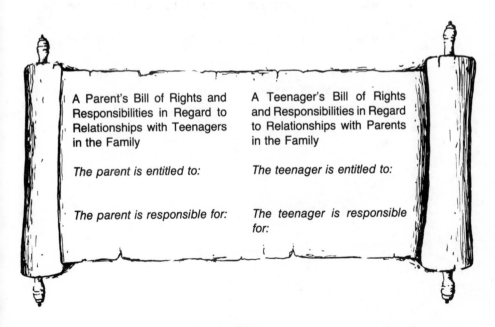

A Parent's Bill of Rights and Responsibilities in Regard to Relationships with Teenagers in the Family

The parent is entitled to:

The parent is responsible for:

A Teenager's Bill of Rights and Responsibilities in Regard to Relationships with Parents in the Family

The teenager is entitled to:

The teenager is responsible for:

To all who may read these statements:

I _____ dedicate this testament to the
promotion of wise and wholesome family life. I affirm that my
attention was focused equally on rights and responsibilities. I also
affirm that my role of teenager was no more than a slight influence
on my enthusiasm as I created the list of my rights and my
parent's responsibilities.

Signed _____

Date   _____

QUESTIONS FOR DISCUSSION

1. In what ways do your parents match the ideal parent role that you have created?
2. In what ways do you match the ideal teenager role that you have created?
3. As you compare your roles to those created by classmates, can you think of any changes in your family relationships that might result in a wiser, more wholesome group?

ACTIVITY 10

A Family Disagreement

This is an activity to help you become aware that people can play a role for the purpose of controlling another person.

In this activity we will demonstrate four roles that are often used in establishing an unwise control over others. These roles are:

1. *Placating:* pacifying, smoothing over differences, being nice, protective, defending others gently, covering up. "Oh, it's not so bad, really." "We agree, basically."
2. *Avoiding:* being quiet, pretending not to understand, changing the subject, playing weak, playing helpless. "I can't help it." "I didn't hear you."
3. *Blaming:* judging, bullying, comparing, complaining. "It's always your fault." "You never . . . ." "Why don't you . . . ?"
4. *Preaching:* lecturing, using outside authority. "You should . . . ." "You must . . . ." Proving that you are right by explaining, calculating, using logic, etc.

To illustrate these roles, form groups of four to role-play a series of family disagreements involving:
- mother
- father
- daughter
- son

This activity has four rounds of five minutes each. In each round, you will play a different member of the family and play one of the four roles: placating, avoiding, blaming, or preaching. For example, in round 1 you might be the placating mother, in round 2 the avoiding father, in round 3 the blaming sister, and in round 4 the preaching brother.

At the end of each round, each person will have one minute to tell what difficulties he or she experienced while playing the role and to hear reactions from the other members of the group.

Choose the family disagreement that your group will role-play from these possibilities, or select another one:
- time when the evening meal is served
- time to be home on Friday and Saturday nights
- use of the family car
- assisting with cleaning the house
- allowance
- daughter's plan to spend spring vacation with friends in Florida
- mother's desire to take a full-time job
- deciding whether or not all four will attend an event (family reunion, ball game, symphony, wedding, etc.)

QUESTION FOR DISCUSSION

What are helpful ways to react to someone who is placating or avoiding or blaming or preaching?

ACTIVITY 11

Feelings About Family Controls

This activity will help you to express and share feelings about family controls.

Make a list of the controls that families use to regulate or limit behavior.

Use a checklist to judge the controls. Recall that a wise control is effective, does no serious or permanent harm to individuals even if the community benefits, and is free from undesirable side effects.

• Place a *W* next to any control that you think is wise.

• Place a *U* next to any control that you think is unwise.

• Write a word or two describing your feelings about each control.

Form small groups and share your lists and feelings. Before the group breaks up, share some "I learned" statements with them. Think about something you learned through this exercise and then say to the group: "I learned _____ about family controls. I was surprised that my family controls are _____. I learned from others _____ about my own family."

ACTIVITY 12

Poll on Family Controls

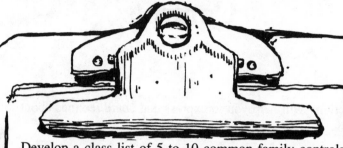

Develop a class list of 5 to 10 common family controls and poll an equal number of parents and students about them. Get responses from at least 20 parents and 20 students. Ask respondents to use the following numerical rating scale to express their opinion of each control:

| Strongly Agree (5) | Agree (4) | Uncertain (3) | Disagree (2) | Strongly Disagree (1) |

Tally the responses numerically for each of the items in the poll. Then analyze the results of the poll by:

- comparing all responses to each of the controls
- comparing responses from students only
- comparing responses from parents only
- comparing and contrasting responses from students and parents

Another way to study the results is to convert responses to each item into percentages. In other words, figure out in percentages how many strongly agree, agree, are uncertain, and so on.

QUESTIONS FOR DISCUSSION

1. How did the responses of the parent and student groups differ?
2. What conclusions can you reach about the adult and the teenage views on family controls?

ACTIVITY 13

Conflict Capsule: A Family Scene

This activity will help you to experience a conflict situation involving family controls.

Select four individuals to role-play the following situation:

"YOU MUST BE HOME BY ELEVEN"

Background

Diana, a high school junior, has been dating occasionally for the last two years. Her parents would not allow her to date until she was 15, and even then they really didn't like the idea. For the past three months she has been dating an older boy, and the relationship seems to be deepening. The conflict situation emerges because the young man, Jim, is a non-conformist. Specifically, he does not conform to Diana's parents' idea of the perfect young man for their only daughter.

Scene

Diana and Jim enter the house at 1:30 A.M. She was to be home by 11:00 P.M. Her mother and father are waiting for her in the living room.

Characters

Father, a man who has come to appreciate the very strict controls he experienced as a teenager. He is concerned about a decline in traditional values that he sees in young people today. He wishes to prevent this from infecting his daughter, at least until she is an adult and is no longer his responsibility.

Mother. Create a role for her.

Diana. Create a role for her.

Jim, the non-conformist. Create a role for him.

You may wish to re-play the scene by changing the characteristics of the mother's, Diana's, and Jim's roles.

QUESTIONS FOR DISCUSSION

1. How do you account for the results of the role play? Which role had the most influence on the results?
2. How do you think the listening or negotiation skills could be helpful in resolving a control conflict in the real world? How could they help in your family?
3. How does the idea of role help you to understand the positions and points of view of different members of the family?

"I keep having this recurring feeling that my parents know what they are talking about . . ."

ACTIVITY 14

Family Controls Wrap-Up

To conclude our study of family controls, complete three or more of the following sentence stems by expressing a feeling.

Permit your thoughts to take shape. What are your present thoughts, feelings, and actions related to family controls? You may wish to refer back to the activities on self-control, wise and unwise external controls, and role and status before completing the sentence stems.

A family is _____.

A parent tries to _____.

A teenager thinks _____.

My family to me means _____.

I think my brother or sister _____.

A family shares _____.

We as a family _____.

As part of this family _____.

At my house a boss is _____.

PEER CONTROLS

PEERS are people who have similar roles and status positions. In the case of a high school student, this means people of the same age, in the same grade at school, etc. Generally peers are subject to a similar set of external controls.

Teenagers are especially vulnerable to the controls set up by the peer group. Your peers often influence your behavior—your clothes, the friends you make or do not make, the places you go for fun. Peer-group controls can be wise if they are effective, protect individual justice, and are free from undesirable side effects. Unfortunately peer controls can also be unwise and may lead to destructive behavior.

ACTIVITY 15

Not Going Along
with the Group

This activity is designed to help you see how your behavior affects your peers and how their response may influence your feelings about yourself or others.

If you are game enough to try, do something for a day that does not conform to the standards of your peer group, something different from what your group would normally do. First determine what some of the unwritten rules of your peer group are, and then break one or more of them. For instance, how does your group feel about borrowing, approaching members of the opposite sex, dating (who pays?), the right way to behave in front of members of the older generation, and wearing out-of-fashion clothes?

At the end of the day, analyze the reactions you got from your peer group:
- How did you feel when you did something that was opposed to the controls of your peer group?
- How did your friends react to your behavior?
- If your friends were upset by your behavior, how did you feel?

ACTIVITY 16

Your Peers and Drinking Habits

According to the 1980 Gallup U.S. Youth Survey, teenage boys are more likely to drink alcoholic beverages frequently (48 percent) than girls are (34 percent). Survey authors defined frequent teen drinkers as those who drink once a month or more often. Younger teens (13–15 years) are half as likely to be frequent drinkers as older teens (16–18 years). Fewer teenagers from the South (34 percent) drink frequently than teenagers from all other sections of the United States (43 percent).

The survey discovered that being with friends who drink is related to the frequency of drinking. Seventy-seven percent of the group who responded that they are frequent drinkers reported that almost all of their friends are at least occasional drinkers. In contrast, only 16 percent of the non-drinkers reported that their friends are at least occasional drinkers.

Almost half of the frequent drinkers (44 percent) reported that most girls and boys would be high by the end of a party where drinking took place. Only 8 percent of the non-drinkers made the same observation.

QUESTIONS FOR DISCUSSION

1. How do the national results compare to your peer group's drinking habits?
2. Is it difficult in your peer group to be a non-drinker or a non-smoker? Why or why not?
3. What needs do you think are being satisfied at a party where most teenagers get drunk?
4. What do you think are the immediate and remote consequences of frequent drinking?

ACTIVITY 17

Peer Status: Leadership

How does one become a leader in your group? What are the resources you look for in a leader? In this activity you will be able to list the qualities you hope to see in your peers and in yourself.

List the resources you think are important if one's goal is to become a leader in your peer group.

Compare your list with the lists of other class members.

QUESTIONS FOR DISCUSSION

1. What resources appear on nearly everyone's list?
2. How many of these resources do you possess?
3. What are the similarities and the differences between the resources needed to become a leader in your peer group and the resources needed to become a leader in the adult community?
4. Do you have a goal of becoming a leader in your school or later in the adult community? If so, what are you doing now to achieve that goal?

ACTIVITY 18

How Do You Feel About Peer Controls?

This is an activity to help you clarify your feelings about peer controls.

Can you express your feelings about peer controls in a creative way? Perhaps you can write a poem about peer control, draw a picture, make a collage, write a song and set it to music, or take pictures of students in situations that show peer control. Explain the pictures orally or in writing. The possibilities are unlimited.

SCHOOL CONTROLS

When school controls are mentioned, your thoughts understandably shift to the rules and traditions that control your alternatives and actions as students. The law requires that you attend school until you reach a certain age. For some of you, school probably is second only to your family as a major influence on your life.

Yet school controls affect people in other roles. The school calendar controls the activities of students' parents. School rules and traditions exercise substantial controls on teachers and administrators.

The buildings and grounds may exercise much control over the mobility of physically disabled students. The IPS of the school includes many different psychological settings. For some of us, the school IPS is supportive of self-esteem. For others, it limits and hinders the growth of self-esteem.

As you experience the following activities, think about how each group in the school is controlled. Are the groups controlled wisely or unwisely? How does an individual's role and status in the school community affect his or her alternatives and actions?

ACTIVITY 19

School Manual

Look at your school handbook, manual, or guide book. What portion of it is devoted to controls? What portion is devoted to pointing out the attractive and satisfying characteristics of the school? For fun, take a section of the school manual devoted to controls and rewrite it in a less negative way. Add some humor if you can.

ACTIVITY 20

Looking at the Rules

School rules and traditions are among your major concerns. Perhaps you question the need for particular rules or traditions. Perhaps you would add other rules or change existing ones.

Form small groups to complete the chart that follows (or use a separate sheet of paper if you are not to write in your book). List school rules or traditions that have substantial effects on you. (A tradition is an unwritten rule or custom passed down from one generation to the next.) For each rule or tradition, indicate its purpose, determine whether you think it is wise or unwise, and recommend changes. If you decide to eliminate a rule or a tradition, suggest other means of achieving the same purpose.

Ask an administrator to talk with the class about school rules and traditions and to respond to the ideas in the chart.

School Rule or Tradition	Purpose	Wise/ Unwise?	Recommended Change

ACTIVITY 21

Students Discuss School Controls

The following activity gives you an opportunity to react to a discussion among students about two school controls. The discussion took place in the winter of 1981.

I. CLASS CUTS[2]

Kelly: "One of the things I disagree with is when kids are caught cutting, they have either an in-school suspension or an out-of-school suspension. Either way, they're not learning anything that day."

Teacher: "Is there any punishment for cutting that will reduce the number of cuts in the future?"

Bob: "Some kids get to the point where they have so many cuts they say, 'Who cares? Let's just cut class today.' I think it almost gets to the point where the student says, 'Oh well, I don't care. One more cut and I'm out of the class. Who cares?'"

Dave: "Parents care once they find out. So it works for some people who have parents who care."

Teacher: "Does anybody else have anything to offer about this particular control?"

Kelly: "Isn't there any other way the school can control cutting? It seems there has to be something better than what's going on, because it's not working."

Teacher: "You all agree with the purpose. The purpose is to encourage you to come to class and to be on time. The question is: what control can do it most effectively with the fewest undesirable side effects?"

Bob: "Improve the curriculum!"

---

[2]From interview with Robert E. Bundy, Eileen Cunningham, Martin Weishampel, and two other anonymous students, January 20, 1981, Lakewood, Ohio.

Kelly: "Yes! That might help a lot. I know classes where it seems like you just go there and you're not learning anything. You're just there."

Bob: "Some of the teaching methods and materials used in some classes—I'm not saying in all—but in some classes there's just no motivation. There's just no pizzaz to it."

Kelly: "Either that, or you get a teacher who has gone stale, talks in a monotone, and doesn't move. It's just the same old thing over and over again."

Teacher: "Do you all think that the curriculum, what is going on in the class, is related to the cutting? Is attendance better in the more interesting classes?"

Marty: "People who cut usually take the attitude 'I don't care.' They're just dropping out, so it might not be the curriculum. Sometimes it's just the mood, definitely the attitude. It's what's happening that day. It depends on a lot of factors."

II. THE SMOKING ROOM

Teacher: "What about smoking: prohibition against smoking, control of smoking? Is that a wise control or an unwise control?"

Marty: "There is really no control on smoking. If you want a cigarette, you can go outside and have one."

Kelly: "But you can't smoke in the school."

Marty: "Well, that's understandable. That limits other people's rights. It would be comparable to a no-smoking section on a bus."

Eileen: "I think they should have something like that in the school. I think they had a very good idea when it came to the smoking room for the students because they would eliminate half of what the security guards are doing. Then they could work on something else that would be more important."

Marty: "In the smoking room they could assign people to clean up the place and keep it."

Eileen: "Well, wouldn't you rather have that than in the bathrooms at this school?"

Teacher: "As students, you support the idea of a smoking room?"

All: "Definitely!"

Marty: "What is the ratio of smoking people in this school to non-smokers? The people who don't smoke probably will say that they don't want people to smoke in our school."

Teacher: "Would the smoking room limit smoking or promote smoking?"

Kelly: "If they're already smoking, it's not going to matter if they have a smoking room or not. They'll go ahead and smoke. They'll smoke in the bathroom. They'll take the chance of getting caught. I know people who get caught smoking a cigarette and the next period are back in the same bathroom smoking another cigarette. So, really, it's not doing any good that way. I think that a smoking room would eliminate a lot of the problems instead of promoting them. It would be brought out in the open. It wouldn't be like a hidden thing."

DISCUSSION

Form into two groups. Each group is assigned to react to one of the control discussions:

- class cuts
- smoking room

Use the Questions for Discussion to guide your reactions. Recorders from each group can share their reactions with the entire class.

QUESTIONS FOR DISCUSSION

1. What needs do you think are reflected in the first control area, class cuts:
   - by the persons who cut classes?
   - by the school officials?
2. What needs are reflected in the second area, smoking:
   - by those who wish to smoke in school?
   - by those who do not wish to have smoking in the school?
3. Do you think that controls on class cutting and smoking are necessary? Why or why not?
4. Do you think the particular controls that were discussed by the students were wise or unwise? Explain.
5. If you thought any of the controls were unwise, what alternatives would you recommend?

ACTIVITY 22

An Administrator's View of Controls

The New Model Me
Teachers and Students
Anywhere, USA

Dear Friends:

I have been a school administrator for the past 16 years in three different positions. I have been a coordinator of pupils for the central administration and a house principal in a very large suburban high school. A house principal is responsible for student discipline, teacher supervision, and assorted other duties. My present position is assistant principal for curriculum in the same high school.

As I examine my job as a school administrator, two controls on my actions make my job quite frustrating. The first is the frustration of limited financing—that is, a lack of money to carry out projects I consider important. Too often worthwhile ideas must be shelved and enthusiasm wasted because the school district is on a tight budget. As the person who must deliver the bad news to teachers and students, I deeply feel their hurt and disappointment.

The second control is placed on me by the law. I am often surprised by the mistaken belief expressed by some teachers and most students that I have a great deal of freedom to exercise my authority. Actually the law has placed unfortunate limits on the extent of my authority. It seems that someone is always looking over my shoulder, watching for a mistake, ready to demand a written explanation or an open hearing. I guess this control resulted from the actions of a few administrators who behaved unwisely or foolishly. When I hear of these actions, I understand the motivations for limitations on the power of administrators. Still, the limitations cause frustrations for me.

Let me present two examples of how the legal system has given education a mixed blessing. Teacher tenure, which was designed to protect good teachers against unwise actions by administrators and school boards, is more likely to protect poor teachers from wise actions against them. Consequently, the education of young people is damaged. Furthermore, the courts have developed "due process" rules for handling student offenses against other people and property. Again, the purpose of the rules is to protect the rights of students, but the effect is often to protect offenders and damage education for the law-abiding student.

Together, the lack of adequate school financing and the many legal controls make my job difficult by limiting and hindering my alternatives and actions.

Regretfully,

J.U.[3]

QUESTIONS FOR DISCUSSION

1. What external controls frustrate the author of this letter?
2. Do you think the administrator believes the controls are wise or unwise?
3. Do you think that they are unwise? Why or why not?

You may wish to designate a class member to interview a school administrator in your building to gain a response to this letter. Share the response with the class.

[3]Letter reprinted with permission of James Ulrich.

ACTIVITY 23

A Teacher's View of Controls

The New Model Me
Teachers and Students
Anywhere, USA

Dear Friends:

Teaching has been a part of my life for 16 years, in a junior high school, in an international school in a foreign country, and in a large suburban high school. I see my role as a facilitator of learning, a person who helps students to acquire knowledge and understanding of themselves and their world.

Sixteen years ago I started out as an idealist. I was full of creative ideas that would change the world of public education for the better. I wished to make it possible for all individuals in my classroom to reach their full potential. The years have made me aware of a number of controls, or obstacles, that will not allow me to be as effective as I dream of being.

One control comes from students themselves. Some of them do not seem to care about learning enough to involve themselves in the work, no matter how hard I try to provide them with a good learning environment. I see a great deal of indifference to education in students.

A second control results from administrative decisions to place too many students together in one classroom. I have been told by administrators that I should be able to teach 40 students as well as I teach 20. But I know from direct experience that the larger my classes are, the more difficult it is to teach all students as individuals.

Class size is only one of the many financial decisions made by principals, superintendents, and boards of education. Because I am a teacher, I do not play any important role in financial decision making, even though every decision directly affects what I can do with my teaching skills. That is another form of control.

Finally I feel controlled by a public that appears not to value education enough to pay for it. When people feel the pinch of inflation and taxes, the solution for many of them is to vote against education. This results in cut-backs that directly affect the programs I can offer to students.

I have tried to describe briefly some of the controls that make my job more difficult by keeping me from effectively reaching all the students who cross my path. Lately, even though I like being a teacher, I have considered leaving teaching because I feel helpless to change most of these controls.

Sincerely,

S.S.[4]

QUESTIONS FOR DISCUSSION

1. What external controls frustrate the author of this letter?
2. Do you think the teacher believes the controls are wise or unwise?
3. Do you think that they are unwise? Why or why not?

You may wish to designate a class member to interview teachers in your building to gain a response to this teacher's letter. Share the response with the class.

[4]Letter reprinted with permission of Shirley Sekarajasingham.

ACTIVITY 24

Paper Cup School

What do you think would be the characteristics of an ideal school? In this activity you will have the opportunity to participate in the creation of such a school—the school that you have always dreamed of attending.

Form groups of four or five.

The plain white Styrofoam cup given to each group will be the base around which your dream school is to be created.

No talking will be permitted once you have been given the cup.

You may do anything you want with your school. One of you may decide to write something on your cup (school); another may want to put something into your cup (school) that represents a feature of an ideal school.

It is important that each member of your group be given at least two opportunities to contribute to your group's school.

Since you will not have a chance to talk during the activity, you will have time afterward to discuss the features of your ideal school with other members of your group.

Select a member of your group to tell the entire class about the school your group has created.

QUESTIONS FOR DISCUSSION

1. What similarities and differences can be identified among the paper cup schools?
2. How does your actual school compare to the paper cup schools? What differences and similarities did you find?
3. What changes would be required if your actual school was to become your ideal school?
4. What controls may get in the way of the creation of the ideal school? How can the influence of these controls be reduced?
5. What features of the ideal schools are not presently part of your school and probably will have to continue to be dreams?

ACTIVITY 25

Controls on the Physically Disabled

There are more than 40 million Americans with physical disabilities. Until recently many of these people were unable to participate fully in everyday activities that are often taken for granted. As a result, their disability became a handicap. Now much has changed. Many of the physical barriers that previously controlled the actions of disabled people have been removed through the passage of new laws and the cooperation of community leaders and private organizations.

How have your school and local communities changed to make it easier for handicapped persons to participate fully? To help you decide, we have prepared the "barrier checklist" that follows.

PARTIAL SCHOOL AND COMMUNITY BARRIER CHECKLIST

Yes *No*

☐ ☐ 1. Do the main entrances of the school and other community buildings have a ramp as well as stairs?

☐ ☐ 2. Are there parking spaces reserved for disabled people?

☐ ☐ 3. Are there cuts in the curbs to enable people in wheelchairs or with baby carriages to move about easily?

☐ ☐ 4. Are there braille markings at curbs to warn blind people?

☐ ☐ 5. If your school has more than one floor, is there an elevator?

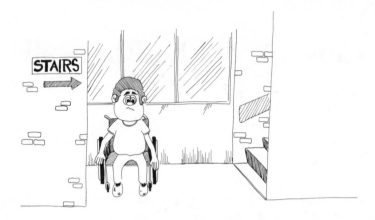

□ □   6. Does the elevator have braille markings to help a blind person select the right floor button?

□ □   7. Can the elevator floor buttons be reached by a person in a wheelchair?

□ □   8. Is the arrival of the elevator at a given floor announced through both a light and a buzzer or bell?

□ □   9. Are the bathroom doors wide enough to accommodate a wheelchair (at least 33 inches wide)?

□ □   10. Are there bars in bathroom stalls to permit people in wheelchairs to lift themselves to the toilet and back again?

□ □   11. Can the telephones be reached by a person in a wheelchair?

□ □   12. Can the water fountains be reached by a person in a wheelchair?

□ □   13. Can the mailboxes be reached by a person in a wheelchair?

□ □   14. Are the fire alarms low enough to permit a person in a wheelchair to signal a fire?

□ □   15. Does the fire alarm signal include a flashing light to warn a deaf person?

FOLLOW-UP

Compare the results of your checklist with those of your classmates.

Talk to physically disabled people to find out what changes in physical controls they have experienced. Ask them how they feel about these changes. Ask them what additional improvements can be made. Find out what you can do to help.

Talk to a school or community leader who is involved in providing access for handicapped people. Ask what changes have been made in the school or community and what improvements are yet to be made.

QUESTIONS FOR DISCUSSION

1. Are there students in your school who are physically disabled?
2. What changes have been made in the school facilities or rules to accommodate students who are disabled?
3. What improvements are yet to be made? What controls have prevented their being made?

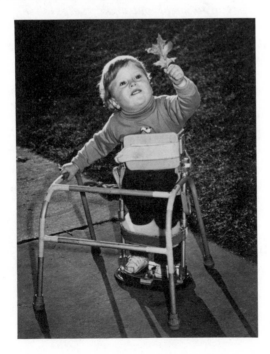

ACTIVITY 26

On Being Handicapped[5]

AUTHOR
WILFRED SHEED

Over the last 10 years, physically handicapped people have become more visible as they participate more fully in community activities. They have also begun to speak out about the psychological controls that reduce self-identity. In this essay, Wilfrid Sheed, a novelist who has a physical disability, tells us what angers him about the way he is treated. Use the PARS System (Worksheet VI) as you read "On Being Handicapped."

Warm Springs, Ga., the very White House of polio, has lately been declared a National Historic Landmark, which sounds like the last throw of the dice. Ever since the Salk vaccine came along, the polio foundation has tried to run along on neuromuscular disorders, but this was strictly a one-disease town, and when polio faded, along with Roosevelt's smiling memory, the famous pools became cracked and boarded over, and the whole place began to resemble the scene of last night's party—or am I imagining things?

I myself rolled up to Warm Springs as a patient in 1945, on waves of ballyhoo. Never was a placebo so publicized. Posters of a wretched little boy in leg-irons followed one everywhere, frightening the life out of my generation. And of course the mighty FDR himself endorsed the place. Since one never actually saw Roosevelt's legs, it was easy to miss the salient point—which was that Warm Springs had done nothing for them at all.

Those hidden legs proved a neat symbol for the whole operation. The public will to believe had instantly turned the place into a shrine like Lourdes, but nobody knew exactly what went on there. In fact, it took me several days on the spot to learn the answer myself: that practically nothing went on there. Fifteen minutes in the pool, being exercised gingerly by buxom nurses, a little walking practice (unauthorized walking was frowned on because it formed bad habits), and that was about it for the day. My parents had pulled every conceivable string to send me there, and all I got for their pains was a so-so knowledge of bridge and the certainty that polio was incurable (at least after the first few months). Incurable by Sister Kenny, Warm Springs, or any of the lesser charlatans.

Movies

It was at least a charming place to learn this. All those dimes had not been wasted. There were at least two-and-a-half staff people to every customer, and they always had time for you, to talk about their golf games or whatever you liked. And we got the same movies as Roosevelt. The boy in the leg-irons was nowhere to be seen, but I do remember some suspiciously healthy-looking servicemen who bribed me to line up for, and smartly hand over, my child's ration of cigarettes every day.

My tour of the dream factory left me skeptical of organized charity, which is correct, but especially about those tear-jerking posters that had roped me in. Later I would find myself working for a missionary society which, for all I knew, distributed the take evenly and well, but we used the exact same tricks. Every month we would riffle through a huge stack of leprosy pictures until we came to the most gruesome, and that's the one we used. Never mind that leprosy societies occasionally asked us to cool it, or that leprosy accounted for little or none of our business: it was box office, a crowd-pleaser, and you use what's there.

Of course the boy in the leg-irons was real enough, even if the promise they held out to him was not. But what any cripple comes most to hate is the use of pity in itself, to raise funds or anything else. Any affliction within reason can be gotten used to. Being treated funny cannot. Cripples do not, as you might suppose, sit around thinking,

"I'm a cripple" all day. It takes other people to remind them—the kind of people who say, "I see you've got a new mustache," in case you'd forgotten.

Real life is comic enough in these respects, without commercial assistance: the little kids who stage-holler, "What's wrong with that man?" (they're OK, as a matter of fact) and their parents who whisper, "Shush" and whisk them away to explain while throwing back anxious glances (they're a downright scream). But for most of the livelong day, the handicapped person is just a human soul at large, facing the world without his feet or his eyes or his ears, as if he'd left them home that day. He does not want to be interrupted by trivia about his health.

So anything that treats cripples primarily as cripples dehumanizes them drastically. And this goes for the retarded Olympics or the spastic hop, skip, and jump classic, or whatever well-meaning freak show they think of next. No human being deserves to be exhibited in this way to pay for his treatment. (And don't tell me how much the creatures enjoy it; they'd enjoy it just as much with the cameras turned off. And don't, while you're up, go on about their damn courage. They are sick to death of hearing about their courage.)

All-Stars

It is not just the contestants who are degraded by these affairs. They are, after all, merely the all-stars of crippledom, the most outstandingly pitiful in the Beauty Parade. In effect, they are sent out there to collect for the whole handicapped gang, who later divide the swag, and are thus implicated. It would be better all around if this form of fundraising went the way of cockfighting, while society came up with some less vulgar way of helping the unlucky.

Not that the handicapped should be kept out of sight: far from it. They should be seen much more than they are—in the buildings they can't enter right now because of swing doors, or climb in because of escalators, or even get to because of transport design—so that people can get used to them. "We can't make the town over for gimps," a waggish friend once said to me, and this may go for Grant's Tomb, St. Peter's Dome, and the Coney Island fun house. But new buildings are something else. Instead of telling the handicapped how plucky they are (there is nothing plucky about being handicapped, it just happens— and if you don't adjust, it's your tough luck), simply let them in the door and up the stairs. That's all they ask. And if this isn't precisely a right—there aren't really all that many rights—it's at least a reasonable tax for the healthy to pay on their luck.

Because, although the handicapped may look different to you, you look exactly the same to them. The only thing that separates you is the rabbit's foot that dangles (and here we Warm Springers would attempt a kind of Vincent Price chuckle) so precariously from your pretty neck.

—*Wilfrid Sheed*

QUESTIONS FOR DISCUSSION

1. What is the author's point of view on organized charity as a way to help the handicapped? Do you agree or disagree?
2. How does the author view such things as the Special Olympics and telethons? Do you agree or disagree?
3. What does the author think about efforts to provide access to public buildings for the handicapped? Does he favor them or is he opposed?
4. How does the essay relate to psychological controls in the school and community? Do you think the author is justified in his point of view? Why or why not?

ACTIVITY 27

A Conversation with Two Friends (Continued)[6]

Remember the conversation with the insurance man, Mitchell Darling, and the teacher, William Kemmett, in Unit II. Do you recall that they have been blind since youth? In our conversation with them, they discussed the idea of physical disability and attitudes toward the physically disabled.

Interviewer: "What do you think high school students ought to know about physical disabilities and physically disabled people?"

Mr. Darling: "Nobody's without physical disabilities. We all have a physical disability in one way or another, because we're not perfect. Just remember that the physically disabled individual is a person—a human being."

Mr. Kemmett: "As Mitch says, we all have physical disabilities of one kind or another. It might bother you or frighten you when you first meet someone who is physically different. Remember that the physically disabled person is another human being who has feelings and needs just as you do. He or she can be hurt just as you can be. Other than the physical disability, the person is no different than you."

Mr. Darling: "Being blind can be an asset. You can't form opinions about persons because they are overweight or underweight or perhaps have a scar on their face. Someone asked me recently how I can stand to talk with a particular person whom I had enjoyed talking with. I discovered that they were unable to talk with this person because her face was horribly scarred as a result of an automobile accident. Until I was told that, I never knew it."

Mr. Kemmett: "Being blind enables you to see the true beauty of the person. Beauty is different for every person. A physical handicap

[6]From interview with Mitchell Darling and William Kemmett, December 17, 1980, Lakewood, Ohio. Used by permission.

or disability is only in the eyes of the beholder. I guess it's what you make of it. People I know sometimes forget that I'm blind. This can be embarrassing, especially when I fall into a lake or run into a tree. We laugh about it."

Mr. Darling: "That's a compliment to you."

Mr. Kemmett: "Yes, it's a compliment. But it's all in the eyes of how people look at you. You can be with a person in a wheelchair and forget that the person is in the wheelchair, or you can dwell on it. It's a totally individual thing."

Mr. Darling: "Some years ago I met a lady who had a very deep voice. She was not at all attractive to me. Then someone told me she was the best-looking woman he had ever seen. Maybe if I had been able to see her I'd have had an entirely different opinion."

Mr. Kemmett: "So we have our prejudices just like everyone else. It's human nature."

QUESTIONS FOR DISCUSSION

1. How do you react to the statement by both Mr. Kemmett and Mr. Darling that we all have physical disabilities?
2. What does this mean: "A physical handicap or disability is only in the eyes of the beholder"?
3. What do you think can be done to help your generation become more understanding of handicapped people?
4. What similarities in point of view do you see between what Mr. Darling and Mr. Kemmett say about disabilities and what Mr. Sheed writes in his essay "On Being Handicapped"? What differences are there?

ACTIVITY 28

School Status

This activity is designed to explore the issue of status in student and teacher roles.

Form into two groups.

The first group is responsible for determining what groups of students have high status in your school. The group may wish to adapt the status experiment (see ACTIVITY 8 in this unit) for use in your school. For example, you may include such groups as the varsity football team, honor roll students, the best looking, the best dressed, and so on.

The second group is to investigate the issue of status differences among teachers. One of the unfortunate characteristics of teaching is that there are few opportunities in most schools for outstanding teachers to be recognized as such. In most schools, salary increases come only through years of service and further education and advanced degrees. Since there is very little opportunity for teachers to assume different roles as teachers, there are hardly any status differences among them. In fact, one of the strongest motivations to become an administrator is related to the lack of status differences among teachers.

The second group might wish to interview teachers and administrators to gain their insights about the issue.

ACTIVITY 29

Psychological Controls in the School Community

Consider again the Cliff Evans story as told in "Cipher in the Snow" in Unit I. Recall how Cliff's resources were diminished by parents, teachers, and classmates. Now recall the "killer statements" activity in Unit II. These two memories should be a constant reminder to us that the Immediate Physical/Psychological Setting (IPS) involves psychological controls as well as physical ones.

Each of us is a part of someone else's IPS. What are you doing to increase self-esteem in others? Are you exercising self-control so that you do not hinder or limit the self-esteem of others? Are you calling others to task when they attempt to use unwise controls on you and the people around you?

Have a class discussion on the progress the group is making in reducing the number of put-downs and increasing the number of put-ups.

Discuss how the IPS differs for teenagers who have it made and for the majority of us who are not ideal physical specimens, who are not A or B students, and who do not always do the right thing. How can the IPS of the school be made better for all?

One of the authors of *The New Model Me* had an unforgettable teaching experience. During the 1960s he was part of a group of 20 teachers from all over the country who met together at a camp for two weeks to discuss teaching and teenagers. With the teachers were 20 teenagers from a suburban school in the Midwest. Of the 20 students, 10 were identified as school leaders—captain of the football team, two cheerleaders, class presidents and other officers, and academic achievers. Ten were students who had problems in school—drugs, alcohol, excessive absences, verbal and physical assaults. At the conclusion of the two weeks, the teachers had formed deeper and more authentic relationships with the problem students than with the school leaders.

QUESTIONS FOR DISCUSSION

1. How do you account for the close relationships between the teachers and the problem students outside the school setting?
2. What do you think might account for the surprising differences between the teacher's relationships with the school leaders and his relationships with the problem students?
3. What do you think would occur if teachers and students in your school were placed in a similar situation?

A SCHOOL IS A WORKPLACE

Have you ever thought of a school as a workplace? Well, it is! To the administrators, counselors, teachers, secretaries, custodians, lunchroom personnel, and others, the school is the place where they work and the source of their livelihood. It is also a workplace for the students and a place to prepare for paid work. The adult community believes that the knowledge, skills, and attitudes learned in school will pay dividends when students enter the work force.

When you enter the work force, you should not be surprised to learn that the controls you faced in school are present in your paid job. Attendance, punctuality, self-discipline, and the attitude you reveal toward your boss and fellow workers are very important. Failure to conform will very likely result in suspension or dismissal.

Skills learned or not learned will also be controls on the job. An article in the business-oriented newspaper *The Wall Street Journal* describes the problems that employers have with poorly prepared

---

RULES

1. The boss is always right.
2. When the boss is wrong, refer to rule 1.

THE WORKER'S DILEMMA

1. No matter how much you do, you'll never do enough.
2. What you don't do is always more important than what you do do.

workers, especially those who cannot read, write, or compute very well.[7] The article includes an actual paragraph written by an applicant for a job at a Chicago bank!

> Well after I graudate from high school I had plan to find me a full time job at a bank as a clerk. I like working with and around people and met new people and see different face. I would love to have a job at this bank because working at a bank meet so much to me and the more important thing in my life.

Would you hire this applicant? The manager of the bank did not. She said, "More and more of the applicants we're seeing straight out of school can't write a complete sentence." Other contributors to the article mentioned the following examples of inadequately prepared workers:

- An insurance company reported that 70 percent of the firm's correspondence must be retyped because typists working from dictation tapes can't punctuate and spell properly.
- In a large industrial equipment company, a worker almost killed several co-workers when a piece of equipment flew apart. He had pieced it together improperly because he was unable to read the packaged instructions.
- Several workers in a defense plant were fired because they could not read the plant's danger warnings.

Meanwhile, word processors and other automated equipment are eliminating the need for simple, relatively unskilled jobs. Employers are looking for people with more skills who can handle more difficult jobs.

WORKPLACE RULES

The following rules were printed in the *Boston Globe* some years ago. They were reported to be the rules posted by the owner of a New England carriage works in 1872, as a guide to his office workers.

---

[7]Carol Hymowitz, "Remedial Bosses: Employers Take Over Where Schools Failed to Teach the Basics," *The Wall Street Journal*, January 22, 1981. Reprinted by permission of *The Wall Street Journal*, © Dow Jones & Company, Inc., 1981. All rights reserved.

ANNOUNCEMENT

1. Office employees will daily sweep the floors, dust the furniture, shelves, and showcases.
2. Each day fill lamps, clean chimneys, and trim wicks. Wash the windows once a week.
3. Each clerk will bring in a bucket of water and scuttle of coal for the day's business.
4. Make your pens carefully. You may whittle nibs to your individual taste.
5. This office will open at 7 A.M. and close at 8 P.M. except on the Sabbath, on which day we will remain closed. Each employee is expected to spend the Sabbath by attending church and contributing liberally to the cause of the Lord.
6. Men employees will be given time off each week for courting purposes, or two evenings a week if they go regularly to church.
7. After an employee has spent his 13 hours of labor in the office, he should spend the remaining time reading the Bible and other good books.
8. Every employee should lay aside from each pay a goodly sum of his earnings for his benefit during his declining years, so that he will not become a burden on society or his betters.
9. Any employee who smokes Spanish cigars, uses liquor in any form, frequents pool and public halls, or gets shaved in a barber shop will give me good reason to suspect his worth, intentions, integrity, and honesty.
10. The employee who has performed his labors faithfully and without a fault for five years will be given an increase of five cents per day in his pay, providing profits from the business permit it.

CONTROLS IN THE POLITICAL COMMUNITY

A political community is a legally defined group of people who are controlled by the same set of customs and traditions and rules and laws. It can be made up of a few people who decide to live together and who agree on the necessary regulations they will follow.

You are a member of several political communities. The village, town, city, county, state, and nation are the most common. Each political community has a set of controls. Controls are of two types:

1. *Common laws and regulations.* Wherever we travel, there are traffic regulations and laws against theft and attacks against other people and their property. These examples of laws and regulations exist in small and large communities almost everywhere in the world.

2. *Controls unique to a community.* All human beings share common characteristics. Yet each of us is unique. The same can be said of political communities. Some customs and traditions and regulations and laws are the product of a community's unique resources and values—its community identity. Social scientists use the term CULTURE to refer to all a community's ways of living. Culture includes such characteristics as a community's language, customs and traditions, literature, and political and economic thought. The more different the culture is from ours, the more different the regulations and laws that control the people will be.

ACTIVITY 30

Controls in Russia: Three Case Studies[8]

THE BLACK RUSSIANS

Serge Kapustin, 31, his wife, Natasha, 23, and her brother Vladimir Schneider, 29, are now living in the United States. They left Russia in 1976 to escape the controls on individual freedom there. In 1980 they signed with Motown records under their group name, Black Russian. In Russia the Kapustins had been members of a community-owned orchestra, and Vladimir was a member of a popular singing group. Vladimir became disheartened by the fact that the singing group had to sing "37 songs about how good the Communist Party is before they could sing one song that they picked, although rock was never permitted."

The community-owned orchestra was even more carefully controlled. All selections had to be approved by a community cultural official. If the music or lyrics did not promote the culture, the song was rejected. Even volume was controlled. Certain instruments were discouraged, including the bass drum. Even though the government could penalize them for doing this, the three Russians listened to forbidden

[8]Based on material that appeared in *The Plain Dealer* (Cleveland, Ohio) in January 1981.

Voice of America radio programs and learned to appreciate rock and soul music.

Finally they gave up the security of careers in Russia for a promise of a freer life in America. Even though life is now sweet, Serge still admits that they have "nightmares that we are back in Russia." (Incidentally, the name Black Russian honors the inspiration that soul music brought to them in their development.)

THE KOZLOVS: DIRECT FROM THE BOLSHOI

In 1979 Valentina and Leonid Kozlov defected from a Bolshoi Ballet tour of the United States. The Bolshoi is the most important ballet company in Russia and is world renowned.

Valentina was influenced to defect by the fact that she would be free to attend church in America. Both Kozlovs dreamed of being free to dance anywhere in the world. Even though they defected, the Kozlovs maintain ties to their families, who remain in Russia. They run up telephone bills of more than 100 dollars a month, although they are afraid that Russian police are listening to the conversations. Leonid is careful not to call people whom the Russian government has called troublemakers for fear that his call will cause them more trouble. The Kozlovs' long-range plan is to arrange for relatives to emigrate to the United States. They believe that if they have a child, the Russian government may allow the grandmothers to come to the United States. As Leonid said, "Valentina have child, so ask Russian government. We would like to have one grandmother. Maybe two! It be nice."

FOUR HAIR STYLISTS FIND FREEDOM IN AMERICA

In a hair-styling salon on the far east side of Cleveland, Ohio, the conversation is constant and lively, but the language is a mixture of English and Russian. The shop employs four hair stylists who have emigrated from Russia to the United States. One of the recent arrivals said, "Russian women do not think about their looks as much as American women, except those in the upper class." She added, "If American women had to work as hard as Russian women, they wouldn't look as good as they do."

In every case, the women left Russia to escape the religious persecution of Jews. Two of the women are Jewish, and the other two are married to Jewish men. The four women explained to a Cleveland *Plain Dealer* reporter in January 1981 that leaving Russia is a long, difficult, and emotionally painful process. During the one, two, or three years of waiting before one is permitted to leave, "you cannot work. The government takes away your documents." One of the women is the daughter of a Russian movie producer. As soon as her family applied to leave the country, her father's name was removed from all of his movie credits. Furthermore, their telephone was disconnected, and they found out later that more than 3,000 telegrams of support from the U.S. film community were never delivered to them.

Although it is difficult for the women and their families to begin a new life in an unfamiliar culture, the four hair stylists are adjusting to life in the United States. They have no choice. They can never return to Russia, even to visit relatives who remain there.

You may wish to learn more about political controls in other countries and compare them to those in the United States. Look at such countries as Iran, Cuba, Chile, China, South Africa, and Uganda.

QUESTIONS FOR DISCUSSION

1. What peculiar controls in Russia are mentioned in the three accounts?
2. What do the accounts suggest about the relative emphasis given to self-identity in Russia as compared to the United States?

ECONOMIC SECURITY VERSUS POLITICAL FREEDOM

One clear difference between Russia and the United States is the way the political community views the conflict between ECONOMIC SECURITY and POLITICAL FREEDOM. In Russia economic security is the first priority of the government. There is very little unemployment. Although wages are low compared with those in the United States, prices for the necessities of life—food, shelter, clothing—are also low. As those trying to leave Russia suggest, the price of economic security is an overbearing control on political freedom.

In the United States, unemployment is a concern for many Americans. When economic times get tough, some people are laid off and have to depend on government help and charity until economic times improve. For the vast majority of Americans who never experience economic insecurity, there are relatively few controls on political freedom. Americans are free to write and speak critically about their government. They are free to pursue their individual self-identities.

What are the consequences of living in a community such as Russia? What are the consequences of living in a community such as the United States?

ACTIVITY 31

Laws and Regulations

In America laws are written by representatives of the people, and people are expected to obey these laws. This does not mean, however, that every law is accepted by every person or that every law is effective in achieving its purpose. Problems do arise, and laws are violated.

In groups of four to six students, consider the reasons why people violate specific laws.

QUESTIONS FOR DISCUSSION

1. Which community laws (local, state, or federal) do individuals or groups often violate?
2. What effect do you think a person's needs have on the decision to violate a law? What effect do resources have on this decision? How is the decision affected by the Immediate Physical/ Psychological Setting?
3. What do you think should be done about laws that are often violated?

ACTIVITY 32

Political Leadership: Role and Status

This is an activity designed to enable you to continue to pursue the nature of leadership. What resources does an individual require to become a political leader and to be successful in that status? Consider the presidency of the United States as an example.

List the resources you think an individual needs to attain the status and to be successful in the role of President of the United States.

QUESTIONS FOR DISCUSSION

1. How do the resources on your list compare with the resources suggested by classmates?
2. What differences and similarities can you find between the resource list for President and the resources you thought were needed to become a leader in your peer group? (See ACTIVITY 17.) How do you account for the differences?

Compare your list of resources with those suggested by Michael Korda in his essay "How to Be a Leader." The essay was written a month after the presidential election of 1980. Use the PARS System (Worksheet VII) as you read it.

ACTIVITY 33

How to Be a Leader[9]

AUTHOR
MICHAEL KORDA

At a moment when we are waiting to see whether we have elected a President or a leader, it is worth examining the differences between the two. For not every President is a leader, but every time we elect a President we hope for one, especially in times of doubt and crisis. In easy times we are ambivalent—the leader, after all, makes demands, challenges the status quo, shakes things up.

Leadership is as much a question of timing as anything else. The leader must appear on the scene at a moment when people are looking for leadership, as Churchill did in 1940, as Roosevelt did in 1933, as Lenin did in 1917. And when he comes, he must offer a simple, eloquent message.

Great leaders are almost always great simplifiers, who cut through argument, debate, and doubt to offer a solution everybody can understand and remember. Churchill warned the British to expect "blood, toil, tears, and sweat"; FDR told Americans that "the only thing we have to fear is fear itself"; Lenin promised the war-weary Russians peace, land, and bread. Straightforward but potent messages.

We have an image of what a leader ought to be. We even recognize the physical signs: Leaders may not necessarily be tall, but they must have bigger-than-life, commanding features—LBJ's nose and ear

[9]*Newsweek* (January 5, 1981). Copyright 1981, by Newsweek, Inc. All rights reserved. Article and photo reprinted by permission. Michael Korda, editor-in-chief of Simon and Schuster, is author of a novel called *Worldly Goods*.

lobes, Ike's broad grin. A trademark also comes in handy: Lincoln's stovepipe hat, JFK's rocker. We expect our leaders to stand out a little, not to be like ordinary men. Half of President Ford's trouble lay in the fact that, if you closed your eyes for a moment, you couldn't remember his face, figure, or clothes. A leader should have an unforgettable identity, instantly and permanently fixed in people's minds.

Special

It also helps for a leader to be able to do something most of us can't: FDR overcame polio; Mao swam the Yangtze River at the age of 72. We don't want our leaders to be "just like us." We want them to be like us but better, special, more so. Yet if they are too different, we reject them. Adlai Stevenson was too cerebral. Nelson Rockefeller, too rich.

Even television, which comes in for a lot of knocks as an image-builder that magnifies form over substance, doesn't altogether obscure the qualities of leadership we recognize, or their absence. Television exposed Nixon's insecurity, Humphrey's fatal infatuation with his own voice.

A leader must know how to use power (that's what leadership is about), but he also has to have a way of showing that he does. He has to be able to project firmness—no physical clumsiness (like Ford), no rapid eye movements (like Carter).

A Chinese philosopher once remarked that a leader must have the grace of a good dancer, and there is a great deal of wisdom to this. A leader should know how to appear relaxed and confident. His walk should be firm and purposeful. He should be able, like Lincoln, FDR, Truman, Ike, and JFK, to give a good, hearty belly laugh, instead of the sickly grin that passes for good humor in Nixon or Carter. Ronald Reagan's training as an actor showed to good effect in the debate with Carter, when by his easy manner and apparent affability he managed to convey the impression that in fact he was the President and Carter the challenger.

If we know what we're looking for, why is it so difficult to find? The answer lies in a very simple truth about leadership. People can only be led where they want to go. The leader follows, though a step ahead. Americans wanted to climb out of the Depression and needed someone to tell them they could do it, and FDR did. The British believed that they could still win the war after the defeats of 1940, and Churchill told them they were right.

A leader rides the waves, moves with the tides, understands the deepest yearnings of his people. He cannot make a nation that wants peace at any price go to war, or stop a nation determined to fight from doing so. His purpose must match the national mood. His task is to focus the people's energies and desires, to define them in simple terms, to inspire, to make what people already want seem attainable, important, within their grasp.

Above all, he must dignify our desires, convince us that we are taking part in the making of great history, give us a sense of glory about ourselves. Winston Churchill managed, by sheer rhetoric, to turn the British defeat and the evacuation of Dunkirk in 1940 into a major victory. FDR's words turned the sinking of the American fleet at Pearl Harbor into a national rallying cry instead of a humiliating national scandal. A leader must stir our blood, not appeal to our reason.

Fallacy

For this reason, businessmen generally make poor leaders. They tend to be pragmatists who think that once you've explained why something makes sense, people will do it. But history shows the fallacy of this belief. When times get tough, people don't want to be told what went wrong, or lectured, or given a lot of complicated statistics and plans (like Carter's energy policy) they don't understand. They want to be moved, excited, inspired, consoled, uplifted—in short, led!

A great leader must have a certain irrational quality, a stubborn refusal to face facts, infectious optimism, the ability to convince us that all is not lost even when we're afraid it is. Confucius suggested that, while the advisers of a great leader should be as cold as ice, the leader himself should have fire, a spark of divine madness.

He won't come until we're ready for him, for the leader is like a mirror, reflecting back to us our own sense of purpose, putting into words our own dreams and hopes, transforming our needs and fears into coherent policies and programs.

Our strength makes him strong; our determination makes him determined; our courage makes him a hero; he is, in the final analysis, the symbol of the best in us, shaped by our own spirit and will. And when these qualities are lacking in us, we can't produce him; and even with all our skill at image building, we can't fake him. He is, after all, merely the sum of us.   —*Michael Korda*

QUESTIONS FOR DISCUSSION

1. What differences and similarities can you find between your list of resources and the list created by Michael Korda?
2. What changes would you now make in your list? Would you be willing to write to Mr. Korda and suggest that one of the resources you listed should have been included in his essay? If so, write to him at the Simon and Schuster Publishing Company.
3. In what ways does Mr. Korda's essay remind you of ideas and skills presented in Unit II, "Self-Identity"?

CONTROLS IN THE ECONOMIC COMMUNITY

An economic community is a group of people who depend on each other to produce and consume goods and services. Because of this dependency, each member of the community exerts some control over all of the other members.

Economic communities can be small, consisting of just a few people. For example, the owner of a small store may need only one employee to serve customers. The owner, employee, and customers form an economic community. Each of the three members exerts some control over the other two: The owner pays the employee, the employee serves the customers, and the customers pay the owner.

Economic communities can be very large, incorporating several smaller communities. For example, the auto manufacturers, the steel companies, and the petroleum industry are economic communities. However, taken together, these three groups form an even larger economic community. The auto manufacturers buy steel and sell their cars to people, who in turn buy gasoline. Finally, in the United States, the government enters the picture to regulate and limit the actions of groups in larger economic communities.

There are three ways to get something done: Do it
yourself, hire someone, or forbid your kids to do it.
—Monta Crane[10]

---

[10]Originally from *Sunshine* magazine. Quoted in *Reader's Digest* (June 1977).

ACTIVITY 34

The Big Apple[11]

This activity will help you to understand how the MARKET forces of supply and demand operate and to explore how prices are set in a competitive market. A competitive market is a physical or psychological setting in which sellers compete to satisfy the wants of many buyers. Sellers try to sell their goods and services at a price that will cover their costs and provide them with a maximum return (profit) on their investment. Buyers attempt to buy the goods or services at as low a price as possible. In "The Big Apple" you will experience the process of setting prices through participating in a competitive market.

HOW TO PLAY "THE BIG APPLE"

Your teacher will divide your class into two separate groups. One group will sell apples, and the other group will buy apples. There will be three rounds for trading bins of apples at various prices. Each round will last eight minutes, and each buyer and seller should make as many transactions as possible during that time.

You will each be given a sell or buy order by an order clerk.

- Sell orders will establish a minimum price for selling a bin of apples. Sellers, however, will be judged on the basis of the difference between this minimum price and the transaction price (the amount of money they actually get for the apples they sell). The higher the price they get, the better their score.

- Buy orders will establish a maximum price for buying a bin of apples. Buyers, however, will be judged on the basis of the difference between this maximum price and the transaction price (the amount of money they must pay to obtain the apples). The lower the price they get, the better their score.

---

[11]Adapted from the "Big Apple" game. Reprinted with permission by Dr. Richard M. Thornton, Associate Director, Center for Economic Education, De Paul University.

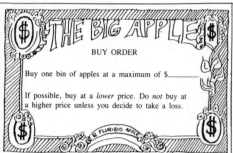

After buy and sell orders are distributed by the order clerk, buyers
and sellers will line up on opposite sides of the room. At a signal
from your teacher buyers and sellers mingle in the "trading pit"
in the center of the room and begin the trading.

- So that no secrecy is possible in the market, buyers and sellers
  must shout out their bids and offer prices for apples (but each
  person should keep the maximum or minimum price on his or
  her orders secret). Buyers and sellers may change their prices
  upward or downward as required to make a trade. However,
  each time they change a price they must shout out the new
  price. In no case may buyers exceed the maximum price on
  their buy order unless they decide to take a loss, or may sellers
  go below the minimum price on their sell order unless they
  decide to take a loss.

- When a buyer and seller agree on a trade, they take their orders
  to the announcer, who shouts out that a trade has been made at a
  specific price. The information is also put on the chalkboard or
  a transparency by the announcer so that students may refer to it
  as the game proceeds.

- Next the buyer and seller take their orders to the record clerk,
  who records the details of the sale.

- The buyer and seller then take their orders to the order clerk and
  exchange them for new orders. They re-enter the "trading pit"
  and resume participation in the game.

After eight minutes, your teacher will announce the end of Round 1. At that time trading will stop. During the break before Round 2, participants who have been unable to make a trade or who have orders with prices they think are too high can go to the order clerk and get a new order. (Buyers and sellers cannot change roles.)

After the break your teacher will announce the beginning of Round 2 and, after eight more minutes and a second break, the beginning of Round 3.

One minute before Round 3 is to close, your teacher will announce that only one minute remains to complete trades. Only trades completed by the end of the session will be recorded. No trades may be completed after your teacher announces the close of the session.

After all trades are announced and recorded, the record clerk will compute the difference between the price on each participant's order cards and their actual transaction prices. The trader who has the highest difference is the winner of the game.

Your teacher will give you further instructions and the materials you will need.

QUESTIONS FOR DISCUSSION

1. At what price were the apples most frequently sold in Round 1? Round 2? Round 3?
2. In which round was there the greatest spread in price?
3. Why do you think the prices became more clustered?
4. Who determined the market price for apples—the buyers or the sellers?

MARKET REGULATIONS

In "The Big Apple" the price of the apples was determined by the forces of supply (sellers) and demand (buyers). Most markets are not as clearly competitive as the one described in the game. In some markets, one seller or a few sellers dominate and are able to set prices. When this occurs, we have a MONOPOLY.

In some of these situations, the government steps in to regulate the market to prevent unwise control over buyers. For example, the government regulates telephone, electric, and gas rates because monopolies exist in these service areas. The correct amount of government regulation over business has become a hotly debated issue during the past 10 years. Regulations often result in a higher product cost, which is then passed on to the public. Some regulations are designed to protect the health and safety of the workers who produce the product or the people who consume it. The question we all must face is how much we are willing to pay to save a few people from sickness, injury, or death.

ACTIVITY 35

Sturdy Steel

This activity will involve you in a controversial case of government regulation. One of the federal agencies that has been the subject of much controversy because of its regulations is the Environmental Protection Agency (EPA). Among its other responsibilities, the EPA monitors and controls the air and water quality in the United States. In this activity you will have the opportunity to examine the possible economic consequences of an EPA ruling.

Read the news item and headlines[12] and then answer the Questions for Discussion.

News item: The Environmental Protection Agency ruled that the Sturdy Steel plant in Alwood must install new equipment to drastically cut the air pollution caused by its furnaces. The estimated cost is $3 million. The new equipment must be installed within three years, or the company will be penalized for non-compliance. The Alwood plant has 3,000 employees.

—Alwood Blabber, April 6

**STURDY STEEL COMPANY EXECUTIVES
MAY CLOSE ALWOOD PLANT**

—Alwood Blabber, April 8

**ALWOOD RETAILERS UPSET BECAUSE
STURDY STEEL PLANT MAY CLOSE**

—Alwood Blabber, April 8

**LOCAL DOCTOR ENDORSES EPA
RULING AS HEALTH MEASURE**

—Alwood Blabber, April 9

---

[12]News item and headlines adapted from *Master Curriculum Guide for the Nation's Schools, Part II, Strategies for Teaching Economics: Basic Business and Consumer Education (Secondary).* © 1979 Joint Council on Economic Education. All rights reserved. Used by permission.

QUESTIONS FOR DISCUSSION

1. Why might the Sturdy Steel Company close its Alwood plant?
2. If the company installs the equipment, what could be the effect on costs and prices?
3. What effect might an increase in the price of steel have on the price of automobiles?
4. Why are retailers in Alwood upset over the possible closing?
5. One of the town's doctors insists that the ruling is a good one. Why do you think the doctor feels this way? Why might the doctor disagree with retailers about the wisdom of this ruling?
6. If you were a manager of the Sturdy Steel Company, would you support the Environmental Protection Agency ruling? Keep in mind both immediate and remote consequences. Explain your answer.
7. If you were a consumer living in Alwood, would you support the EPA ruling? Keep in mind both immediate and remote consequences. Explain your answer.

CONTROLS THROUGH THE MASS MEDIA

Sixty million Americans purchase a daily newspaper. Four to eight million of us read *Time, Newsweek,* or *U.S. News and World Report* each week. There are more than 340 million radios in the United States, and 97 percent of all American homes include at least one television set. Newspapers, magazines, radio, and television are examples of media—channels or routes by which information is presented. Face-to-face contact is another example of a medium. We label this segment of the unit "Controls Through the MASS MEDIA" because the media we will examine are used to present information to great numbers of people.

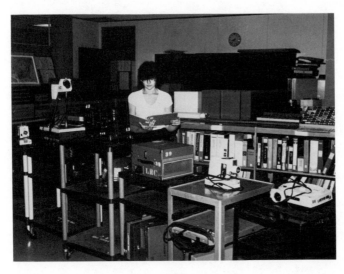

What is the impact of the mass media on each of us? Possibly we do not realize how much the media influence us because the influence is constant and unseen. Yet it is possible and important to discover how we are affected by the media and the techniques used to get the message across.

We will examine how the mass media—especially television—can control actions and alternatives. PROPAGANDA, the major tool of those who use the mass media to persuade, will also be studied. Propaganda is a conscious effort to persuade people to think or feel a particular way.

The mass media are powerful tools to inform, to educate, to entertain, and to persuade. They can be tools for good or for bad. We can learn what is going on in the world, participate in great events and unique entertainment experiences, and become exposed to new products and services. We can also be manipulated and used by unscrupulous businesses, unprincipled politicians, and many other special interest groups. Whether the power of the mass media is used for good or for evil, it is always a power for control.

ACTIVITY 36

Mass Media

Attending school, sleeping, eating, studying, working, playing sports, and engaging in miscellaneous activities may use up 103 hours of the 168 hours in your week. Do you know what portion of the 65 remaining hours of your week are devoted to the mass media? Do you really know?

The following activity will help you find out just how much the media enter your life.

Use the following chart to add up the amount of time, in hours and minutes, that you spend on the various media. First figure out the time you spend during one week. Then multiply the time spent per week by 52 to determine how much time you devote to these activities in one year. Assume that you will live for 50 more years and continue to devote the same amount of time as you do now to mass media. Determine, in years, how much time you will devote to the media during the next half century.

Medium	Time per Week (in Hours & Minutes)	Time per Year (in Hours & Minutes)	Time in 50 Years (in Years)
Television			
Radio			
Movies (not on television)			
Comic books and magazines			
Books			
Newspapers			
Records and tapes			
Total			

The information about the time you spend with media can now be used to determine whether you feel it is time well spent.

Complete the following sentence stems.

    1. I learned that . . . .
    2. I was surprised that . . . .
    3. As the result of what I learned, I plan to . . . .

ACTIVITY 37

Propaganda and Its Techniques

The following activity will help you recognize propaganda, identify its techniques, and become aware of how it can control and affect people.

Propaganda is a systematic attempt to influence opinions or beliefs. Advertisements, commercials, and political speeches are the most common forms. Propaganda techniques include pictures, printed words, talks, debates, and documentaries. All appeal to emotions, but they are disguised as an appeal to logic. All seek to control human beings in one way or another.

> "A timely gift of beauty to be treasured now—and in years to come—the First Lady's Inaugural Pendant."

Under this caption you would see a beautiful sterling silver neck chain and a solid sterling silver pendant. The appeal to the need for self-esteem is powerful, and the propaganda technique used is that of transferring the prestige of the First Lady to you or your lady. *You* will be giving or wearing this extraordinary object.

What do you think of the following candidate and his political advertisement?

> "John Plain is for lower taxes, a strong military establishment, and lower government spending."

This is a propaganda technique called "card stacking." All of the things listed are good and favorable to the candidate. But they may not be consistent with one another—how do you reduce taxes, reduce spending, and still build a strong military? Something else must go. What will it be?

The following list identifies some other propaganda techniques:

1. *Name calling:* A negative label is applied to a person or an idea without concern about whether or not it is accurate. A political candidate could be called a tool of the mob or a fat cat.

2. *Transfer:* This technique associates something most people consider good with a person or product—for example, restaurants display "home cooking" signs and hotels have names like Caesar's Palace. Political candidates may use slogans like "he is a real American hero."

3. *Glittering generalities:* This technique uses vague words that sound good but are meaningless without explanation. They are used to enhance the person or thing referred to—for example, "Our candidate is honest, loyal, moral, and charming" or "WOW Cereal makes you feel like WOW!"

4. *Testimonial:* Someone has a well-known person say good things about him or her, or a famous person is paid to speak highly of some product.

5. *Plain folks:* This technique makes a person appear to be just like us or the man on the street. It can also be used to show that some product is used or bought by people like us.

6. *Band wagon:* This technique creates the impression that everyone is doing a particular thing and, therefore, we should join the crowd.

7. *Card stacking:* All the things said about a person or product are favorable. Only one side of an issue is presented.

Using the propaganda techniques just explained, select the one that is represented by each of the following statements. (Use a separate sheet of paper, lettered a to g, to record your choices.)

_____ a. My opponent has the support of people associated with organized crime, radical groups, and subversive activities. He has appeared in the company of those who would destroy our way of life.

_____ b. Don't be left behind. Join the crowds buying American cars.

_____ c. Joe Namath says Brut is great for the real man!

_____ d. Abe Lincoln was known as the railsplitter, Jimmy Carter as a peanut farmer, and Ronald Reagan as a cowboy.

_____ e. "Good for Chicago!" was a banner statement used by Mayor Richard Daley.

_____ f. Keep cool with Kools.

_____ g. Television is a wondrous invention. It gives us news, beauty, new ideas, great drama and music, and documentaries.

ACTIVITY 38

Propaganda Collage

To practice recognizing propaganda techniques that you see every day, complete the following activity:

Look through magazines, newspapers, journals, or any other printed materials and find examples of the seven propaganda techniques used to control us.

Cut out the examples and place them on a large piece of construction or art paper. Label each example. Make a heading or title at the top of the paper.

ACTIVITY 39

Advertising and Our Needs

In Unit I you learned about Maslow's five basic needs: physical requirements (air, water, food, etc.), safety and security, love and belonging, esteem, and self-fulfillment. Advertisers appeal to these needs in their presentations.

The following advertisements have appeared in magazines. Construct a chart similar to the one that follows. In the first blank column, name Maslow's need to which each advertisement appeals. In the other column, explain how the advertisement appeals to this need.

Advertisement	Need	Appeal
"Heart to Heart. Messages of Love. Families, friends, and sweethearts will never forget this Valentine's Day surprise! Run a greeting in our Valentine feature."		
"Is your *hair* physically fit?"		
"Shield helps stop cavities before they start."		
"The eternal secrets of skin beauty from India will help you look years younger."		

QUESTIONS FOR DISCUSSION

1. In what way does an understanding of advertising help you decide what to purchase?
2. Examine a series of automobile advertisements. What needs do they appeal to? Explain.
3. Self-fulfillment is the highest need we have. It is the something within us that makes us want to be more human, to grow, and to strive for perfection. It is difficult to find advertising that appeals to this need. What kind of advertisement would appeal to the desire for self-fulfillment?

ACTIVITY 40

Role and Status on Television

Each of us watches television many hours every week. We derive both entertainment and knowledge from it. What we learn is a concern of sociologists and educators. Are we learning useful information? Are we getting an accurate view of American life, or are the media controlling that view, either by design or by accident?

To gather evidence on these issues, we will view situation comedies on television.

Make a list of the prime-time television situation comedies on the three major networks. Use only prime-time shows to make sure you are getting a current view of America. (Prime time is defined in the East as the hours from 8:00 to 11:00 P.M.)

Choose five of these shows by picking numbers from a bowl or flipping a coin. If the entire class participates, try to watch all of the shows.

On a chart similar to the one on the next page, answer the questions about roles and status in the family, the work setting, male/female relationships, and racial and ethnic groups.

QUESTIONS FOR DISCUSSION

1. What did you conclude about Americans and their roles as portrayed by television?
2. What kinds of people seem to have high status as seen through the television lens? What kinds have low status? How does this information compare with the information about status presented in ACTIVITY 8?
3. What television portrayals of roles and racial and ethnic groups support stereotypes about them? What portrayals seem to differ from the stereotypes?
4. In general, what conclusions can you draw about the accuracy of what television teaches about American roles and racial and ethnic groups?

233

Questions	Responses
1. FAMILY Does this show portray family life? If so, how is each member of the family portrayed? Is he or she smart or stupid? pleasant or unpleasant? someone to envy or to pity?	
2. WORK SETTING Does this show portray a work setting? If so, is the work setting pleasant or unpleasant? How is each person in the work setting portrayed? the boss? the workers? the customers? Are they smart or stupid? pleasant or unpleasant? people to envy or to pity?	
3. MALE/FEMALE RELATIONSHIPS How does the show portray male and female relationships? How are the men and women portrayed? Are the men and/or women portrayed as smart or stupid? pleasant or unpleasant? people to envy or to pity?	
4. RACIAL AND ETHNIC GROUPS Are any characters identifiable as black, Oriental, Hispanic? as Italian, Irish, Jewish, Polish, etc? If so, how would you describe these identifiable characters? Are they smart or stupid? pleasant or unpleasant? people to envy or to pity?	

Television show_____

Date viewed _____ Time of day _____

ACTIVITY 41

How Much Violence Is There on Television?

The following activity will help you determine how much violence is portrayed on television. View at least two hours of drama (police, mystery, soap opera, disaster). For each program you watch, make up a chart similar to the one shown below to share your findings with the class. We have provided a sample analysis of one episode of *Hart to Hart*.

Television show	*Hart to Hart*		Channel 5
Date viewed *1/13/81*		Time of day *10–11 P.M.*	

Use of Physical Force to Hurt or Kill (Describe what occurred, why)	Number Hurt or Killed	Weapon Used
Man shot. He was a spy for Russia.	*1*	*Handgun*
Karate fight between two men—U.S. and Soviet agents	*2*	*Gun and hands*
Hart threatens a man.	*0*	*—*
TOTAL NUMBER OF INCIDENTS *3*		

QUESTIONS FOR DISCUSSION

1. In 1973 it was estimated that every hour there appeared on television an average of eight incidents in which physical force was used. How does this compare with the findings of your class?

2. How do you think violence on television affects the amount of violence in your school and political communities?

3. Would you agree or disagree with a policy to reduce or even eliminate the use of physical force to hurt or kill on television? Explain.

IMPACT PEOPLE:
A POSITIVE CONTROL

Before this unit on controls is completed, we think it is appropriate to move in an upbeat direction. Until this point, the discussion of wise and unwise controls has had a taste of medicine about it. Medicine may or may not be helpful, but it usually tastes awful. Many of the laws, rules, and traditions we encounter throughout our lives feel awful as we experience them. The unwise controls leave a bitter taste in our mouths. In a few cases, the bitterness remains for a lifetime.

However, all controls are not distasteful. Some controls are not only wise; they are even pleasant if they come from a source we respect and admire. Such controls guide us rather than manipulate us. They set examples for us to examine rather than force us to behave in a particular way. They permit us to exercise self-control as we become capable of doing so. People who influence us in these ways often become our IMPACT PEOPLE. We admire impact people. We want to please them and be like them. We learn from them.

Impact people are parents, older brothers and sisters, other relatives, teachers, clergymen, counselors, friends, and acquaintances. People we have not met can be impact people. People who have lived in the past can be impact people. Even characters in fiction and fantasy can be impact people. As we age, our impact people change. We may drop some and add others, but, in any case, we are fortunate to have them.

ACTIVITY 42

My Impact Person[13]

AUTHOR
JOE WRIGHT GRIGGS

We are fortunate to have a friend of The New Model Me *who was willing to share his impact person with us. Use the PARS System (Worksheet VIII) to read his essay.*

Never have I felt so afraid as I did the day I walked into a sixth-grade classroom in Brownsville, Texas, to begin my first teaching assignment. I had completed only two years of college, had taken none of the required education and psychology courses, and was myself still a teenager, having celebrated my 19th birthday only two months before.

The only reason I was teaching school instead of returning to college was that my dad, himself a Texas school superintendent with a very strong personality, had decided that I should teach school for a few years before I finished college and went on to law school—another part of his plan for my life. Through Dad's influence with one of his fellow superintendents, I was given a position in a large inner-city elementary school with all Mexican-American pupils.

---

[13]Written especially for *The New Model Me* by Joe Wright Griggs.

So, on that first day of school, I staggered across the classroom, close to collapse, and fell heavily into the teacher's chair. I stared at the 47 curious faces of my pupils. They stared back. For several minutes I achieved what I never had again in my entire teaching career—absolutely perfect classroom control!

Finally a little girl near the front broke the silence with a question. "What's your name, Mister?"

I gasped my name in a high-pitched, squeaky voice. It must have sounded to them like "Mr. Greese" because that's what they called me until I finally calmed down enough to write "Mr. Griggs" on the chalkboard.

Because of my feelings of fear and inadequacy, I did some pretty bad things in the classroom. I listed a number of strict rules covering everything from gum chewing to whispering and severely punished each infraction—usually with a paddling. I made sure that they had a heavy load of homework to do each day in every subject, and warned that anyone who had not finished his homework would stay after school the next day until it was finished. More often than not, my entire class was forced to stay extra hours after school.

My pupils were naturally extremely upset by my harsh teaching methods. They sought an advocate—someone who had the interest and the authority to plead their cause.

The person they chose was a very warm Mexican-American woman named Mrs. Gonzales, who taught directly across the hall from me. Since she had been the fourth-grade teacher for many of my pupils, they knew her to be kind, fair, and compassionate—someone who would really listen and respond to them.

When problems arose, as they often did as a result of my strict disciplinary methods, delegations of pupils from my class sought the advice and help of Mrs. Gonzales.

I have often thought about what could have happened if Mrs. Gonzales had been as insecure and fearful as I was. She might have come storming across the hall, shaken a finger under my nose, and called me a bigot. She might have said, "Mr. Griggs, you're prejudiced against these Mexican children—that's why you treat them the way you do." And she would have been wrong. I was not prejudiced, I was afraid. I would have been just as fearful if I had been facing 47 white children.

But Mrs. Gonzales knew who she was and was always sensitive to my feelings of insecurity and inadequacy. When a problem had been related to her, she waited until I was alone before paying me a visit. The first thing she did after greeting me warmly was to "brag on me"—tell me about something that I was doing well. I have often thought that she must have lain awake at night trying to think what positive things she could say to me the next time a problem arose.

And it really worked! When she had affirmed me, both as a person and as a teacher, I was relaxed and ready to hear whatever she wanted to say. When she had me feeling good about myself, she approached the problem at hand—but always in a positive, never a judgmental, way. She helped me to understand the needs of the child or children with whom I was having trouble, and then suggested ideas or methods she thought would help me be a more effective teacher.

Then one day an incident occurred in my class that literally changed my life. A shabbily dressed little girl named Paula, whom I had always viewed as a real troublemaker, turned in her spelling words written on two sheets of toilet paper.

I immediately became angry and defensive. I felt that this was a deliberate insult. Obviously there was an implied message here, and I did not like the message!

Enraged, I waved the two sheets of toilet paper in front of the class, and screamed at Paula, "Paula, why did you do this?"

Paula immediately burst into tears, and between sobs she gasped, "Mr. Griggs, that's all I had to write on."

That afternoon while the children were out for recess, Mrs. Gonzales came to see me. As usual, I was very happy to see her. (Most of us like to be with people who make us feel good about ourselves.)

As always, following her warm greeting, Mrs. Gonzales had words of praise for something I was doing well. After she had built me up, Mrs. Gonzales said, "I heard about the problem you had with Paula this morning. Mr. Griggs, do you know anything about Paula and her family?"

I had to confess that I knew very little about any of the children in my class. I was so occupied with my own problems that I had not bothered finding out about theirs.

Mrs. Gonzales then told me about Paula and her family. Paula's father had been unable to find work to support his family in his home town, the Mexican border city just across the river from Brownsville.

So one dark night, in order to avoid the border patrol, he and his family had waded across the Rio Grande and illegally entered this country.

Mrs. Gonzales always visited the children in her class at home so that she might meet their families. She had gotten directions on how to get to Paula's home. "I had great difficulty locating it, Mr. Griggs," she said. "It was a two-room, tar-paper shack in an isolated patch of trees near the bank of the Rio Grande."

The eight children slept in one room and the parents slept in the other, which also doubled as a living room. There was no plumbing in the house; the family went to the river for their drinking water. Mrs. Gonzales said that the house was full of lice. "If you will look closely at Paula's hair, you will see it is alive with nits, and there is nothing she can do to get rid of them." She also told me that she had heard that Paula's father had tuberculosis and was not expected to live out the year.

"Since there is no one working and they are hiding out from social services, they just don't have any money, Mr. Griggs." She told me that Paula would continue to wear the same thin cotton dress all year. She had no coat or shoes and would continue to come to school barefooted.

"So, when she told you she had nothing to write on except two sheets of toilet paper, she was probably telling you the truth."

I stared at Mrs. Gonzales but said nothing. The story of Paula showed me a lot about Paula—and a lot more about me. I had been terribly unfair to condemn her behavior without attempting to understand the underlying causes. Wasn't this what I had been doing with all of the children in my class?

A seed was planted that day which has been growing and developing ever since. I resolved that from then on I would get to know my pupils and become aware of their needs and feelings.

The change was slow. I still needed the kind, supportive visits from Mrs. Gonzales. But toward the end of the school year, the visits were much less frequent. I felt better about myself, as both a person and a teacher. As I became more accepting of my pupils, they became more accepting of me—and, more importantly, of themselves.

I realize now that Mrs. Gonzales was not just trying to salvage Mr. Griggs as a person and a teacher. Her primary concern was that I should have a positive influence on the lives of the pupils in my class.

But I also know that Mrs. Gonzales's influence goes far beyond that one classroom in Brownsville, Texas. Indirectly, she has helped every person in my life since that time. And, after all, isn't that what a true impact person always does?

—*Joe Wright Griggs*

QUESTIONS FOR DISCUSSION

1. What are the needs of each person in this story?
   - Mr. Griggs
   - Mr. Griggs's father
   - Mrs. Gonzales
   - Paula
2. What characteristics made Mrs. Gonzales an impact person?
3. Who are some impact people in your life?
4. Why do you see them as impact people?
5. Do you feel you have been an impact person in the life of anyone?
6. In your response to the other person, what did you do that you feel made an impact on his or her life?
7. Is it possible to be an impact person in the lives of everyone with whom we come in contact? Why or why not?

ACTIVITY 43

Impact People: My Board of Directors

This activity will help you to become aware of your impact people—the people who have the greatest influence on you.

Draw a rectangle. The rectangle will contain the names of the board of directors of your company. The company is you. Your impact people make up your board of directors.

List all the people who presently sit on your board of directors. Look for people you admire and respect—people whose ideas are important to you when you must make major decisions. Remember, impact people can be real or imaginary, living or dead, relatives or people whom you have never met.

Put a *C* next to the person who is chairman of your board.

Rank the members of the board, assigning the highest number to the chairman and proceeding down to 1.

Put an *M* next to each board member whom you have met.

Put a *W* next to each board member whom you see or talk to at least once a week.

Put a *D* next to all who are deceased.

Put an *I* next to all who are imaginary.

Put a *V* next to all persons who were on your board five years ago.

Think of some major decision you have made in the last month. Put a check mark next to all board members who helped you to make this decision.

QUESTIONS FOR DISCUSSION

1. Are there people who are not on your board of directors, but who you think might like to be? Why did you not include them?

2. What qualities would you like to see in a member of your board of directors? Does each member of your board possess these qualities?

3. On whose board of directors do you sit? On whose board of directors would you like to sit?

A Review of the Objectives

Now that you have completed the activities in Unit III, can you:

1. Describe the differences between self-control and external controls and between wise and unwise controls?

2. Explain how role and status can act as controls on self-identity?

3. Describe how controls are used in the family, school, peer group, and political and economic communities?

4. Explain how the mass media can be both ways we learn about controls and controls in themselves?

5. Recognize the impact people who guide and influence your decisions?

6. Tell what each WORD or PHRASE means?

7. Use the WORD or PHRASE correctly in a sentence?

UNIT IV

DECISION MAKING

CONTENTS

**Aggressive Behavior: Constructive
and Destructive**

Looking Ahead

WHY STUDY DECISION MAKING?

Should I go on to college after high school? Should I take a job or become involved in a job training program instead? What about marriage and child rearing? Three years in one of the branches of the U.S. armed forces might be best for me. Why not take a year off and drift along like a twig in a quiet stream, moving when the need is irresistible and stopping here or there when necessary?

Each of these thoughts represents an alternative choice or path to an immediate future. Choosing one alternative forces us to forego the others, at least temporarily. When the choice is made, a decision is reached.

Although many situations in previous units required decisions, in this unit we focus directly on DECISIONS and DECISION MAKING for the first time. All through our lives we make decisions. Many are ordinary and relatively unimportant. Then, without much warning, we suddenly face a critical decision that requires considerable thought.

Both everyday and critical decisions require a choice among alternatives. Critical decisions often involve not only alternative paths to a goal, but also a choice among competing goals. In critical decision situations, one or more of the alternatives may have serious immediate or remote consequences. These consequences can increase personal resources, and they can also diminish them. The consequences may increase your freedom to exercise self-control or place you in a physical setting where external control on your actions and alternatives is powerful and ever present.

We hope that this unit will help to increase your decision-making skills and expand the resources you need to deal with frustrations and

problems. The unit will re-emphasize the BEHAVIOR EQUATION as
an aid in decision making.

As you participate in the decision-making activities, write down
your reactions and feelings in your JOURNAL NOTES.

OBJECTIVES

When this unit is completed, we are confident that you will be able to:

1. Recognize the similarities between the BEHAVIOR EQUATION
   and the process of decision making.
2. Distinguish between immediate and remote consequences.
3. Use a decision tree to analyze a critical decision situation.
4. Explain the relationship between responsibility and decision
   making.

5. Explain the relationship among needs, frustration, aggression, and violence.
6. Discuss alternative methods of punishment for violent crime.
7. Recognize some essential facts about the destructive alternative of suicide.
8. Use the decision-making skills presented to improve your own decision-making ability.
9. Tell what each WORD or PHRASE means.
10. Use the WORD or PHRASE correctly in a sentence.

WORDS AND PHRASES

Critical Decisions

Decision Tree

Responsibility

Indoctrination

Aggressive Behavior

Aggression

Reinforce

Vandalism

MAKING DECISIONS

IMMEDIATE AND REMOTE CONSEQUENCES

Needs interact with resources and the immediate physical/ psychological setting to produce behavior.

Behavior has not only causes, but also consequences, for oneself and others. These consequences are of two kinds:

1. *Immediate consequences*—the immediate effects of an action or decision on oneself and others. For example, the immediate effects of speaking harshly to someone may satisfy your needs, but the hurt and anger produced in that person may have immediate consequences for you.
2. *Remote consequences*—the effects that are not readily visible or known. For example, in the above situation, the remote effect may be that you lose a friend or make an enemy.

Decision making involves knowing the causes of a situation, the available alternative behaviors, and the likely consequences of each alternative.

ACTIVITY 1

Needs, Feelings, Decisions

This is an activity designed to help you see how the decisions you make are related to your needs and feelings. Complete each of these thought starters in your JOURNAL NOTES. Use only one word to express how you feel, and try to use no word more than once.

When I am with a friend, I feel _____, and I usually _____.

When I am alone, I feel _____, and I often _____.

When I meet new people, I feel _____, and I usually _____.

When I am with my family, I feel _____, and I often _____.

When I am someplace I have never been before, I feel _____, and I usually _____.

When I don't know what I want to do, I feel _____, and I often _____.

When I am with people older than I am, I feel _____, and I usually _____.

When I am with people younger than I am, I feel _____, and I often _____.

When I have a problem I can't solve, I feel _____, and I usually _____.

QUESTIONS TO ASK YOURSELF

1. In each of the preceding situations, what needs are you trying to satisfy?
2. How might you satisfy the same needs in ways other than the ones you listed?
3. What resources are you using to satisfy your needs?

QUESTION FOR CLASS DISCUSSION

What is the relationship of each of the following to decision making?
- needs and feelings
- resources
- immediate physical/psychological setting
- immediate and remote consequences of behavior

ACTIVITY 2

Impact People Interviews:
Decisions and Goals

It may be useful for you to interview people who are significant to you and who have made constructive decisions to reach their goals. This activity offers you an opportunity to do this.

The idea of impact people was introduced at the conclusion of the previous unit. You will recall that these are people whom you respect and admire, and who set positive examples. Impact people in your life have made many decisions as they achieved their goals. In fact, you may be seeking goals that some of them have reached.

Interview two of your impact people who have accomplished goals to which you aspire. Prior to the interview, make up some questions that will help you (1) state your goal clearly and precisely; (2) determine what decisions the people you interview had to make in order to accomplish their goals; (3) decide *how* they made the decisions; and (4) identify some of the values that were significant in the decisions they made and the accomplishment of their goals.

Practice interviewing in class before you meet with your impact people. You may want to consider using a tape recorder for your interviews.

AFTER THE INTERVIEWS

Write a summary of each interview and add it to your JOURNAL NOTES.

Discuss in class the kinds of decisions the impact people had to make and how they made them.

Complete the following statements in your JOURNAL NOTES:
- By interviewing these impact people, I discovered that . . .
- This interview helped me with decision making by . . .
- Now my goals . . .

ACTIVITY 3

Making a Decision to Get Involved

This project on decision making is designed to encourage you to make a contribution to the class. Make a decision to get involved in this unit by participating in one or more of these projects:

1. Create a collage about decision making.
2. Develop a class bulletin board display based on decision making.
3. Report on five current news events involving significant decisions.
4. Do a brief report on how a historical decision was made. For example:
   - the Supreme Court's 1954 decision on desegregation—*Brown* v. *Board of Education of Topeka, Kansas*
   - President Truman's decision to drop the atom bomb
   - the southern states' decision to secede from the union
   - President Nixon's decision to resign
5. Share a record in class that has a decision-making theme. Be sure to have a copy of the words of the song to give each class member.
6. Watch a television program in which a critical decision is the central theme and report on it to the class.
7. Invite a community decision-maker to class to talk about the process of making good decisions.
8. Ask 10 adults to tell you the most significant decisions they ever made, and report their responses to the class.
9. Decide to do some other activity of your choice that will be appropriate for this unit on decision making. Check out the activity with your teacher before you begin working on it.

THE DECISION-MAKING PROCESS

The following six steps go into the process of making effective personal decisions:

1. Think about the goal you are trying to reach. What needs are you trying to fill?
2. Examine the probable immediate and remote effects of selecting different goals or alternative behaviors.
3. Consider the goals and alternatives in light of your own personal standards—your values and philosophy of life.
4. If possible, eliminate one or more of the various choices.
5. Make a decision. Select the choice that holds the most promise of reaching your most highly prized goal and satisfying your needs, while being consistent with your values.
6. Examine the results of your decision. If it has failed to do what you desired, return, if possible, to step 4 and re-think your choices.

USING THE DECISION-MAKING PROCESS

People do not use the whole decision-making process described above for every decision. Decisions become more difficult as we move from everyday choices to a concern for basic needs. Decisions can be grouped into three types, ranging from such everyday choices to CRITICAL DECISIONS.

1. *Everyday choice*. Daily life is filled with many choices. Often they are made according to the habits of the individual and are relatively easy. There may not even be any feeling of having made a choice.

Two roads diverged in a yellow wood...
Robert Frost

2. *Choice between two paths to the same goal.* In these situations, it is important to the individual to reach the goal, but how it is reached is *not* important. For example, a woman may try to decide which pair of shoes to wear to a party where it is important that she make a good impression. Or a man may try to decide whether to drive his car or take a bus to work. The goal matters, but the method of reaching the goal does not. A student may have difficulty deciding whether to take geometry this year and history next year or vice versa. In each of the above cases, the individual normally considers the consequences of each available alternative and then makes a choice. However, the decision is relatively easy.

3. *Critical decisions.* This type of situation requires us to consider several important goals and alternative courses of action in making a decision. The choice is very difficult and often means giving up something of value. Here the need to go through the decision-making process is most important. Serious thought about the matter helps an individual identify the needs involved, consider the alternatives and their probable consequences, relate the needs and their alternatives to personal values, and ultimately make a choice.

Some people refuse to make critical decisions and therefore suffer the internal conflict created by indecision. Others make their choice on impulse, without considering needs or consequences, and regret their decisions later in life. Both of these methods tend to have serious effects upon everyone involved.

Sometimes one can find an alternative that will take care of all the needs involved. The search for this kind of alternative takes time, energy, and thought, but the results are usually worth the effort.

As a class or in small groups you may wish to:

identify examples of each of the three types of decisions
examine critical decisions and discuss in detail:
- the needs involved
- the available alternatives and their immediate and remote consequences
- the values that are involved in the decision and that may be in conflict
- the alternative you feel you would select if faced with the situation

ACTIVITY 4

Torn Between Family and Community

As you sit in the witness chair in a court of law, the judge asks you to explain what you think is best for you. You are 12 years old. You, your parents, and your 7-year-old sister are Russian citizens who have been permitted to travel to the United States in order to visit relatives. It is now time to return home to the Soviet Union. After a pleasant month-long trip, your parents are prepared to do so.

You are torn between love for your parents and sister and a growing feeling that life in the United States is preferable to life in the Soviet Union. In America there is more joy, better food and clothes, more laughter, and a spirit of freedom.

An aunt and uncle have invited you to stay in America with them and their children. They have urged the court to appoint them as your guardians and to grant you political asylum in America. Your parents are determined that you will return with them to the Soviet Union. They argue that your place is with them and that you are being attracted by the wasteful wealth of the United States.

QUESTIONS FOR DISCUSSION

1. What needs should you consider as you respond to the judge's questions?
2. What alternatives should you consider? What are the immediate and remote consequences of each alternative?
3. What decision did you reach after consideration of your needs, your alternatives, and their consequences? Will you stay in America or return to the Soviet Union? Explain.

ACTIVITY 5

A Crusading Warden's Critical Decision

In a film released in 1980, a young, intense, reform-minded warden assumes control over a scandalous prison in a southern state in the United States. The prison has been the scene of one violent incident after another: fights between inmates, sexual attacks, and beatings of prisoners by guards. Money for prison maintenance has been skimmed off by prison officials, and barely livable conditions are the result. The prison food is unhealthy. The prison hospital lacks drugs and other medical supplies because they have been sold for profit. Because a local contracter used inferior materials, the prison roof leaks. Prison inmates are being loaned out to local businessmen and farmers. Although the inmates do the work, the prison guards, some privileged

prisoners, and the warden have received "under the table" money.

During the year that the reform-minded warden is in charge, things begin to change for the better. The massive corruption ends, and conditions at the prison improve. A prisoners' council meets regularly with the warden to discuss items of common concern. The food is better; the prison is cleaner and safer.

Suddenly the warden discovers that dozens of former inmates are buried in a nearby woods. He learns that they were murdered by the small gang of guards and prisoners who ran the prison prior to his arrival. From a state legislator, the warden learns that these murders were hushed up to keep the situation from exploding into public view. The legislator reminds the warden that the dead men were all convicted criminals who were serving long prison sentences. He also declares:

> "If you leave the dead alone, we are prepared to meet any reasonable requests for changes at the prison. Your ideas designed to make the prison a showplace for your principles of prison administration will be quickly acted upon. If, on the other hand, you choose to continue the investigation, we will use our power to destroy you and return the prison to leadership that will be different from the kind you believe in. Your reforms will quickly disappear."

QUESTIONS FOR DISCUSSION

1. What needs do you think are involved in the warden's decision?
2. What alternatives does he have? What are the immediate and remote consequences of each alternative?
3. Assume the role of a prison inmate. What needs are important to you as the warden prepares to make a decision? What decision would you recommend that he make?
4. Assume the role of the warden. What will your decision be? Be prepared to discuss it with other members of the class.

DECISION TREES

A helpful way to plan for a critical decision is to use a DECISION TREE. A decision tree will help you to visualize the goals you are trying to reach.

As you look at this decision tree, begin at the bottom:

The trunk represents the critical decision-making situation.

The large branches represent the alternatives the decision-maker
   must consider.

Moving up through the branches, we encounter the possible
   immediate and remote consequences of each alternative.

At the top of the decision tree are the needs to be satisfied and the
   goals sought.

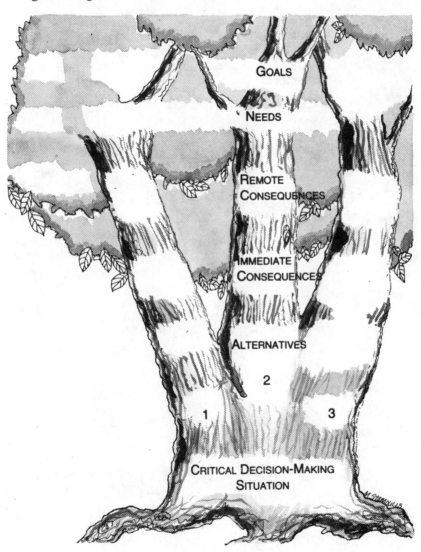

Application

To see how to use the decision tree, read the case study on page 265, which presents a problem requiring a solution, and then study this completed decision tree. (Don't forget to start at the bottom.)

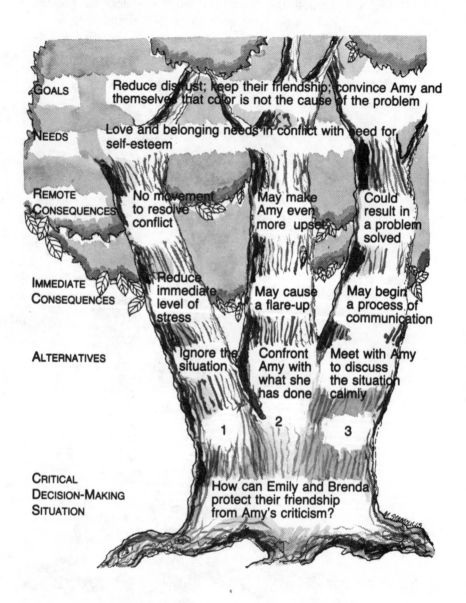

GOALS Reduce distrust; keep their friendship; convince Amy and themselves that color is not the cause of the problem

NEEDS Love and belonging needs in conflict with need for self-esteem

REMOTE CONSEQUENCES
No movement to resolve conflict | May make Amy even more upset | Could result in a problem solved

IMMEDIATE CONSEQUENCES
Reduce immediate level of stress | May cause a flare-up | May begin a process of communication

ALTERNATIVES
Ignore the situation | Confront Amy with what she has done | Meet with Amy to discuss the situation calmly

1   2   3

CRITICAL DECISION-MAKING SITUATION
How can Emily and Brenda protect their friendship from Amy's criticism?

Brenda and Emily, teenagers living in the same community, are best friends. They attend the same school, are active in dramatics, and enjoy spending leisure time together. Brenda is white and Emily is black.

Amy, a white classmate of the girls, is very critical of Emily behind her back. She seems to be trying to break up the friendship between Emily and Brenda.

What should Emily and Brenda do to protect their friendship against Amy's criticism? A completed decision tree for the two friends might look something like the one on page 264.

Bear in mind that a decision tree will not automatically solve every problem. It will, however, increase the likelihood that all alternatives will be carefully considered before a decision is reached.

ACTIVITY 6

A Decision Tree for You

This activity will permit you to develop your own decision tree. You should begin by tracing the tree from your book or, preferably, by drawing your own larger tree. Print what each part of the tree represents to the left of the tree, as done on the tree on page 264. You may use either of two approaches to start your tree.

The first approach is to state, clearly and precisely, a goal that you wish to achieve. For example:

I wish to become more popular with the "right" people.
I wish to improve my grades.
I wish my conversations with my father and mother were more pleasant.
I wish to help a friend who is using drugs.

If you choose this approach, your decision tree will begin at the top, and your next step will be to think of a critical decision-making situation.

The second approach is to think of a decision-making situation in which you are now involved or may be soon. For example:

You get the feeling that when you try to get involved in a conversation with a group of popular kids, they reject you.
You get an F in English III.
It seems as if every time you talk to your parents about any subject, the conversation turns to your smoking habit.

If you choose this approach, your decision tree will begin at the trunk. Your next step will be to think of your goals and the needs of those involved in the decision-making situation.

Whether you choose the first or second approach, after you have begun your tree, continue by filling in the alternatives and consequences. Before your tree is completed, discuss it with a friend to be sure that you have included all of the alternatives. Have your friend also look at the consequences you have listed for each alternative.

Then act on your decision tree. Make the decision.

Finally, add the decision tree you drew to your JOURNAL NOTES.

DECISION MAKING AND RESPONSIBILITY

It would be nice if we could make decisions and reach goals just by completing decision trees. We all know that more is involved. An essential ingredient in decision making is RESPONSIBILITY.

As used by people today, "responsibility" has several meanings. When the soldier falls asleep on guard duty, we say that soldier has failed his or her responsibility. Each of us has the responsibility to carry a driver's license when we drive a car.

However, the word "responsibility" as used here has quite a different meaning.

It means taking ownership of one's feelings and alternative actions. When you say, "You make me so angry!" you pass the responsibility for your anger on to someone else. By refusing to accept ownership of your feelings, you contribute to your own sense of helplessness.

Most of us do not recognize that we have the freedom to *select* a feeling and an action in response to another's behavior. Suppose someone tries to provoke you into a fight by insulting you in front of others. You can get angry, you can make fun of the insult, or you can ignore both the person and the insult.

What does this discussion of responsibility have to do with decision making? When we take ownership of alternatives and feelings, we can follow through on the decisions we choose to make. We are able to combine our thoughts and feelings to satisfy our needs and reach our goals. We are no longer helpless and acted upon. Our behavior is no longer controlled by others, and we become increasingly self-controlled. As a result, the alternatives we select are likely to be of the most benefit to ourselves and others.

ACTIVITY 7

Willingness to Take Responsibility

You may know quite a few people who are willing to accept responsibility for what they say or do. Throughout history, individuals have stood out from the group because of their commitment to ideas and action and their willingness to take responsibility for them.

Roger Williams, Susan B. Anthony, Thomas Jefferson, Mother Teresa, Mohandas Gandhi, Eleanor Roosevelt, and Martin Luther King are examples of such individuals: men and women who promoted the dignity and worth of each person. Their non-violent, thoughtful, and reasonable actions were consistent with democratic ideals.

Find out what these people did that shows that they took responsibility for their actions. Share what you learned with the class.

QUESTIONS FOR DISCUSSION

1. What issues do you feel strongly about?
2. Have you acted on your feelings?
3. Why did you decide to take action on those particular beliefs?
4. What were the immediate and remote consequences of your actions?

ACTIVITY 8

An "I Urge" Telegram

Acting is the next step after deciding. This activity is designed to help you move your decisions into action.

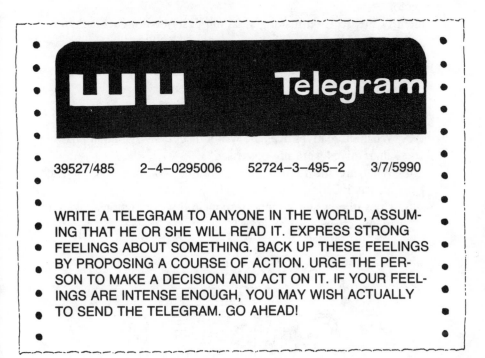

W U Telegram

39527/485   2–4–0295006   52724–3–495–2   3/7/5990

WRITE A TELEGRAM TO ANYONE IN THE WORLD, ASSUMING THAT HE OR SHE WILL READ IT. EXPRESS STRONG FEELINGS ABOUT SOMETHING. BACK UP THESE FEELINGS BY PROPOSING A COURSE OF ACTION. URGE THE PERSON TO MAKE A DECISION AND ACT ON IT. IF YOUR FEELINGS ARE INTENSE ENOUGH, YOU MAY WISH ACTUALLY TO SEND THE TELEGRAM. GO AHEAD!

ACTIVITY 9

Letters to Columnists

Bring a selection of "Dear Abby" and "Dear Ann Landers" columns to class. Outline each of them on the blackboard or on an overhead projector.

Identify the decision-making situation described in each column.

QUESTIONS FOR DISCUSSION

1. What needs are involved in the situation?
2. What goals does the letter-writer wish to reach?
3. What alternatives does the writer discuss? What other possible alternatives were not discussed?
4. What are the immediate and remote consequences of each alternative?
5. Does the writer accept responsibility for actions taken or blame others for problems?

ACTIVITY 10

A Schoolboy Prank?

This activity is based on a true incident. It is designed to stimulate your thinking about needs and feelings, help you consider why people behave as they do, and give you some insights into individual and group responsibility.

A high school football team has a record of 10 wins and no losses. They lead their conference and will go to the state tournament if they win their final game on the weekend.

On Wednesday after practice, five members of the starting team are in the locker room. They begin kidding around with the student trainer. The team members tie him up, blindfold him, and tape him to a wheeled cart, which they then start spinning like a top. They lose control of the cart and the student trainer's head hits a locker. He is knocked unconscious, and his head is severely cut. The five team members get out of the locker room fast!

The student trainer is found by the custodian and rushed to a hospital. Although he requires 50 stitches in his scalp and has a concussion, the doctor declares him out of danger.

The next morning the five students involved in the incident report the whole story to the principal. The story also appears in the morning paper. In the paper, the principal says he does not know what his decision regarding the incident will be.

Assume that you are the principal and must decide what action to take.

QUESTIONS FOR DISCUSSION

1. What alternatives come to mind?
2. What are the immediate and remote consequences of each alternative?

3. What comments about responsibility would you make to the five participants in the prank?
4. What difference does it make that the students told you what they had done? Explain.
5. What action will you take in this case? Be prepared to defend your decision.

INDIVIDUAL RESPONSIBILITY IN A GROUP

In the preceding activity, five members of the football team were involved in the prank and the resulting injury to the trainer. What if one of the five had only stood around and watched? Would he share the blame for the consequences equally with those who were active participants?

An important theme of this unit is the idea that you, and you alone, must take responsibility for your decisions. Going along with others is often the same as fully participating in the planning and execution of the decision. In fact, this is a rule that is often applied in criminal cases. Ask yourself:

How responsible do you think an individual is for decisions made by a group that he or she belongs to?

What responsibility do you take for decisions made by the groups of which you are a part?

What consequences should you expect from alternatives chosen by the group?

The Holocaust during World War II was one of the most tragic atrocities we can think of. It was caused in part by the many minor Nazi officials who went along with others. After the war, when they were asked why they had participated in unspeakable atrocities, they replied, "I was only following orders," or "I was only a clerk. Although I witnessed acts of violence, I never touched anyone."

ACTIVITY 11

A Controversial Issue

Imagine yourself in the role of the social studies department chairperson. Ms. Marjorie Green began teaching in your social studies department six months ago. You recommended that she be hired just two weeks after you were appointed chairperson. Her experience in the Peace Corps, her potential for reaching out to students with reading problems, and her ability to relate to students with low self-esteem impressed you. Although your principal and superintendent expressed some concern about her dedication to campaigns and causes, they went along with your recommendation.

Since September, you have made a special effort to observe her teaching and talk to her students. Everything you have learned has supported your original decision; all of your hopes and expectations have been more than realized. Her classes are lively and informative. She has formed tutoring groups for less able readers and has enlisted caring students from all over the school to help out as tutors. The students you have met with have praised her as an exceptional teacher and a warm human being.

It is now the middle of March, and suddenly everything appears to be crashing down upon Ms. Green and upon you, too, as her sponsor. During the last two weeks, 20 parents have called to complain about her. The fury has been so intense that the school board is meeting tonight to consider the alternatives and take some action.

When you first heard the complaints, you were protective of Ms. Green and skeptical about the charges against her. But you began to investigate quietly. You are quite confident now that you have discovered the truth. This is what you learned:

> During her service in the Peace Corps, Ms. Green became disillusioned with governments and government programs. She thinks that the best government is the smallest possible government. She believes that people ought to take care of themselves and not expect the government to provide for them. She also believes that other nations should take care of themselves without looking to the United States for protection.

Ms. Green's goal is to bring back all our troops and equipment from overseas and close down all American bases in foreign countries. She and others have formed a new political party to promote these ideas. The cornerstone of her program is a call to slim down the U.S. government to one-third of its present size and reduce all taxes by two-thirds.

You have also learned that more than 100 of her students—nearly 80 percent—have agreed to work for her new political party. They are running around the community making mini-speeches, circulating petitions, and gathering more converts. Of course, opposition to her ideas has reached the school board. She is accused of INDOCTRINA-TION—planting her ideas in students rather than teaching them to think for themselves.

The school board has asked you to appear before them and to recommend a course of action. What will you decide to recommend?

Before making a decision, you should try to answer the following: Did Ms. Green consciously set out to indoctrinate her students, or did she reveal her political philosophy only after students questioned her? Were they converted to her views because of her personal impact on them, or as a result of a deliberate effort on her part?

You may wish to do a decision tree to enable you to select from as many alternatives as possible.

QUESTIONS FOR DISCUSSION

1. What needs of the following people must be considered as you decide what to recommend to the board of education?
   - Ms. Marjorie Green
   - Ms. Green's students
   - the board of education
   - the parents who are upset
   - your fellow teachers
   - you, as the social studies department chairperson
2. Assume that Ms. Green did attempt to indoctrinate her students. What alternative will you recommend to the board?
3. What if the indoctrination happened by accident rather than on purpose? Will your recommendation change?
4. Do you think indoctrination is wrong regardless of what is being taught? Is indoctrination ever justified? Why?
5. How does the problem of responsibility fit in with the facts of this case?

ACTIVITY 12

The School Board Meets

This activity is a role play of a critical decision-making situation that deals with a contemporary educational issue. First read the background information that follows. Before the role play can begin, some players will need to explore various aspects of the issue, as described under the ground rules.

Situation

Controversy over sex education in the junior high school has the board of education, school administrators, students, teachers, and the entire community in an uproar. A parents' advisory committee has studied the issue for a year. At this point the members are equally divided over the value of a sex education curriculum for the junior high school.

Setting

The advisory committee has decided to ask the board of education to make a decision at its next meeting. At that time the five-member board is to decide the issue by majority vote. Prior to the vote, advocates and opponents of sex education in the junior high school will select spokespeople to summarize the arguments before the board.

It is now the evening of the board of education meeting. Develop a plan to simulate this community dilemma.

The Players

- a spokesperson for members of the parents' committee who oppose sex education in the junior high school
- a spokesperson for members of the parents' committee who are in favor of sex education in the junior high school
- the president of the board of education, who presides at the meeting
- four other members of the board of education

- the audience at the board of education meeting (class members who are not playing one of the above seven roles)

Ground Rules for the Role Playing

- The two peop' speaking for and against sex education must gather inform: on to support their positions. Seek help from your teacher a ou prepare your statements.
- All members of the board of education must also gather information on the topic. Again, seek assistance from your teacher.
- The president of the board of education is to conduct the meeting in a fair, efficient, and businesslike manner.
- All members of the board of education are encouraged to respond to or question comments made by the spokespeople and the audience.
- Members of the audience may speak at the meeting only if they have asked to do so in writing to the president of the board of education prior to the meeting. Anyone speaking from the audience must have gathered information to support his or her statements.
- The board of education is to vote after all the people with permission to speak have expressed their opinions.

QUESTIONS FOR DISCUSSION

(Note: These may be discussed during and/or following the role playing, or both.)

1. Do you think sex education should be approved as a subject in American schools? If not, why not? If so, in what form?
2. What goals would be reached by approving or rejecting sex education in the schools? What needs would be satisfied by each alternative?
3. What are the immediate and remote consequences of each alternative discussed?
4. How does responsibility relate to the issue of teenage sexual behavior?

AGGRESSIVE BEHAVIOR: CONSTRUCTIVE AND DESTRUCTIVE

AGGRESSIVE BEHAVIOR is an alternative in critical decision situations. It has two definitions.

Aggressive behavior can be behavior that is positive, energetic, assertive, and necessary to reach a goal. Most of society views this as constructive behavior and approves of it. The purpose of this type of behavior is *not* to hurt or harm people or property. Some individuals argue that if we do not act aggressively in this sense of the word, we could die.

One of the goals of this course is to help you channel your aggressive energy into the positive, constructive actions this definition suggests.

Aggressive behavior is also defined as "behavior aimed at the injury of some person or object, or behavior which would affect another person in a harmful way." We use the term AGGRESSION in *The New Model Me* to refer to aggressive behavior that fits this second definition. Most people in our society view this kind of aggressive behavior as destructive and disapprove of it. The intent of this kind of behavior *is* to hurt or harm people or property.

Regardless of the immediate physical setting, one of the causes of aggression appears to be frustration that escalates to an explosive point, like a steam radiator with a defective valve. There is no way to relieve the excess pressure. When this happens with human beings, a full set of alternatives is not examined, and appropriate constructive alternatives are overlooked.

Aggression (destructive aggressive behavior) in the form of violence in our society is a major concern in the 1980s. Many magazines have published feature articles about violence in America. Major metropolitan newspapers contain lengthy articles about crime in the streets. Television programs document the increasing numbers of people who buy guns because they fear for their lives. Aggression and violence occur everywhere—on playgrounds with three- and four-year-olds, in school vandalism and fighting, through abusive behavior in homes, on big city streets, and in rural areas, and in wars where nations battle.

All of society is affected when individuals and groups make a decision to use aggression and violence to meet their needs and resolve frustration. Because it is such a significant problem, we devote the remainder of this unit to the study of aggression and violence in America. You will have the opportunity to discuss the severity of the problem, its causes and consequences, and constructive alternatives for reducing its destructive effects.

Consider the following questions as you begin the final section of this unit on decision making: Why do people decide to commit acts of aggression? Are we born with aggressive traits, or are they acquired through cultural experiences? Are men naturally more aggressive than women? Although aggressive behavior has been the subject of much serious research, apparently there are no clear answers to these interesting questions.

ACTIVITY 13

The Fruits of Aggression

This activity introduces you to an important study of aggression.

A few years ago, a group of three- and four-year-old children in each of two middle-class nursery schools was observed for about 60 sessions during a 26-week period. The investigators were watching for acts of aggression. When one was seen, the investigators recorded the responses of the victim of the aggression and the teacher. The investigators predicted that if the victim did not stand up to the attack, the aggressor would be likely to attack the same child again. However, they believed that if the victim counterattacked or the teacher intervened, the aggressor would direct the aggression toward other children.

The results of the study strongly supported the investigators' predictions.

QUESTIONS FOR DISCUSSION

1. What do you think is the significance of this research study?
2. Do you think that human beings are born aggressive, or do you think aggressive behavior is learned? Explain.
3. If either of these is true, what alternatives do we have to lessen the amount of aggression in society?

REINFORCEMENT

The investigators who designed this study concluded that immediate consequences—the rewards gained from aggressive actions—REINFORCE the tendency toward aggression. For some people and in some situations, the aggression works, at least temporarily. This may be a reason people select the alternative of aggression.

Nations, as well as individuals, sometimes achieve their goals through aggression. Students of recent world history know of the aggressive demands and actions taken by Adolf Hitler and the weak responses of France and England. From 1936 to 1939 Hitler gobbled up Austria and Czechoslovakia. He was finally challenged when he tried to devour Poland as well. A similar pattern was seen in Asia as Japan struck in Manchuria and then in China.

Aggressors seek to identify victims who lack the actual strength to resist or who think they are unable to resist. This is a good argument for individuals and nations to develop the capability to protect themselves.

AGGRESSION AND VIOLENCE

Aggression and violence go hand in hand. We see violence around us in many forms. Some forms are generally approved of in the community, some forms are controversial, and some are not approved of by most people.

Generally Approved Violence

violence in sports that is within the rules of the game
violence in war after attack
violence by the police in subduing an aggressive suspect
violence by a citizen who is acting to protect family or self

Controversial Violence

violence by a person who is unjustly accused
violence by a country in attacking before it is attacked
violence in the form of capital punishment
violence by soldiers or police in anticipating attacks by civilians

Generally Disapproved Violence

violence in war to gain territory, power, or riches
violence done to innocent people
violence by police that is unnecessary to subdue a suspect

VANDALISM

The Vandals were a Germanic people who lived in the area south of the Baltic Sea between the Vistula and Oder rivers. In A.D. 455 they plundered and looted Rome. VANDALISM as we know it in the 20th century got its name from the kind of behavior exhibited by the Vandals more than 1,500 years ago.

According to *Webster's New Collegiate Dictionary*, vandalism is defined as "willful or malicious destruction or defacement of public or private property." It is a significant problem in the 1980s.

Evidence of vandalism is all around us. Graffiti on public buildings, deliberately damaged playground equipment in parks, public telephones tampered with so that they are not usable, and broken windows in school buildings are but a few examples of vandalism.

Why do you think people decide to vandalize? What do you think are the effects of vandalism on the individuals whose property is vandalized, on the vandal, and on society in general? What do you think would be some effective methods of eliminating vandalism?

ACTIVITY 14

Vandalism: Causes, Consequences, Prevention

This activity is intended to encourage you to get involved in an investigation of vandalism: its causes, consequences, and prevention. Read through the list of suggested projects and choose no more than two in which you want to participate. Perhaps you have a similar project in mind that you would like to do. If so, be sure to clear the project with your teacher before you begin.

1. Three or four students can tour the school building and look for equipment and facilities that have been vandalized. Make notes during the tour so that you can give an accurate report to the rest of the class. Discuss with the class what you think the causes and consequences of the vandalism are and what you think might be done to prevent similar acts of vandalism in the future.

2. Survey students, teachers, administrators, and other adults in your school about the causes and consequences of vandalism, their feelings about it, and their suggestions on how to cut down the amount of school vandalism. Some suggested survey questions are:
   - What needs do you think a vandal is trying to satisfy?
   - What do you think causes a person to vandalize?
   - What evidence of vandalism have you noticed around our school?
   - Why do you think this vandalism occurred?
   - How do you think such acts of vandalism can be prevented?

3. Organize an anti-vandalism campaign in your school. Design posters, make announcements on the public address system, publicize the campaign in the school paper, and generally make it known that your group is concerned about the senseless destruction of school property. You might want to turn this into a school

spirit campaign and suggest that there are many positive, constructive reasons for treating the school building and equipment
with respect.

4. Depict the causes and consequences of vandalism and constructive
   alternatives to it by having individuals or groups:
   • develop bulletin boards
   • make collages
   • draw cartoons
   • take pictures

5. Four to six students can prepare and present a panel discussion on
   the causes and consequences of vandalism. Consider the consequences of vandalism for the victim, the vandal, and society in
   general.

6. Discuss incidents in which members of the class or the teacher
   were the victims of vandals. Talk about how you felt when the
   vandalism happened, why you think it occurred, and what you did
   about it.

7. For two weeks, clip articles about vandalism from current newspapers and magazines. Share them with the class. Consider the
   needs of the vandal, the vandal's resources and immediate phys-
   ical/psychological setting, and the short- and long-term consequences of the vandalism.

8. Invite adults to class to discuss their ideas about vandalism.
   Appropriate individuals to invite would be parents of students in
   your class; teachers, counselors, and administrators in your
   school; and law enforcement officials and school district personnel who have information on the amount and cost of vandalism in
   your school.

9. Brainstorm the following topics in groups of four or five:
   • causes of vandalism
   • consequences of vandalism
   • alternatives to vandalism
   • techniques to prevent vandalism
   After the small groups have discussed each of the topics, share the
   groups' comments with the class.

10. Ask the advisor and editor of the school newspaper to develop a
    series of articles on vandalism. Offer to supply them with infor-
    mation and ideas from your study of the topic.

VIOLENT CRIME

Violent crime is a serious concern for Americans. It is nothing new, however, for people have committed acts of crime and violence since the beginning of time. Muggings and assaults were common in colonial America. The sagas of the western marshals and villains of the 19th century are well known.

Crime is a common occurrence today, especially in America's cities. It is difficult to tell whether the number of violent crimes in America is increasing each year because reporting of such crimes as murder, assault, rape, and robbery is inconsistent from place to place and from year to year. But there is no doubt that the fear of violent crime is increasing in America, not only in the big cities, but also in the suburbs and rural areas.

ACTIVITY 15

Fear of Crime

What are your feelings and thoughts about violent crime? This activity will permit you to compare them with those of experts in this field.

The following statements were made by people who are active in law enforcement. Read the statements and decide whether you agree or disagree with them. After you have decided how you feel, discuss the statements with the rest of the class.

1. "Crime is as American as Jesse James." Charles Silberman, author of *Criminal Violence/Criminal Justice*
2. "There is a reign of terror in American cities." Warren Burger, Chief Justice of the U.S. Supreme Court
3. "The fear of crime is slowly paralyzing American society." B. K. Johnson, Houston, Texas, Police Chief
4. "Within four or five years every household in the country will be hit by crime." Harry Scarr, former Director of the Bureau of Justice Statistics
5. "We're in a state of civil war between the criminals and the law-abiding community." Henry W. Chmielinski, Judge from Massachusetts
6. "There does not appear to be a deterrent to violence." William T. Hanton, Cleveland, Ohio, Police Chief

RESPONSES TO CRIME

How are innocent people responding to their growing fear of crime? In the spring of 1981, *Newsweek* magazine had the Gallup Organization poll a sample of the American people to determine their reactions to what is thought to be the quickening pace of violent crime. Their responses are contained in the activity that follows.

A NATION AFRAID

The Curse of Violent Crime

Drug culture intertwined with violent crime, spawning devastation and despair

Security in an Age of Fear

Crime leap spurs third grand jury

Violent crimes surge 38% in city

Violence slithers into rural life

The Duel over Gun Control

Anger at a would-be assassin, prayers for a much loved Pontiff

Mystery surrounds suicide of twins

Death penalty near approval

'No, I would not mind killing anyone who has no business being in my place.'

Learning to fight back: Security business booms

What Crime Does to the Victims

ACTIVITY 16

Responses to Crime

Examine the responses of Americans to these questions concerning crime in our country.[1]

Is there any area within a mile of your home where you would be afraid to walk alone at night?

Yes	53%
No	46%
Don't know	1%

Which of these precautions against crime have you taken?

Try not to go out alone at night	64%
Never carry very much cash	79%
Avoid certain areas even during the day	60%
Avoid wearing expensive jewelry	64%
Keep a gun or other weapon	31%
Keep a dog for protection	44%

Is there more crime in your area than there was a year ago?

More	58%
Less	14%
The same	24%
Don't know	4%

What is most responsible for the increasing rate of crime?

Unemployment	37%
Courts too lenient	20%
Breakdown of family, society, values	19%
Punishment not severe enough	13%
Drugs	13%
TV violence, movies	3%

[1]Poll from "Spreading Fear, Changing Lives," *Newsweek* (March 23, 1981). Copyright 1981, by Newsweek, Inc. All rights reserved. Reprinted by permission.

Which of the following have happened to you in the past 12 months?

Property vandalized	20%
Money or property stolen	21%
House broken into or attempt made	14%
Assaulted or mugged	3%
Car stolen	3%

Do you think criminals today are more violent than they were five years ago?

Yes	75%
No	21%
Don't know	4%

Choose any one of the questions asked in the poll and search for more information about it or the responses to it.

Choose a response to any question and defend or criticize it. Explain why you think the response is wise or unwise, useful or useless.

QUESTIONS FOR DISCUSSION

1. Are there any surprises in this poll? If so, what are they?
2. How would you have answered each question? You may wish to compare your responses with those of your classmates.
3. If the questions were asked about your school rather than the larger community, how would you answer them?

ACTIVITY 17

Guns and Their Control

On Monday, March 30, 1981, in Washington, D.C., a scene was played that has been repeated hundreds of times in recent American history. Innocent people were seriously injured by a violent, mentally unbalanced individual who fired a handgun several times at a crowd. The only unusual feature of this tragedy was that one of the injured persons was Ronald Reagan, the President of the United States. The wounding of the President added emphasis to the question of what to do about the number of handguns owned by Americans. More than 50 Americans were killed with handguns on the same day that President Reagan was shot.

There are an estimated 55 million handguns in America today. A handgun is sold in the United States every 13 seconds. Some of those guns are in the hands of criminals and people who are mentally ill. Yet most are in the possession of law-abiding persons who wish to protect themselves and their families from the criminals' guns. As the fear of crime has increased, more and more households are turning to guns for protection.

Although few people dispute the conclusion that guns contribute to the violent crime statistics, there is much disagreement about what alternative course of action should be taken.

Some people argue that gun ownership is a personal right in a free society. These people also say that to have a gun in a home or business is necessary for their protection. Without a gun, the lawful citizen is at the mercy of the violent criminal, who will get a gun regardless of any laws against gun possession. Finally, this argument is made: "Guns don't kill people; people kill people."

Opponents of the widespread ownership of handguns argue that many violent crimes began as verbal fights between husband and wife, or between neighbors, or between people who meet under the influence of alcohol or drugs.

The possession of a gun changes the fight into a shootout in which one or both persons are injured or killed.

There are three basic approaches to the ownership of handguns and their use in violent crimes:

1. Permit free and easy access to handguns, but increase the punishment of criminals who use guns. Make punishment harsh and sure for anyone using a gun while committing a crime.
2. Register handguns. Police would then be able to check on prospective buyers and establish tests or requirements, such as a safety course or a passing score in marksmanship.
3. Ban the manufacture and sale of handguns. Such a ban would gradually reduce the number of guns in people's hands.

You may wish to gather more information about this controversial issue. It may surprise you to learn that each year there are nearly 10 murders for every 100,000 people in the United States. In Japan, Great Britain, and West Germany, the murder rate is less than 2 for every 100,000 people.

QUESTIONS FOR DISCUSSION

1. Which of the three approaches to the ownership of handguns do you prefer? Be prepared to defend your preference.
2. What needs are satisfied by the ownership of a handgun?
3. What are the immediate and remote consequences of widespread ownership of guns?
4. In what ways does a responsible person show others that he or she takes proper care of handguns?

ACTIVITY 18

Why Nick?[2]

**AUTHOR
JEANNE SHIELDS**

A personal tragedy that involved a gun prompted the author to write the essay that follows. Use the PARS System (Worksheet IX) as you read the essay.

If the telephone rings late at night, I always mentally check off where each child is, and at the same time get an awful sinking feeling in the pit of my stomach.

Four years ago, April 16, we had a telephone call very late. As my husband answered, I checked off Pam in Long Beach, California, Nick in San Francisco, David in New Brunswick, New Jersey, and Leslie outside Boston. The less my husband spoke, the tighter the knot got in my stomach. Instinctively, I knew it was bad news, but I wasn't prepared for what he had to tell me. Our eldest son, Nick, 23, had been shot dead on a street in San Francisco.

Nick was murdered at about 9:30 P.M. He and a friend, Jon, had come from lacrosse practice and were on their way home. They stopped to pick up a rug at the home of a friend. While Jon went in to

[2]*Newsweek* (May 8, 1978). Copyright 1978, by Newsweek, Inc. All rights reserved. Article and photo reprinted by permission. Jeanne Shields lives in Wilmington, Delaware.

294

get the rug, Nick rearranged the lacrosse gear in the back of their borrowed Vega. He was shot three times in the back and died instantly, holding a lacrosse stick.

Nick was the fourteenth victim of what came to be called the "Zebra killers." Between the fall of 1973 and April 16, 1974, they had randomly killed fourteen people and wounded seven others—crippling one for life. Four men were subsequently convicted of murder in a trial that lasted thirteen months.

My son was tall, dark, and handsome, and a good athlete. He was particularly good at lacrosse and an expert skier. Nick was an ardent photographer and wrote some lovely poetry. He was a gentle and sensitive man with an infectious grin and the capacity to make friends easily. It was hard for me to believe he was gone.

Overwhelming Response

The generous support and love of our friends gave us the strength to go on during those days. The calls and letters that poured in from those who knew Nick were overwhelming. In his short life, Nick had touched so many people in so many ways. It was both heartwarming and very humbling.

But always, running through those blurred days was the question, Why? Why Nick? My deep faith in God was really put to the test. Yet nothing that I could do or think of, or pray for, was ever going to bring Nick back.

Because Nick was shot two days after Easter, the funeral service was filled with Easter prayers and hymns. Spring flowers came from the gardens of friends. The day was mild, clear, and beautiful, and a kind of peace and understanding seeped into my aching heart.

No matter how many children you have, the death of one leaves a void that cannot be filled. Life seems to include a new awareness, and one's philosophy and values come under sharper scrutiny. Were we just to pick up the pieces and continue as before? That choice became impossible, because a meaning had to be given to this vicious, senseless death.

That summer of 1974, the newspapers, magazines, and television were full of Watergate. But I couldn't concentrate on it or anything else. Instead I dug hard in the garden for short periods of time or smashed at tennis balls.

On the other hand, my husband, Pete, immersed himself in a study of the gun-control issue. Very near to where Nick had died, in a vacant lot, two small children found a gun—the gun. It was a .32-caliber Beretta. Police, in tracing it, found that initially it had been bought legally, but then went through the hands of seven different owners— most of whom had police records. Its final bullets, fired at close range, had killed my son—and then it was thrown carelessly away.

Ineffective Laws

Pete's readings of presidential commission recommendations, FBI crime statistics, and books on the handgun issue showed him that our federal laws were indeed weak and ineffective. He went to Washington to talk to politicians and to see what, if anything, was being done about it. I watched him wrestle with his thoughts and spend long hours writing them down on paper—the pros and cons of handgun control and what could logically be done about the proliferation of handguns in this nation.

Through friends, Pete had been introduced in Washington to the National Council to Control Handguns, a citizens' lobby seeking stricter federal controls over handguns. As Pete became more closely associated with the NCCH as a volunteer, it became increasingly obvious that he was leaning toward a greater involvement.

Consequently, with strong encouragement from me and the children, Pete took a year's leave of absence from his job as a marketing executive so that he could join NCCH full time. A full year and a half later, he finally resigned and became the NCCH chairman.

The main adversaries of handgun control are members of the powerful and financially entrenched National Rifle Association, macho men who don't understand the definition of a civilized society. They are aided by an apathetic government which in reality is us, because we citizens don't make ourselves heard loud and clear enough. How many people are in the silent majority, who want to see something done about unregulated sale and possession of handguns? Why do we register cars and license drivers, and not do the same for handguns? Why are the production and sale of firecrackers severely restricted— and not handguns?

A Grim Litany

I now work in the NCCH office as a volunteer. One of my jobs is to read and make appropriate card files each day for a flood of clippings describing handgun incidents. The daily newspapers across the country recount the grim litany of shootings, killings, rapes, and robberies at gun point. Some of it's tough going, because I am poignantly aware of what a family is going through. Some of it's so appalling it makes me literally sick.

Some people can no longer absorb this kind of news. They have almost become immune to it, because there is so much violence. To others, it is too impersonal; it's always something that happens to somebody else—not to you.

But anybody can be shot. We are all in a lottery, where the likelihood of your facing handgun violence grows every day. Today there are 50 million handguns in civilian hands. By the year 2000, there will be more than 100 million.

So many families have given up so much to the deadly handgun. It will take the women of this country—the mothers, wives, sisters, and daughters—to do something about it. But when will they stand up to be counted and to be heard? Or will they wait only to hear the telephone ringing late at night?

—Jeanne Shields

QUESTIONS FOR DISCUSSION

1. What is your reaction to reading about the random killing of 14 people?
2. Why do you think Jeanne Shields says people become immune to violence in society and let it become impersonal?
3. How do you think members of the National Rifle Association would respond to the author's statement that they don't understand the definition of a civilized society?
4. What is the National Rifle Association's position on gun control? What is the reasoning behind it?
5. How effective are organizations like the National Council to Control Handguns and the National Rifle Association?

SUICIDE

We now move from aggression and violence directed against others to the increasing rate of violence turned inward—suicide. During the last 25 years, the rate of suicide for Americans between the ages of 15 and 24 has more than tripled. Approximately 5,000 Americans between 15 and 19 die at their own hands each year. Suicide is the second leading cause of death among teenagers; only accidents exceed it. Consider also that some deaths labeled as accidents are actually suicides. Furthermore, it is estimated that suicide attempts number in the hundreds of thousands each year. It is not surprising that the destructive alternative of suicide is an alarming problem in America.

Who are the people who commit suicide? Why do they choose it as an alternative? How can you recognize a person who is considering suicide? What can you do to help prevent it?

ACTIVITY 19

A Suicide Quiz

Indicate whether you think each of the following statements about suicide is true or false by placing a *"T"* or an *"F"* in the blank preceding the statement. If you are not to write in your book, number a sheet of paper from 1 to 10 and write your answers next to the numbers.

T or *F*

_____ 1. Suicide is a serious problem for both males and females, for both teenagers and senior citizens.

_____ 2. There is little or no connection between suicide and the use of alcohol and drugs.

_____ 3. Authorities believe that divorce and poor family relationships contribute to suicide among teenagers.

_____ 4. Most suicide threats can be dismissed as just talk.

_____ 5. Rarely does any single event trigger a suicide attempt.

_____ 6. When a person has decided to commit suicide, no one can stop him or her.

_____ 7. It is best not to talk about suicide, because it may plant the idea in someone's head.

_____ 8. Once a person has attempted suicide and failed, he or she will be ashamed and will tend not to repeat the attempt.

_____ 9. Often you can observe signs in a friend that he or she is considering suicide.

_____ 10. We assume that many suicide attempts are actually cries for help. In fact, there is little help available.

The answer key, with explanations, appears on the following pages.

SUICIDE QUIZ: ANSWER KEY

___T___ *1. Suicide is a serious problem for both males and females, for both teenagers and senior citizens.* It surely is! In fact, it is a serious problem for almost everyone. For example, in the group of actual suicides, men outnumber women between two and three to one. However, in the group who attempt suicide, women outnumber men three to one.

In regard to age groups, children under 15 are least likely to commit suicide. All other age groups have much higher rates of suicide. Each age group has its own stresses and challenges. Teenagers may have family and love concerns. The elderly may face serious health challenges and the frustration of living with pain and dependency.

___F___ *2. There is little or no connection between suicide and the use of alcohol and drugs.* False. Alcohol and drug abuse are often associated with suicide. It sometimes looks as if suicide comes out of a bottle. As many as 40 percent of suicide victims are alcohol- or drug-abusers. Bear in mind, however, that although the abuse may bring on a suicide attempt, it is rarely a basic cause. The abuse of drugs or alcohol is a consequence, just as the suicide attempt is.

_T_   *3. Authorities believe that divorce and poor family relation-ships contribute to suicide among teenagers.*   True. According to a study conducted by the director of youth services at the Los Angeles Suicide Prevention Center, two-thirds of suicidal youths are on poor terms with their families. Divorce also adds stress, for the parent with custody often has too little time for the teenager.

_F_   *4. Most suicide threats can be dismissed as just talk.*   Abso-lutely false! Although threats differ in their degree of seriousness, every one should be taken seriously. Authorities suggest that two-thirds of those who commit suicide announce to others that they are planning to do so. The announcement is a disguised call for help.

_F_   *5. Rarely does any single event trigger a suicide attempt.*   False! Although the basic causes behind the suicide are complex and difficult to identify, the actual suicide attempt is usually triggered by one event—death in the family, a broken love affair, loss of freedom, etc.

_F_   *6. When a person has decided to commit suicide, no one can stop him or her.*   Absolutely false! Suicide attempts are often calls for help. If help is provided before the attempt, there may not be any attempt. In many cases the potential suicide victim is confused and uncertain. A friend or family member can provide wise counsel, building up the individual's self-esteem and helping him or her find constructive alternatives.

_F_   *7. It is best not to talk about suicide, because it may plant the idea in someone's head.*   False! It's dangerous not to talk about it. This is especially true when a suicide occurs within a group. This is the time to emphasize the destructive and final nature of suicide. After suicide there are no more opportunities to find constructive alternatives.

_F_   *8. Once a person has attempted suicide and failed, he or she will be ashamed and will tend not to repeat the attempt.*   False! Once an attempt has been made, the barrier between thought and action is broken. Unless help is provided, there may be more attempts. Eighty percent of those who commit suicide have attempted suicide before.

___T___   *9. Often you can observe signs in a friend that he or she is considering suicide.*   Yes, there are signs. These signs only suggest the possibility of a suicide attempt. They certainly are not a guarantee that suicide is being considered. The following are some of these signs.

Diminished Resources

Recall what effects the loss of resources can have on a person. Sickness, accidents, and emotional pain can trigger suicide.

Dramatic Changes in Behavior

A usually happy person suddenly becomes sad.
Someone withdraws from contact with others.
There are destructive outbursts from a person who is usually quiet.
Someone suddenly lacks energy and has trouble sleeping.
A good student suddenly stops caring.

Making Final Arrangements

Someone starts giving away prized possessions.
A person repeatedly talks about wills or discusses funeral procedures.

Frequent References to Death and Suicide

Does the person refer to how awful life is? How little there is to look forward to?
Does he or she indicate that suicide is being considered?

Unusual Stress

The greater the stress, the greater the danger. Events such as a broken love affair, failure to achieve a cherished goal, and living under a threat of violence or punishment can bring suicide to mind as an alternative.

Loss of Support

Death in the family, financial disasters, and serious family breakdowns are causes for concern.

Remember that these signs only suggest the possibility that suicide is being considered. Most people who possess sufficient resources can find constructive alternatives. With the assistance of others, everyone ought to be able to find an alternative to suicide.

___F___   *10. We assume that many suicide attempts are actually cries for help. In fact, there is little help available.*   False. You might be surprised to learn how much help is available:

You can help by getting involved. There is no substitute for close friends and family members who care and give of themselves.

Try to discuss suicide and point out its destructiveness. Look for constructive alternatives. Build up the person's self-esteem.

Seek help from parents, a teacher, counselor, administrator, clergyman, or mental health facility.

Look up "Mental Health" in the Yellow Pages of the telephone book. Find the Suicide Prevention Center or the Crisis Intervention Team.

Call your community hospital and ask for psychiatric assistance.

If you become concerned about a friend, seek help. Even if you are wrong, you did your friend a service by speaking out. As someone has said, "Killing a friendship is better than standing by while a friend is killed."

VIOLENCE AND AGGRESSION: ANOTHER VIEWPOINT

The activities you have just completed paint a grim picture of aggression and violence in our society. You might wonder if it is safe to be on the streets any place in the United States! Is there a chance that the media overemphasize acts of violence and aggression? Are things really as bad as they seem? Is the situation hopeless?

To close out this unit, we have included an essay by Gary Moore that suggests that America may not be as dangerous as many people think and a final activity that gives you an opportunity to suggest constructive alternatives to violence and aggression.

ACTIVITY 20

What America Is Really Like[3]

AUTHOR
GARY MOORE

Use the PARS System (Worksheet X) as you read this essay.

A 3,600-mile walk has proved to me that America is not as dangerous as many people think.

Last May, I set out on foot from Boston. Eight months later, I
walked into San Diego, having accepted no rides en route. But it was
not the hike's length that astonished many of the back-porch and
lunch-counter acquaintances that I made along the way; it was the fact
that I had not been mugged.

Said a waitress in North Texas: "You mean you don't carry
no gun?"

In town after town I was warned that the citizens of the next county
or the next state or the next region were likely to fall upon me and do
me harm. Yet invariably when I arrived at these alleged no man's
lands, I would feel that I must have taken a wrong turn and wound up
somewhere else, for my wary glance was never met with violence.

[3]*Newsweek* (April 10, 1978). Copyright 1978, by Newsweek, Inc. All rights reserved. Article and photo
reprinted by permission. Moore is a free-lance writer in San Diego, California.

Often it was met with open hospitality. In fact, the whole nation turned out to be amazingly, gratifyingly friendly.

Many times, in crowded suburbs as well as on isolated farms, I was invited into people's homes for meals or lodging. At no time did anyone attempt to run me over with a car, or to steal my backpack, or to stab, stomp, or strangle me. I repeat, they did not even try.

Banjos and Home Cooking

Though it had been predicted that my long hair and beard would bring me to a sad end in Texas, the Lone Star State besieged me only with repeated helpings of home cooking. The mere fact that I was a stranger was supposed to spell my doom in the Missouri Ozarks, yet I was greeted there with backwoods banjo concerts and invitations to go water-skiing.

In the all-white rural parts of Illinois that surround East St. Louis, it was begrudgingly admitted that I might get through the predominantly black inner city alive—but certainly not without four or five huge junkies ordering me to hand over my backpack. Yet when I persisted in my suicide mission and entered East St. Louis, I got only a few stares and an offer from a black businessman to buy me lunch.

Could there possibly be two Americas existing simultaneously in the same space—one, the rather amiable country that is accessible to those who will see it, the other, the menacing landscape that imprisons those who see only their fears?

Those who live in the second America—the menacing one—seem to feel that it is jam-packed with one or the other of two groups: murderous "red-necks" or murderous "crazies."

Sufferers of red-neck phobia are usually city dwellers or longer-haired young people who do not realize that in the last five or ten years the countryside has undergone an important change. Vanished are the days in the sixties and early seventies when hirsute travelers were thrown into sheep-dip vats in Wyoming and shot at in Georgia. Perhaps Watergate and Vietnam have humbled us, for an extraordinary atmosphere of restraint has settled upon the land. I saw repeated evidence that America's mayhem-minded bigots have turned to dissipating their energies in grumbling.

Murderous Lunatics

"If you'd a come through here five years ago," I was told by a friendly Oklahoma housewife who invited me in for lunch, "they'd a got you down and cut your hair. But now, all them that was doin' it, they have long hair themselves."

This same restraint seems also to have affected other prejudices. In most parts of the country that I crossed, racist attitudes were flourishing—but without the consistent violence of decades past. As I discussed the sudden decrease in volent racism with a Texas newspaper editor, I mentioned that I had grown up in Mississippi. He looked at me thoughtfully, then replied, "You're from the South. You know how it used to be. Don't you think it says a lot about this country—that we can go through a change like that without a revolution?"

But the fears of "Easy Rider"-type bigots account for only half of American paranoia. For every anxious suburban long-hair there is an equally distraught small-town beautician or auto mechanic. The bugaboo of these people is murderous lunatics. Sometimes the fears are only of "drug-crazed" lunatics, but often they are more general—embracing all manner of ax-murderers and stranglers, who are seen as the natural product of a society gone crazy. Like the political assassins of the sixties and seventies, for instance, or that former Eagle Scout who killed all those people with a high-powered rifle from atop an observation tower.

Newspapers and television may be partly to blame for the spread of this kind of anxiety. The same media overkill that made the violent racists shudder from exposure and reconsider their impulsive deeds has made violent psychotics seem as abundant and as inescapable as tabloid headlines about them.

The fallacies of the murderous-lunatic syndrome can be summed up by an incident that happened to me in St. Louis, on a bus-stop bench. I had stopped there to rest my pack, and was soon joined by a small man of middle age. He was wearing a football-referee's cap.

He seemed to think that because I carried a backpack, I was hitchhiking, and he told me that he just did not see where I got the courage to get into other people's cars. Why, every day he saw bus seats that had been carved on with knives. I should watch my step, he said, for the world was definitely full of dangerous weirdos.

Shock
This rankled me, and I gruffly told my new companion that he was wrong—especially about the abundance of weirdos. The rebuff seemed to stun him like a physical blow—sending him into shock. For

a moment, he stared into space; then suddenly he whipped off his referee's cap, snatched a silver whistle from underneath it, blew the whistle, replaced the whistle on his head, replaced the cap on the whistle, and after another pause he began, as if nothing had happened, to talk cooperatively about how safe the country was.

Slowly I realized that when he had first sat down, he had been afraid of me. His unusual behavior was just his way of coping with the hostility he expected to find. But in fact, I was really rather harmless, and so was he.

You see, some rather extraordinary people do exist out there, but they are as benign as the bus-stop referee—if only we would see them as they are, rather than as we fear they will be.

—*Gary Moore*

QUESTIONS FOR DISCUSSION

1. What does the author mean when he suggests that there may be two Americas existing simultaneously in the same space?
2. According to Gary Moore, what changes took place in America between the early seventies and the late seventies?
3. Why do you think Americans are anxious and fearful of people they do not know?
4. What do you think Gary Moore is saying about people when he wishes, "If only we would see them as they are, rather than as we fear they will be"?
5. What alternatives do we have to help us become less fearful of others and more able to see people as they are?

ACTIVITY 21

Buzz Groups on Violence and Aggression

What alternatives are there to violence and aggression in our society? This final activity is intended to help you think of some.

Each person is to bring to class three current news items about aggression and violence in America. These items can include articles from recent magazines or newspapers, as well as notes made from radio or television programs.

Share these items in groups of three or four. As the items are discussed, suggest alternatives that might have prevented the violence or aggression, or that might prevent it from occurring again. Be sure someone in each group records the suggested alternatives.

After the group lists are complete, the group recorders are to compile a class list of alternatives to violence and aggression.

QUESTIONS FOR DISCUSSION

1. How many different alternatives to aggression and violence did your class develop?
2. How practical are the suggested alternatives?
3. Which of the alternatives does your class think would be the most effective?

A Review of the Objectives

Now that you have completed the activities in Unit IV, can you:

1. Recognize the similarities between the Behavior Equation and the process of decision making?
2. Distinguish between immediate and remote consequences?
3. Use a decision tree to analyze a critical decision situation?
4. Explain the relationship between responsibility and decision making?
5. Explain the relationship among needs, frustration, aggression, and violence?
6. Discuss alternative methods of punishment for violent crime?
7. Recognize some essential facts about the destructive alternative of suicide?
8. Use the decision-making skills presented to improve your own decision-making ability?
9. Tell what each WORD or PHRASE means?
10. Use the WORD or PHRASE correctly in a sentence?

UNIT V

CHANGE: THE NEW MODEL ME

CONTENTS

Looking Ahead

WHY STUDY CHANGE: THE NEW MODEL ME?

TELEVISION COMMERCIAL

Billy: "Mommmmmmmmmm! I can't find my sneakers."
Mom: "Look under your bed."
Billy: "I AM under my bed!"

The dialogue between mother and young son never seems to change. However, most things do change. You and your world have changed in the time that you have been taking this journey.

In the preceding four units you have grown in confidence and self-identity through:

- greater understanding of why people behave as they do
- an increase in personal resources
- learning to accept and use wise controls and, at the same time, to work through democratic means to change unwise controls
- expanding the number of constructive alternatives you consider when involved in a critical decision situation

This growth has led you to your destination, Unit V, "Change: The New Model Me."

In Unit V we will concentrate on the changes that you may experience in the future. However, before examining the future, we will look at how you have changed during this course. After this brief evaluation our attention will shift to the future, since change and the future go hand in hand. How you prepare for this future is important, but some images of the future cannot be clearly seen at present. We can make at least four predictions about the future, however:

1. *An information explosion is in progress*, and it will accelerate in the future. In many areas of learning the amount of new information

will double every 15 years. Science provides marvelous techniques for spreading this information—radio, television, movies, computers, records, and others.

2. *Change will come at an increasing pace.* For example, there are 90,000 different occupations in our society today, and the number is increasing every year. During your lifetime, you may have to change your career more than once.

3. *The problems of human interdependence, or social problems, will be of the utmost importance.* We must learn to live effectively with ourselves and other people. Problems of poverty, ecology, pollution, overpopulation, food distribution, use of energy, war and peace, and human rights are all essentially social; they involve all of us.

4. *Personal fulfillment will be a critical concern.* The needs for food, safety, belonging and love, achievement and esteem must be met to allow people to be all that they can be.

OBJECTIVES

When this unit is completed, we are confident that you will be able to:

1. Develop and use planning and evaluation skills to direct changes in your life.
2. Judge alternative views of immediate and distant futures involving such topics as:
   • technological change
   • education
   • rebuilding after disaster
   • living environments in space
   • money and credit
3. Recognize the effects of "future shock" on individuals.
4. State the relationship between life changes and stress.
5. Demonstrate the knowledge you have gained from *The New Model Me* by: (a) planning an activity that fits one of the five units in the text and (b) re-designing the cover of the book
6. Demonstrate growth in your ability to resolve your frustrations by use of the Behavior Equation.

7. Tell what each WORD or PHRASE means.
8. Use the WORD or PHRASE correctly in a sentence.

WORDS AND PHRASES

Life Line

Turning Point

Technology

Suppress

Consequence Standards

Innovations

Future Shock

Transience

Novelty

Diversity

ACTIVITY 1

Let's Re-Design the Cover

This is an activity to help you see how you have changed since you began this course.

Remember the front cover you drew in Unit I? Re-do that cover, basing your design on all the activities and experiences in this course. What pictures, messages, ideas, symbols, thoughts, and questions come to mind as you begin to decorate the cover?

ACTIVITY 2

"I Think I've Changed"

In a course like this, strong and warm feelings often develop among class members. This activity will give you the opportunity to share with the class the changes you have experienced during this course.

Form a circle in the center of the room. People may start by telling how they feel they have changed since the course began. Anyone who wishes to may speak. Begin with "I think I have changed because . . . ." Take no more than five minutes. When you are finished, you can find out how you have changed (or not) in the eyes of the others.

ACTIVITY 3

How Do You Now Handle Your Frustrations?

Understanding your needs and building your resources can help change your behavior in the face of frustration. This activity will show you how this works.

In Unit I you participated in activities that involved frustration. They may have helped you discover constructive alternatives that enabled you to satisfy your needs. We hope your resources have grown to the point that the frustration you analyzed on the frustration flow chart in ACTIVITY 6 of Unit I can be resolved more easily now.

Look at the frustration you analyzed originally and plot it again on another frustration chart. (If you are permitted to write in your book and the flow chart in Unit I is completed, copy it on a separate sheet of paper.)

QUESTIONS FOR DISCUSSION

1. In what ways were you better able to identify your needs?
2. Name some additional things you wished you had done beyond those named on the original frustration flow chart.
3. Were your alternatives more constructive on this chart than on the original chart? Why or why not?

ACTIVITY 4

How Do You Use Your Resources?

How have you used, or can you use, the resources you have developed during this journey to THE NEW MODEL ME? This summary activity will help you to answer this question.

Draw a rough sketch of your family on a large sheet of paper.
On the reverse side of the paper list people in your family and identify their relationship to you. After each person's name write the services he or she performs for your family: bringing in the family income, providing transportation, doing the dishes, taking out garbage, baby sitting, and so on.

QUESTIONS FOR DISCUSSION

1. What resources must each family member have to perform these services?
2. Who performs the largest number of services in your family? Why do you think this happens?
3. What services do you perform? How do they compare with those performed by other members of the family? What resources must you have to perform these services? Are you satisfied with your service contributions to your family? If not, what further services could you contribute?
4. In groups of three compare and contrast responses you wish to share.

ACTIVITY 5

Life Lines and Turning Points

The next two activities are designed to help you develop and use planning and evaluation skills as you experience change in your life. Form a working group with two other students with whom you work well and complete the following activity. The three of you should pull your chairs together so you can face one another.

PHASE I. LIFE LINE REVIEW

Draw a horizontal line across the middle of an 8½ by 11 inch blank piece of paper. This is your LIFE LINE, the line representing your life from birth (at the left end) to the present (at the right end).

Privately review the years you have lived. Along the line, label the events that were TURNING POINTS in your life.

You may wish to discuss some of the events with your group. What caused or led to the turning points? Did frustration often precede or follow them? How did you deal with this frustration? Are many of the turning points in your life similar to those of other group members?

PHASE II. LIFE LINE PREVIEW

Draw a horizontal line across the middle of another 8½ by 11 inch blank piece of paper. The line represents your expected life from the present (at the left end) as far into the future as you wish (toward the right).

Privately imagine the years you have ahead of you. Along the line label the events you believe will be turning points in your future life.

You may wish to discuss some of the events with your group. What will you need to do now to make your expected future become your probable future? What frustrations do you foresee?

PHASE III. THE UPS AND DOWNS OF LIFE

A turning point can mean a change upward toward a more fulfilling life or a change downward, a step away from life goals. Think for a moment of a business chart of your life—past, present, and future. Mark upward and downward turning points that represent your feelings of personal fulfillment and lack of fulfillment.
Write a brief explanation of your "line."
Share with your group any ideas or feelings you want to discuss.

PHASE IV. WHAT DO I WANT TO ACHIEVE?

Make a list of some of the career goals you would like to achieve. For example, you might want to be a teacher, an Air Force pilot, a diesel truck driver, or a member of an Olympic team. Share a goal from this list with the members of your group of three.

Make a list of some of the goals you would like to achieve in your relationships with your family and friends. For example, you might want to get married and have children, go out on a date with a famous movie star, get along better with your parents, or become better acquainted with one of your friends. Share a goal from this list with the members of your group.

Make a list of some of your goals for personal happiness and fulfillment. For example, you might want to become more self-confident and courageous, or thoughtful and generous. Share a goal from this list with the members of your group.

PHASE V. A PLAN FOR MY FUTURE

Establish a planning program to help you reach several of your most important goals or build on your achievements. List the steps that must be taken in order to reach each goal. Set a timetable for achieving each step.

Consider developing and signing written contracts with the other members of your group, indicating that you all agree to work toward your individual goals.

Share with your group any ideas or feelings you want to discuss.

Make some "I learned" statements in your JOURNAL NOTES:

• I learned that . . .

• The goals I consider most important are . . .

ACTIVITY 6

Personal Change

Change can be difficult. This decision-making task will help you understand the roadblocks that get in the way of change and the ways in which you can plan to overcome them. The task will involve a number of choices:

Divide a plain sheet of 8½ by 11 inch paper into six equal squares. Number the squares 1 through 6.

You will receive six slips of paper with choices that you will have to make in the next five to ten years. Place these slips on the numbered squares in the order of their importance to you. After you have done this, wait for additional instructions from your teacher.

At the completion of the activity, list in order from 1 (most important) to 6 (least important) the choices you have made.

QUESTIONS FOR DISCUSSION

1. What do your choices tell you about yourself?
2. How difficult was it to make your choices?
3. How do you plan to obtain the things you have selected?
4. What might prevent you from obtaining these things?

TECHNOLOGY AND CHANGE: PROS AND CONS

Americans have traditionally thought of the future in a positive way. Very often we visualize the future in the form of wheels, gears, and other advances in technology. TECHNOLOGY is the application of scientific principles to the solution of practical problems. For example, the successful landing of Americans on the moon was the result of technological advances.

As a result of technological changes, new sets of words may come into use. Dictionary editors keep an eye on new words entering our

GREENLEE '82

vocabulary, accepting those that appear most often in print. Then the editors add those words to the next edition of their dictionary. In 1975–1976, some of the words being considered were "digital watch," "flextime" (a system that allows employees to choose their own starting and finishing times), "brown-out," "ultrasuede," "agricorporation," "cyborg," and "cybernetics."

Look up these words in a current dictionary. Did they become popular enough to be entered?

Americans also think of technological advances as something to hate or fear. Countless science fiction novels, short stories, and films have dwelled on the love/hate relationship between man and machine. The character of Hal the computer in Stanley Kubrick's film *2001: A Space Odyssey* reflects these mixed feelings about technology. In this film the computer actually shows such human emotions as love, jealousy, and hate. Another example of feelings that are mixed is the ease with which we use credit cards and the frustration or hate we feel when the computer fouls up our account.

A technological future is coming with all of its pluses and minuses, and only we can decide where it is going. The human community must make choices. These alternatives and actions will affect all of us.

ACTIVITY 7

The House of Solomon[1]

One way to examine the technological future is from the point of view of the past.

Sir Francis Bacon, the Renaissance scientist and scholar, wrote of a mythical island community that he called New Atlantis. He placed himself among a ship's crew wrecked on the coast of New Atlantis in the year 1625. Befriended by the island's royal governor, the crew was instructed daily on the history of the island and the culture of the people who resided there. Of particular interest to the crew was the governor's discussion of a magnificent building, Solomon's House. Here is a part of what the governor revealed:

> "Ye shall understand, my dear friends, that among the excellent acts of our king, one has stood above all others. It was the erection of Solomon's House. We think it the noblest foundation that ever was upon the earth; it is our lantern.
>
> "The facilities and instruments contained within Solomon's House go far beyond anything you can have imagined. We have a system of large caves sunk to a depth of nearly seven kilometers. These caves have in turn been divided into a series of chambers, each housing a different sort of scientific inquiry."

The governor spoke of the many marvels in these chambers. The scientists of New Atlantis have discovered how to:

- cure rare and terminal diseases and, through special potions, restore youth to an aging body
- create new forms of food through the science of grafting and growing them in great gardens
- apply the principles of anatomy to the study of human bodies by means of dissection of all sorts of birds and beasts

[1]Adapted from David W. Adams, David Cornelius, and Marvin Pasch, "The House of Solomon: A Lesson in Ethical Responsibility," *The Science Teacher* (December 1976). Reprinted with permission from *The Science Teacher*, published by the National Science Teachers Association.

- develop great furnaces and engines for the manufacture of goods for its citizens
- invent ships that both fly in the air and swim under the sea

The governor continued:

"Some of you may wish to know how this magnificent foundation is governed. Solomon's House has developed a most ingenious means of overseeing its work through the creation of a governing group called the Merchants of Light. This is a committee of 12 of the kingdom's noblest scientists, and they have absolute say regarding the direction of scientific inquiry.

"The committee also has responsibility for deciding whether scientific discoveries and inventions are to be made known to the general public or kept secret, even from the king himself. The reason for this is simple. We believe that scientists should be responsible for the consequences of their work. Thus, when a particular investigation has yielded findings that are potentially dangerous to the citizens of New Atlantis, the findings are suppressed. The committee looks upon its role in this area as most important for the island's welfare. I am told that the committee sessions on such matters are enthusiastic and sometimes quite heated."

INSTRUCTIONS

Imagine yourself a member of the Merchants of Light in the year 1625. Remember, you have the power to release a discovery or invention to the island's citizens or to SUPPRESS it (hold it back, hush it up).

You and your committee must make a decision on the two proposals on pages 329–330. Your decision should be based on whether the particular invention or discovery will bring good or harmful consequences to the citizens of New Atlantis. Consider both immediate and remote consequences. Different people have different standards about the degree of harm they will tolerate from a new discovery. That is, they have different CONSEQUENCE STANDARDS. Here are three standards.

- *Standard A.* Release if the invention or discovery will result in good consequences for New Atlantis, even though serious harmful consequences can also be expected.

- *Standard B*. Release if the expected good consequences will outweigh the expected harmful consequences.
- *Standard C*. Release if the invention or discovery will result in good consequences only; otherwise suppress it.

THE PROPOSALS

HOUSE OF SOLOMON EVALUATION FORM: PROPOSAL I

DEPARTMENT SPONSORING: Physiology

SUBJECT: Eternacol

DESCRIPTION: After many years of experimenting, several scientists of the House of Solomon have discovered a serum that can cause human beings to live twice the normal life span maintaining their youthful appearance and health. In a year's time it will be possible to produce enough serum to inject all the men on the island. Sufficient experiments have shown that no harmful effects are caused to the body as a result of the serum. It is important to understand, however, that the serum is effective only on males.

SIGNIFICANCE

1. All males will be guaranteed a life span twice the one they could normally expect.
2. This discovery will enable the male inhabitants of the island to extend their lives while the Department of Physiology continues to search for a similarly effective serum for women, as well as a serum that will give everlasting life to citizens of New Atlantis.
3. As a result of the serum, overcrowding on the island will become a problem in the near future, requiring some form of population control or a plan of colonization that will deprive the island of its isolation.
4. Use of the serum will mean that males will greatly outnumber females on the island. This will no doubt require a change in the institution of marriage.

COMMITTEE DECISION: Release ☐   Suppress ☐

HOUSE OF SOLOMON EVALUATION FORM: PROPOSAL II

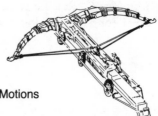

DEPARTMENT SPONSORING: Forces and Motions

SUBJECT: Giant Ballista

DESCRIPTION: By the application of known scientific principles, the Department of Forces and Motions now has the capacity to construct a giant ballista, an enormous crossbow mounted on six wheels in three parts. This mechanism fires a shrapnel-loaded fireball, which, upon reaching the ground, ignites and causes considerable destruction. It is estimated that this fireball has a range of up to one mile.

SIGNIFICANCE

1. This weapon has greater capacity for destruction than any known weapon in the world.
2. The giant ballista would be a most useful weapon for defending the kingdom should it be assaulted.
3. The island's isolation seems to be coming to an end, as is indicated by the recent increase in visitors from ships "lost" at sea.
4. Construction of the ballista would change what up to now has been the non-military orientation of the kingdom.
5. Construction of the ballista would enable the department to experiment with weapons even greater in destructive power.

COMMITTEE DECISION: Release ☐   Suppress ☐

QUESTIONS FOR DISCUSSION

1. Do you believe scientists should be responsible for the consequences that result from their inventions and discoveries? Why or why not?
2. Do you think a group similar to the Merchants of Light should be formed in America? Who should be on this committee? Explain.
3. What inventions or discoveries of the 20th century would you have voted to suppress? Why?

ACTIVITY 8

The Merchants of Light and the Future[2]

Assume that you are a member of the Merchants of Light assigned to review technological advances in America today. Your committee has the power to provide financial backing for a limited number of INNOVATIONS—new products or processes that accomplish desired goals. What is your judgment about the value of the ideas listed under "Innovations to Consider"? Follow these procedures:

Consider both the immediate and the remote consequences of each innovation.

Use the consequence standard you selected in the last activity to guide your judgments.

Read and consider the 20 innovations that follow. On a sheet of paper write vertically the numbers from 1 to 20 and record your judgment about each next to the numbers. Use this rating scale:

a. I am eager to see it developed.
b. I wish to see it developed with certain controls.
c. I am uncertain about it.
d. I do not wish it to be developed.
e. It makes no difference to me.

INNOVATIONS TO CONSIDER

_____ 1. extensive and intensive worldwide use of high-altitude cameras for mapping, prospecting, census, land use, and geological investigation

[2]Adapted from Ibid. Reprinted with permission from _The Science Teacher_ (December 1976), published by the National Science Teachers Association.

_____ 2. new methods of water transportation (large submarines, flexible and special-purpose container ships, more extensive use of large, automated single-purpose bulk cargo ships)

_____ 3. extensive use of cyborg techniques in medicine (mechanical aids or substitutes for human organs, including sense organs, limbs)

_____ 4. new or improved uses of the oceans for mining and extraction of minerals from seawater

_____ 5. use of nuclear explosives for excavation and mining, generation of power, creation of high-temperature/high-pressure environments, or as a source of neutrons or other radiation

_____ 6. new and possibly more widespread techniques for surveillance, monitoring, and control of individuals and organizations

_____ 7. some control of weather or climate

_____ 8. the practical use of direct electronic communication with the brain

_____ 9. cheap and widely available or excessively destructive weapons and weapons systems

_____ 10. genetic control or influence of the intellectual, physical, and emotional characteristics of children

_____ 11. more extensive use of human organ transplants

_____ 12. extensive use of robots and machines "enslaved" to humans

_____ 13. chemical methods for improved memory and learning

_____ 14. improved chemical control of some mental illness and some aspects of senility

_____ 15. mechanical and chemical methods for improving human analytical ability more or less directly

_____ 16. more widespread use by businesses of computers for the storage, processing, and retrieval of information

_____ 17. space defense systems

_____ 18. extensive genetic control of plants and animals

_____ 19. new biological and chemical methods of identifying, tracing, incapacitating, or harassing people for police and military uses

_____ 20. new and possibly very simple methods for waging deadly biological and chemical warfare

QUESTIONS FOR DISCUSSION

1. Judging from your answers, would you describe yourself an optimist or a pessimist about technological and scientific innovations? Explain why.

2. In groups of five or more, share your answers. One person in the group should be a recorder. Tally the group's judgment on the Group Total Sheet that will be given to you. A class recorder should then combine each group's tally on a final Group Total Sheet to determine the class viewpoint.

3. Take two of the possible technological innovations that you are eager to see developed and indicate what one immediate or remote consequence of their development might be. Do the same for two of those you do not wish to see developed. For example: *innovation*—some control of weather or climate; *consequence*—specific individuals decide about the kind of weather or climate (but who gets to decide?).

ACTIVITY 9

Does Change Shake You Up?

More than 10 years ago, Alvin Toffler wrote a book that became so popular that its title, *Future Shock*, entered our everyday vocabulary. FUTURE SHOCK is a kind of mental paralysis that strikes some people during a period of rapid change. In his book, Toffler argues that Americans are going through just such a period. He believes that the conditions that cause today's future shock are clear and can be described easily. First, there is TRANSIENCE—the temporary nature of relationships with friends, acquaintances, fellow workers, neighbors, and communities. Second, there is NOVELTY—the desire to participate in new experiences and be the first person on the block to have a color television or a home computer terminal. The third condition is DIVERSITY—having too many alternatives from which to select.

Thus, transience, novelty, and diversity are potentially shocking conditions. Some people react by denying that change is occurring. Others hang on to what used to be successful, even though they recognize conditions have changed. Still others try to keep up with only the changes in their narrow area of interest. Finally, some people look for simple answers to account for everything. They think the cause of every trouble is bad diet or permissiveness or politicians or communists or the signs of the zodiac.

The following activity is designed to make you aware of the trends of transience, novelty, and diversity in your own life. Respond to the following questionnaire in your JOURNAL NOTES.

Transience

1. How many different houses have you lived in?
2. How many different cities have you lived in?

3. How many different schools have you attended?
4. Were you born in the city or town in which you now live?
5. Were you born in the town or city where one of your parents was born?
6. Do you still have friends that you met 10 years ago?

Novelty

1. Name machines that now do what human beings did 10 years ago.
2. How many electronic games have you played? Name or describe them.
3. Which of these forms of transportation have you used?
   - horse and buggy
   - automobile
   - trolley car
   - train
   - ship
   - subway
   - airplane
   - motorcycle
   - snowmobile
   - hang-glider
   - glider
   - hot air balloon
   - hydroplane
   - monorail
   - blimp
   - other: _____
4. What do you think is the most valuable invention in your lifetime?
5. What do you think is the least valuable invention in your lifetime?

Diversity

1. What is your greatest fear?
2. Name three consumer products that were once readily available but are no longer manufactured.
3. Name the sports, entertainment, and political figures you most admire now. Who were the ones you admired two years ago? Five years ago?
4. How many channels are available on a cable television hookup in your area?
5. How many options are available on a sub-compact Ford, Datsun, Chevrolet, or Plymouth automobile?
6. How many makes of calculators are on the market?

Thinking about your answers, complete the following sentence stems:

- I was surprised that . . .
- I learned that . . .

ACTIVITY 10

To Move Is to Change

Change can be dramatic. We all have to cope with major changes that affect the future of life on earth and beyond, such as advances in medicine, transportation, education, agriculture, and construction.

We all have to cope individually with smaller changes, too. A common event, like moving to another apartment or home within a city or moving to another town or to another country, can make a big change in a person's life. Transience is a way of life for many people in the United States. Approximately 45 million Americans move yearly. How many times have you moved during your lifetime?

Experts tell us that moving can result in stress. It can be a contributing cause of physical and emotional illness. As one person has said, moving may be hazardous to health. However, it can also be challenging and valuable and result in a family growth experience.

The chart on page 338 lists many of the changes that accompany relocation to another community. To determine how your moves affected you, place checks under "Unhappy" or "Excited." In the third column write a few words or a sentence describing the changes in your behavior that resulted from each change in your surroundings.

QUESTIONS FOR DISCUSSION

1. Which of the changes in the Relocation Chart do you think are most important? Draw a line like the one that follows, with "Little Effect" at one end and "Great Effect" at the other. Write the number of each item in the chart on the line wherever you think it fits, according to that change's effect on you.

Little   Great
Effect_____Effect

2. Select three items and explain the adjustments you made to reduce the effects of those changes.

RELOCATION CHART

Change	Unhappy	Excited	Behavior
1. Changing homes			
2. Leaving old friends			
3. Making new friends			
4. Altered schedules (in school, work, recreation)			
5. New food and eating habits			
6. Change of climate			
7. Change of wardrobe			
8. Leaving relatives			
9. Financial changes			
10. Status and role changes			

ACTIVITY 11

Education Should Be . . .

You are currently as close to education as anyone can be. Six or more hours a day and five days a week of your life are spent in formal education. This has been going on for nine to twelve years. Forecasters tell us that you will continue some type of formal education beyond high school because of the need to upgrade your competencies, just to keep up with changes that will be occurring. Change has been going on in education, as in everything else. Sometimes the change has been more rapid than people wish and sometimes not as rapid.

The thirteen recommendations for education for the 1980s given on pages 340–341 were made at the end of 1979. Study them and indicate

whether or not you think each listed change should be supported. Vertically number a sheet of paper from 1 to 13 and respond with "OK" or "Not OK" by the number of each item.

OK or
Not OK

_____ 1. Train students in biofeedback to put them in a frame of mind that is receptive to teaching. (Biofeedback is a technique whereby one seeks to consciously regulate a bodily function thought to be involuntary, like heartbeat or blood pressure, by using an instrument to monitor the function and signal changes in it.)

"Will this help me to cope with a high-technology computer-oriented society?"

OK or
Not OK

_____ 2. Support research into drugs that enhance brain function and memory to aid the advanced student.

_____ 3. Support research into drugs that enhance brain function and memory to aid slow learners.

_____ 4. Provide more opportunities for students to participate in out-of-school educational experiences.

_____ 5. Increase the use of computerized devices, teaching games, and video technology in instruction.

_____ 6. Use computer technology for instruction at home.

_____ 7. Have companies pay the private school tuition of employees' children.

_____ 8. Abolish compulsory education.

_____ 9. Decrease the amount of time spent in education on social issues and student involvement in community service.

_____ 10. Include more vocational/career education, science, and basic skill/remedial courses.

_____ 11. Reduce the number of art, music, and modern language courses.

_____ 12. Require all students to pass standardized comprehensive tests in order to graduate.

_____ 13. Encourage the growth of private schools by providing tax credits for people who send their children to them.

QUESTIONS FOR DISCUSSION

Meet in groups of five and discuss the following questions:

1. What would be one possible consequence of each of the recommendations listed above?
2. Can you think of constructive alternatives leading to the same end result for five of the recommendations?

ACTIVITY 12

Change

Social studies and science classroom teachers in Iowa identified 12 issues as the most important ones affecting American society in the 1980s.

In your JOURNAL NOTES rank these 12 issues as follows: *1* is most important, *2* is next in importance, and so on. You may also add others that you consider more pressing.

Rank

_____ a. The politics of energy (conflict between the oil-producing and oil-consuming nations)

_____ b. Nuclear power (use and safety)

_____ c. Alternative energy sources (availability, costs, environmental effects)

_____ d. The politics of food (using food as a weapon in international affairs)

_____ e. Air pollution (standards set by federal, state, or local governments)

_____ f. Pesticides (possible dangers to humans and other living things)

_____ g. Human medical experiments (could or should question)

_____ h. Soil conservation (responsibility of individuals, industry, or government?)

_____ i. Drugs and narcotics (use and abuse)

_____ j. Abortion (individual or government decision?)

_____ k. Bioethics (the making of such decisions as whether or not to use artificial life-sustaining measures and who should decide)

_____ l. Genetic counseling (using new medical techniques to predict certain birth defects and diseases)

QUESTIONS FOR DISCUSSION

1. How much instruction have you received about each of these issues?
2. Do you think the amount of instruction was:
   • too little?
   • about right?
   • too much?
3. How much instructional time do you think should be devoted to these topics during the four years of high school?

ACTIVITY 13

Credit Cards: A Cashless Society

Should you or shouldn't you carry and use credit cards? Many people carry cards for department stores, car service, travel, dining, and various other business dealings. In fact, eight of ten people who make a purchase do so with a credit card. People sometimes joke that clerks are confused when a customer pays cash.

There are conflicting views about the use of credit cards. Some people say that credit cannot be ignored. The whole economy of the United States is based on it. If you do not have it, you are lost. Another view is that you do not have to have credit. It is not really good. You do not have to have it in later life.

It is estimated that one in 35 teenagers has a credit card. Therefore it is worthwhile to determine whether credit is controlling you or you are controlling credit.

How does a teenager get a credit card? You can be what is called an "authorized user"; that is, you can have a duplicate card in a parent's or guardian's name. This is easy to obtain. In fact, at the time this activity was written, in California the Bank America VISA had no age restrictions on its accounts; in Cleveland Ameritrust/VISA stated that one must be 18.

Experts offer the following recommendations to teenage credit card users:

1. Have a credit limit or "line." Begin with $50–100.
2. Follow a set of rules on which you and your parents agree.
3. Make a record of all purchases.
4. Open a savings account before you get a credit card. This will provide a reserve to meet monthly payments.
5. Limit your purchases to necessary items.
6. Pay for your purchases in full at the end of each month.
7. Be aware of your responsibilities. If your parents are legally responsible for your debts, consider their welfare.

344

The widespread use of credit cards is a relatively recent technological change. In fact, your parents can probably remember when credit cards first began to be used. This activity is intended to help you understand how the extensive use of credit cards may be controlling you now or may tend to control you in the future. To help you understand the situation, fill out the sample application for a credit card. (Unless you are permitted to write in your book, copies will be distributed.)

Reprinted with permission of the AmeriTrust Company, Cleveland, Ohio.

QUESTIONS FOR DISCUSSION

1. It is estimated that more than 500,000 teenagers have credit cards. Have you ever used a credit card? How often?
2. Do you know of anyone who has *(a)* one or more, *(b)* five or more, *(c)* ten or more credit cards in his or her wallet or purse?
3. What kind of information does a store or bank require when you complete a credit card application such as the one shown above?
4. Could the information listed on the application be used for any other purpose?
5. Do you think that the information asked for on an application would allow someone to invade your privacy? If so, how?

STEPPING INTO THE FUTURE

THE IMMEDIATE FUTURE

How old will you be in the year 2000? Most of you will be in your thirties.

Think of the immediate future as the time from now until then. Formerly it was not too difficult to imagine and cope with the changes that might occur over that span of time.

In recent years change has occurred more rapidly. Our reaction to this rapid change, as we said above, has come to be called future shock. It has affected some people so dramatically that they have been unable to function.

Dramatic changes in the future need not be overwhelming if you are prepared for them. The following activities are designed to stimulate your thinking about the immediate future—the time between tomorrow and A.D. 2000.

ACTIVITY 14

Rituals and Ceremonies

It is fun to imagine how life events in the immediate future may differ from those common today. Write an essay of no more than 100 words on what you think one of the following activities will be like in the year 2000:

- a trip to a supermarket
- a homecoming football game
- a senior prom
- a wedding ceremony and reception
- a funeral
- a basketball game

Exchange essays and read them in groups of four. Discuss the changes you anticipate.

ACTIVITY 15

Fifteen Years from Now

What will your life be like 15 years in the future? This activity is designed to help you to answer that question and to examine your present and future needs, resources, immediate physical and psychological setting, aspirations, and values.

Write a short autobiography for your JOURNAL NOTES focusing on how and where you see yourself 15 years from today. Answer the following questions as you write:

1. Where do you live?
2. What education have you had since high school?
3. What kinds of jobs have you had?
4. What job do you have now? How do you feel about it?
5. What are your goals in relation to your work?
6. Are you single? Married? Are you living alone or with others?
7. Do you have any children? If so, what are their ages? If not, do you plan ever to have a family?
8. What are your favorite sports, hobbies, and forms of recreation?
9. How do you feel about your life?

ACTIVITY 16

Headlines: January 1, 2000[3]

Imagine that it is New Year's Day in the year 2000. Write five
headlines that you think might appear in the newspaper that day.
Sections of the newspaper to consider as you develop the headlines are:

- national news
- international news
- politics
- sports
- entertainment
- education
- business
- human interest
- travel

After you have written your headlines, you can:

discuss them in small groups
display them on a bulletin board
write stories to accompany them
publish a newspaper for New Year's Day, January 1, 2000, using
    the headlines and stories you have written

---

[3]Reprinted with permission of John A. Bowen, Lakewood High School, Lakewood, Ohio, who originated
this activity.

ACTIVITY 17

Changing Status and Role

In Unit III we studied the status and role of various occupations and professions in American society. This activity will help you examine how groups of people are arranged in what are called social classes. It will also help you project what changes in social class structure are possible in the future.

Americans are generally grouped into social classes based on occupation, source of income, and place and type of residence. For example, one social class is called the "upper-upper class." These people have inherited wealth and therefore do not have to work; if they do work, they often choose the areas of investment and finance. Frequently they enter politics. Such names as Rockefeller, Roosevelt, Kennedy, and Taft are familiar to most Americans. Since their wealth is inherited, the source of most of their income is dividends on stocks and interest on bonds and other investments in business and industry. The upper-upper class people live in very large and elaborate houses, which may have belonged to their families for generations. They are likely to have homes in more than one place: a town house, a country estate, and a vacation retreat. Their houses are all built in very exclusive areas, which are recognized as upper-upper class neighborhoods.

Social class descends in a series of steps from upper-upper class to what has been called the "lower-lower class." These people are at the lowest wage levels or are unemployed, and they live in slums.

Social class in the future may be an entirely different matter. A whole new group of people may occupy the "upper-upper class"—for example, those who control energy resources or have expertise in the medical field, or even professional athletes and entertainers.

QUESTIONS FOR DISCUSSION

1. What social classes do you think exist in the United States today? How do you think the social class structure developed?
2. If someone is unhappy with his or her social class, what alternatives are available to change it?
3. How might social class structure in the year 2000 differ from the present structure?

THE REMOTE FUTURE

Forecasting the future beyond 20 years is always risky. Numerous surveys show that young people as well as older people feel they have little control over the future. They seem to accept the notion that it just happens.

It seems vital to us, however, that people concern themselves about the future and their place in it.

The activities that follow examine the remote future in terms of the causal approach to human behavior. The causes and the short- and long-term consequences of behavior must be considered if constructive alternatives for the future are to be chosen.

ACTIVITY 18

Four Views of the Future[4]

One way to think about your values as they are related to the future is to examine four different views of the future.

1. The future is a great roller coaster on a moonless night. We know that the track exists, twisting ahead of us in the dark, although we can only see each part as we come to it. We can make estimates about where we are headed and sometimes see around the bend to another section of track, but looking ahead doesn't do us any real good because the future is fixed and determined. We are locked in our seats, and nothing we can find out or do will change the course that is laid out for us.

2. The future is a mighty river. The great force of history flows along, carrying us with it. Most of our attempts to change its course are mere pebbles thrown into the river. They cause a momentary splash and a few ripples, but they make no difference. The river's course can be changed, but only by natural disasters like earthquakes or landslides or by massive human efforts on a similar scale. On the other hand, we are free as individuals to adapt to the course of history, either well or poorly. By looking ahead, we can avoid sandbars and whirlpools and pick the best path through any rapids.

3. The future is a great ocean. There are many possible destinations and many different paths to each destination. A good navigator takes advantage of the main currents of change, adapts his course to the unpredictable winds of chance, keeps a sharp lookout posted, and moves carefully in fog or uncharted waters. A navigator who does these things will get safely to his or her destination, barring a typhoon or some other disaster that no navigator can either predict or avoid.

[4]Reprinted with permission of Bruce T. Beebe and John A. Bowen, Lakewood High School, Lakewood, Ohio, who originated this activity.

4. The future is entirely random, a colossal dice game. Every second, millions of things happen that could have happened another way and produced a different future. A bullet is deflected by a twig and kills one man instead of another. A scientist checks a spoiled culture and throws it away, or he looks more closely at it and discovers penicillin. Since everything is chance, all we can do is play the game, pray to the gods of fortune, and enjoy whatever good luck comes our way.

FOR YOUR JOURNAL NOTES

First rank the four views of the future, from the one you think is the most accurate (1) to the one you think is the least accurate (4). Be prepared to explain your ranking.

Then write your own view of the future in five sentences or less. It can be similar to one of the four you just read, a combination of two or more of them, or your original viewpoint.

ACTIVITY 19

Survival: Can We Adapt to Change?[5]

The survival story printed here was written to help you:

- think about the future and long-range planning
- refine your group task skills
- learn to cope with frustrations and resolve them positively
- develop decision-making skills

Read "Red River" and the rest of this activity. Then develop a three- or four-page written conclusion to the story. You may work in groups of five or six, or your entire class may want to work together to complete the story.

RED RIVER

You and your 12 companions have just arrived by jeep in Red River, a small town in the foothills of the Canadian Rockies. For the past three weeks your group has been high above the timber line on a high school outdoor endurance project. During that time you have had no contact with the outside world.

You have just learned that within the past 24 hours a mysterious killer virus has wiped out virtually every person in Western Canada—and quite possibly the world. Just three hours ago the two adult advisers of your group contacted fevers, became delirious, and suffered painful deaths. Scores of dead bodies are lying on the streets of Red River and in the hospital. It is obvious that these people died as your advisers did.

No one in your group feels ill. Your group concludes that there is a good chance that none of you will be infected by the killer virus.

[5]Reprinted with permission of Bruce T. Beebe, Lakewood High School, Lakewood, Ohio, who originated this activity.

This, then, is your present situation:

- Not a living soul, other than your group members, is in sight.
- You assume that all other human beings are dead.
- All lower animals appear to be unaffected by the virus.
- Electricity is working, and all electrical applicances are operating.
- Radios and telephones are working, but you are unable to contact anyone.

Working from this information, you and your companions must plan for the immediate and long-range future. Make careful, specific, and detailed notes on the future you envision. Think of your group's needs and resources as you discuss and complete the story. Locate your immediate physical setting on a map. Be sure to consider the short- and long-term consequences of your behavior as you plan for the future.

Now write the conclusion to "Red River."

QUESTIONS FOR DISCUSSION

1. If your class developed more than one conclusion for "Red River," how were they similar and how were they different?
2. What needs and resources of your group were discussed in the conclusion(s)?
3. Why does it seem to be easier to plan for the immediate future than the long-range future?
4. What characteristics must we possess to be able to adapt to change successfully?

ACTIVITY 20

Time Capsule[6]

What would you say are the meaningful and significant elements of our culture—our total way of life? What elements do you value?

Here is one way to determine those elements. The class will select items to place in a time capsule to be opened 50 years from now. The contents of the capsule should be carefully chosen to represent today's culture and values to future generations. Either the representative items themselves or symbols of them are to be placed in the capsule.

No living thing can be put in the capsule. The dimensions of the capsule are to be determined by the class. It can range in size from a small container to the entire classroom.

FIRST DISCUSSION SESSION

1. Students form groups of five.
2. Each student brings a minimum of three items (or symbols of three items) for possible inclusion in the capsule.
3. The group selects by consensus one item from each group member.
4. Group members should be encouraged to justify the value of their contributions and convince others of it.
5. An elected recorder in each group notes how and why final items are selected.
6. Items not selected are saved for possible future use.

[6]Reprinted with permission of John A. Bowen, Lakewood High School, Lakewood, Ohio, who originated this activity.

SECOND DISCUSSION SESSION

1. The entire class participates in this discussion.
2. The whole class discusses and decides on the size of the class time capsule.
3. A class recorder lists the final choices of each group on the board.
4. Class members decide by consensus what is ultimately to be placed in the class time capsule. It may be necessary to reconsider choices, to debate, to advocate items, or to remove some or replace them with items set aside earlier.
5. When the final list of items is compiled, the recorder should write a reason for the choice beside each item.

QUESTIONS FOR DISCUSSION

1. How similar were the items you originally suggested to those that were finally included in the class time capsule?
2. Why do you think it is difficult to reach consensus?
3. Judging from the contents of your class time capsule, what are the characteristics of our culture that your class values?

TECHNOLOGY AND VALUE DILEMMAS

In Unit I the activity "A Renewed Chance for Life" dealt with the mythical dying planet of Prospero. To give some of the people of Prospero a chance to survive, you were to nominate eight people to be transported to another planet, where they would be safe and could multiply. The key problem was a value dilemma that had to be resolved. In this activity we turn to a similar value dilemma.

A scientist has proposed colonizing space and believes such colonies would be so attractive that the earth's population would choose to live in space rather than on earth. This could occur, he suggests, within the next 100 years. The value dilemma this proposal raises is closer to us than Prospero's because of technological developments already in operation. The 1981 space shuttle is but one example.

Use the PARS System (worksheet number XI) as you read the following essay. Be prepared to complete the tasks at the end of the article.

ACTIVITY 21

Humanity Unlimited[7]

**AUTHOR
TOM PAINE**

Imagine, if you can, a future five centuries from now in which mankind has increased to 20,000 times its current population. Impossible, scoff the currently fashionable doomsters, who claim that if we are not atomized in a nuclear holocaust, we will soon be impoverished by the exhaustion of earth's resources. But there are other, more optimistic scientists today who are looking into another, more expansive future—and believe that it can work.

One of these is Dr. Gerald K. O'Neill, a Princeton physics professor, who calculates that humanity could achieve a good life, even at 20,000 times its present size, by colonizing space. O'Neill stresses that he is not prophesying the future, but he is weighing its possibilities.

By moving into space, man could increase his cultural diversity and environmental quality, he argues, while decreasing poverty and territorial wars. He believes that the people left on earth itself might eventually dwindle to the 1900 level of about a billion, restoring our planet to a pristine condition free of industrial contaminants. Earth would be a great place to visit, but with more desirable abodes available, most people wouldn't want to live there.

Although I must take issue with Dr. O'Neill's timetables and cost estimates, his bold proposals are based on a realistic appraisal of potential space progress over the next hundred years and deserve serious consideration. I know what well-managed industrial and government organizations can achieve on the frontiers of technology, and I've visited development groups around the world that are already working on the basic technical advances and cooperative international programs required to begin work on Dr. O'Neill's plans. Let's consider his vision of the year 2075 after man's first century in space and then review the development programs of the next 25 years that might convert his far-out proposals into a serious option for mankind.

Human Settlements in Space

The sun irradiates space with unlimited clean energy. Gravity and an atmosphere can be provided in two ways: on the convex surface of a massive planet or on the concave interior of a rotating space community, where centrifugal force simulates gravity. Most space-colonization proposals have concentrated on the planets, but the space pioneer Tsiolkovsky suggested that artificial habitats also be considered. The Princeton proposal envisions a number of man-made space communities in the vast region between Venus and Mars, each containing several million people living on a hundred square miles of habitable acreage within a pair of cylinders about 4 miles in diameter and 20 miles long.

A rotation rate of half a revolution per minute would simulate earth's gravity. The sparkling atmosphere inside the cylinders would include a blue sky fleeced with white clouds and occasional sprinkles of rain. Three long mirrors with matching windows along the sides would flood the interior with sunlight. Opening and closing the mirrors on a 24-hour cycle would move the reflected sun across the sky as in a normal earth day, with seasonal variations as desired. Animals, birds, flowers, and trees would share the parklike environment with people, but agricultural production of natural fresh foods would be carried out in attached nonrotating pods so zero gravity and continuous sunlight could enhance productivity. Similar pods would be available for astronomical observatories, hospitals, sports arenas, and industrial and recycling processes. Steam-turbine generators energized by solar boilers would furnish abundant clean power; electric vehicles and bicycles would provide transportation.

Reproducing Earth's Terrain

To increase the attractiveness of the environment, Dr. O'Neill suggests lakes for fishing, swimming, and sailing and sculptured end caps of the cylinders reproducing features of the earth's mountain terrain for hiking and skiing. Mountaineers would find one difference, though—as they scaled the peaks in space, they'd notice the simulated gravity progressively weakening, with complete weightlessness achieved at the peak. At a lesser altitude, weight would decline to the point where people with artificial wings could fly.

With no friction or gravity to overcome, space travel between communities would be relatively simple. Low-cost family-recreation vehicles consisting of pressurized shells with living quarters and recirculating atmospheres could visit other communities of diverse cultures across the solar system. The construction of new habitats to house immigrants from earth and also future generations would be a major activity on the space frontier. At first, the equipment and critical supplies would be furnished from earth, but raw materials needed for expansion could be supplied at lower cost from a small moon colony. For example, 89 percent of the weight of the water required in space would come from oxygen extracted from lunar soil, the remaining 11 percent being supplied as liquid hydrogen from earth.

Is 2075 Too Far Out?

It's hard enough to predict tomorrow, but a few men with technical vision have looked a century ahead with remarkable clarity. A hundred years ago, Jules Verne foresaw the Apollo program in extraordinary detail by consulting creative scientists and imaginatively projecting the future developments that their work implied. The best way to judge the potential of the Princeton proposal, then, is to assess relevant work now under way in the avant-garde of space technology.

In Palmdale, California, U.S. space technicians are assembling the powerful new delta-winged space shuttle. This reusable rocket will initiate economical round-trip service to orbit in the 1980s. Apollo was the Viking ship of space, capable of daring voyages for brief forays, but the shuttle will be the practical caravel that opens space for permanent settlement and economic development. In Noordwijk, Holland, the European Space Agency's $400 million Spacelab program is well under way. The U.S.-U.S.S.R. Apollo-Soyuz project provides further foundations for the international space-transportation systems and orbital facilities of the 1980s required to begin work on Dr. O'Neill's far-out proposals. In the 1990s these could readily be extended to establish and support the required lunar base. There is no reason to believe that the technology will not be ready to launch the next exciting phase in man's evolution.

Far-out is not far-fetched.

—Tom Paine

DISCUSSION: WHAT IS POSSIBLE?

The tremendous advances that have occurred during your lifetime make it easy to believe in other technological possibilities:

Visualize the 4-mile by 20-mile cylinders or pods suspended in space that were described in the essay.

Draw or construct models of these space communities.

The human problems that accompany these technological advances are of equal or greater magnitude:

Consider a number of the technological predictions in the essay. Select a minimum of two and write an imaginary description of the human outcomes of them. Make the outcomes both positive and negative. For example, the effects of establishing a number of space settlements might be as follows:

• Positive: There would be a great variety of cultures to visit easily.

• Negative: The establishment of settlements could be controlled by powers that want only certain cultures to exist.

ACTIVITY 22

You Design a Final Activity

Until now you have been involved in activities that *we* developed for *The New Model Me*. These activities have been concerned with five basic themes:

Human Behavior— Unit I	The Behavior Equation was introduced to help you understand how needs, resources, and the physical and psychological setting interact to cause behavior.
Self-Identity— Unit II	Emphasis was on recognizing and increasing your personal resources—the abilities, knowledge, attitudes, and energy that support your values.
Controls— Unit III	Inner and external forces that regulate, limit, and shape your actions were stressed.
Decision Making— Unit IV	The Behavior Equation was applied as you considered a range of alternatives in critical decisions.
Change: The New Model Me— Unit V	You were encouraged to review and evaluate changes in your needs, resources, and values as a result of studying *The New Model Me*. The unit also provided you with a look at the future.

Now is the time for *you* to design a concluding activity for *The New Model Me*:

Divide into groups of five.
Develop with the other members of your group an activity that you think will lead to the achievement of the objectives for any one of the five units.

365

Write out a detailed description of the activity after you have thoroughly reviewed it to be sure everything is clear.

Prepare a plan to lead the activity in one of the final classes of *The New Model Me*.

A Review of the Objectives

Now that you have completed the activities in Unit V, can you:

1. Develop and use planning and evaluation skills to direct changes in your life?
2. Judge alternative views of immediate and distant futures involving such topics as:
   - technological change?
   - education?
   - rebuilding after disaster?
   - living environments in space?
   - money and credit?
3. Recognize the effects of "future shock" on individuals?
4. State the relationship between life changes and stress?
5. Demonstrate the knowledge you have gained from *The New Model Me* by: (a) planning an activity that fits one of the five units in the text? (b) re-designing the cover of the book?
6. Demonstrate growth in your ability to resolve your frustrations by use of the Behavior Equation?
7. Tell what each WORD or PHRASE means?
8. Use the WORD or PHRASE correctly in a sentence?

About the Authors

JOHN R. ROWE, an educational consultant, was Project Director of "Curriculum for Meeting Modern Problems" in Lakewood, Ohio. He now resides in Asheville, North Carolina. His B.S. and M. Ed. degrees are from Bowling Green State University. He has 31 years of experience in education as a social studies teacher, counselor, assistant principal, principal, coordinator of a Title III curriculum writing project, director of a curriculum dissemination project, and educational consultant. He led the writing team that developed the first edition of *The New Model Me*. As Director of a Developer/Demonstrator Project in the U.S. Department of Education's National Diffusion Network for eight years, he conducted awareness-training activities based on the first edition of *The New Model Me* in 35 states. He is available to conduct awareness and training workshops on the text.

MARVIN PASCH led the writing team for this second edition. He has been Professor and Chairman of the Department of Curriculum and Foundations at Cleveland State University. A former social studies teacher, Dr. Pasch taught for 11 years in secondary schools in Illinois. He is the author of articles, monographs, and other books in the areas of both curriculum design and evaluation and is an evaluation consultant for *The New Model Me* dissemination project, as well as for other projects across the country. His present position is Head of the Department of Teacher Education at Eastern Michigan University.

WILLIAM F. HAMILTON was from 1977 to 1981 Project Associate of "Curriculum for Meeting Modern Problems" in Lakewood, Ohio. His B.S. is from Wittenberg University; his M.A., from the University of Chicago. He is a John Hay Fellow and Coe Fellow. He has 32 years of experience in education as a social studies teacher, coordinator of humanities and social studies, and principal. He was a consultant for the development of the first edition of *The New Model Me*. As Project Associate of a Developer/Demonstrator Project in the Department of Education's National Diffusion Network, he conducted awareness-training activities based on the first edition of *The New Model Me* in 29 states. He is currently an Educational Consultant with the Martha Holden Jennings Foundation and College Board, Advanced Placement Program. He is available to conduct awareness and training workshops on the text.

Bibliography

UNIT I

Ford, Edward E., and Zorn, Robert. *Why Be Lonely?* Niles, Ill.: Argus Communications, 1975.
   Offers practical advice for individuals who have become afraid of involvement with others.
Grace, Miriam S., et al. *Your Self: An Introduction to Psychology.* New York: A&W Publishers, 1976.
   A humanistic approach to basic principles of psychology designed for high school seniors and college freshmen. Applies psychological concepts to common experiences.
Hall, Elizabeth. *Why We Do What We Do: A Look at Psychology.* Boston: Houghton Mifflin, 1973.
   Examines principles, techniques, and experiments in modern psychology to help young people understand the nature of human behavior.
Human Behavior Series. Alexandria, Va.: Time-Life Books, 1976.
   Adams, Virginia. *Crime.*
   Bailey, Ronald. *Violence and Aggression.*
   Campbell, Robert. *The Enigma of the Mind.*
   Murphy, Richard W. *Status and Conformity.*
   Tanner, Ogden. *Stress.*
Hyde, Margaret O., and Marks, Edward S. *Psychology in Action.* New York: McGraw-Hill, 1967.
   Updated descriptions of the work of all types of psychologists.
Johanson, Donald C., and Edey, Maitland A. *Lucy: The Beginnings of Humankind.* New York: Simon & Schuster, 1981.
   The story of Lucy, the hominid whose 3.5 million-year-old remains were found in Ethiopia.
Le Shan, Eda. *What Makes Me Feel This Way: Growing Up with Human Emotions.* New York: Collier Books, 1974.
   "An invitation to explore, understand, and enjoy your own feelings." Helps one to understand that these feelings are natural and are shared by just about everybody else in the world.

Lifton, Robert Jay. *The Life of the Self: Toward a New Psychology*. New York: Simon & Schuster, 1976.
   Articulates concepts and principles developed by Lifton through various studies and writings.

Massey, Morris E. *The People Puzzle: Understanding Yourself and Others*. Reston, Va.: Reston Publishing Co., 1980.
   Examines the factors that govern people's actions and shape their perceptions of the world.

Morris, Desmond. *The Human Zoo*. New York: Delta Books, 1969.
   Explains the ways in which the behavior patterns of modern, urban man resemble those of wild animals caged in a zoo.

Rubinstein, Joseph, and Slife, Brent D. *Taking Sides: Clashing Views on Controversial Psychological Issues*. Guilford, Conn.: Dushkin Publishing Group, 1980.
   One of a series of volumes prepared to provide readers with well-developed, carefully considered, and sharply opposed viewpoints on enduring issues.

Sagan, Carl. *The Dragons of Eden: Speculations on the Evolution of Human Intelligence*. New York: Random House, 1977.
   A survey by the well-known astronomer and astrobiologist of current knowledge about the development of intelligence on earth in various forms of life.

Weinstein, Grace W. *People Study People: The Story of Psychology*. New York: Dutton Publishing Co., 1979.
   Provides basic facts about psychoanalysis, behaviorism, humanism, and the theories of Piaget and describes the influences in our daily lives.

UNIT II

Borland, Hal. *When the Legends Die*. New York: Bantam Books, 1976.
   Young Thomas Black Bull knows the songs and ways of his Ute ancestors. Following his parents' deaths, he is dragged into the white people's world, where he gains fame as a rodeo star.

Cormier, Robert. *I Am the Cheese*. New York: Pantheon Books, 1977.
   A young person's journey through the mysteries of the mind.

Greenberg, Joanne. *Rites of Passage*. New York: Holt, Rinehart & Winston, 1972.
   Stories that speak about the experiences of adolescence.

Greene, Bette. *Morning Is a Long Time Coming*. New York: Dial Press, 1978.
   A sequel to *Summer of My German Soldier*. Patty Bergen graduates from high school and travels to Europe, where she must make major decisions.

Greene, Bette. *Summer of My German Soldier*. New York: Bantam
    Books, 1974.
    A friendship between a Jewish girl and a German prisoner of war in the
    United States.
Hinton, S. E. *That Was Then, This Is Now*. New York: Viking Press, 1971.
    Bryon confronts the problems of drugs, alcohol, and betrayal when he
    faces losing his best friend.
Kerr, M. E. *The Son of Someone Famous*. New York: Harper & Row, 1974.
    Adam hides from the fame his father gained as a presidential advisor who
    dates starlets, and Brenda fights her mother's concept of what a woman
    should be.
Kerr, M. E. *Is That You, Miss Blue?* New York: Harper & Row, 1975.
    After her mother runs off with a younger man, Flanders Brown is sent to
    an Episcopalian boarding school by her father. There, Flanders begins to
    work out her mixed feelings about herself and her unusual parents.
Knowles, John. *A Separate Peace*. New York: Bantam Books, 1966.
    Gene, the narrator, both admires and envies Finney, his athletic and
    handsome friend. One summer during the early years of World War II,
    Finney is injured in a fall from a tree and Gene has to face himself and
    his involvement in the accident.

UNIT III

Berne, Eric. *What Do You Say After You Say Hello? The Psychology of
    Human Destiny*. New York: Grove Press, 1972.
    Reveals the ways in which each person's life is governed by parental
    programming.
Brancato, Robin F. *Blinded by the Light*. New York: Alfred A. Knopf, 1978.
    A story of religious cults and their control over young people.
Brancato, Robin F. *Come Alive at 505*. New York: Alfred A. Knopf, 1980.
    Danny Fetzer has the senior-year shakes. He is tugged in three direc-
    tions—by his parents, by a girl, and by his own hopes for a career as a
    disc jockey.
Butler, Beverly. *Gift of Gold*. New York: Pocket Books, 1973.
    Cathy Wheeler, blind since she was 14, is stunned when her college's
    speech department chairman suggests that she abandon her plans to
    become a speech therapist.
Bylinsky, Gene. *Mood Control*. New York: Scribner, 1978.
    A report on biochemical psychiatry. Details the availability, uses, and
    effects of the newest drugs, diets, and mind-control techniques and
    reviews their potential for good and evil.

Cormier, Robert. *The Chocolate War*. New York: Pantheon Books, 1974.
A combination of *Lord of the Flies* and *A Separate Peace*.

Packard, Vance. *The People Shapers*. Boston: Little, Brown, 1977.
Surveys the current work, projects, and ambitions of geneticists, behavioral psychologists, psychosurgeons, technologists, marketing professionals, and others involved in reshaping and controlling people and their behavior. Examines the moral implications of their activities.

Pines, Maya. *The Brain Changers: Scientists and the New Mind Control*. New York: Harcourt Brace Jovanovich, 1973.
A report on what is being done in a unique area of controls.

Schrank, Jeffrey. *Snap, Crackle, and Popular Taste: The Illusion of Free Choice in America*. New York: Delacorte Press, 1977.
Examines some of the usually invisible factors that shape our everyday decisions.

Sullivan, Tom, and Gill, Derek. *If You Could See What I Hear*. New York: Harper & Row, 1975.
By a young, blind husband and father. Recounts his lonely childhood, education, and early adulthood, his refusal to submit to his handicap, and his struggles to succeed in sports, music, and life.

UNIT IV

Angell, Judie. *Ronnie and Rosey*. Scarsdale, N.Y.: Bradbury Press, 1977.
The problem involved in facing family death and other conflicts.

Bosse, Malcolm J. *The 79 Squares*. New York: Thomas Y. Crowell, 1979.
A gang member meets and becomes friends with an old man. Offers some good insight into old age, friendship, prejudices, nature, and family relationships.

Eyerly, Jeannette. *See Dave Run*. Philadelphia: J. B. Lippincott, 1978.
Running away from an intolerable home situation, a 15-year-old boy finds he has nowhere to go and no one to turn to.

Holland, Isabelle. *The Man Without a Face*. Philadelphia: J. B. Lippincott, 1972.
A readable novel for teenagers. Reveals the friendship that can grow between a young person and a disfigured man.

Johnson, A. E. *A Blues I Can Whistle*. New York: Four Winds Press, 1969.
After an unsuccessful attempt at suicide, Cody is hospitalized and tries to figure out who and what and why he is.

Mitchell, Joyce Slayton. *Free to Choose: Decision Making for Young Men*. New York: Delacorte Press, 1976.
Provides information and advice on personally determined careers and

life styles, encouraging young men to value their own experiences, feelings, and goals.

Potok, Chaim. *The Chosen*. New York: Fawcett Publications, 1967.
Two Jewish boys grow up in Brooklyn, one Hasidic, one Orthodox. Danny and Reuven are good friends but live in different worlds.

UNIT V

Asimov, Isaac. *Change! Seventy-One Glimpses of the Future*. Boston: Houghton Mifflin, 1981.
Discusses the developments in technology, computers, robots, and genetic engineering that lie in the future.

Beitz, Charles, and Washburn, Michael. *Creating the Future: A Guide to Living and Working for Social Change*. New York: Bantam Books, 1974.
A catalogue of opportunities for people concerned with social change.

Dunstan, Maryjane, and Garlan, Patricia W. *Worlds in the Making: Probes for Students of the Future*. Englewood Cliffs, N.J.: Prentice-Hall, 1970.
Written especially for young people interested in future studies. Includes a variety of illustrations, forecasts, and articles that challenge the reader.

Maddox, John. *The Doomsday Syndrome*. New York: McGraw-Hill, 1972.
Contradicts those who believe that the problems created by world population, pollution, and new biology cannot be solved. A very optimistic view.

Mead, Shepherd. *How to Get to the Future Before It Gets to You*. New York: Hawthorn Books, 1974.
Provides a daring and amusing antidote to doomsday prophets who believe man will destroy himself and the earth.

O'Neill, Gerard K. *The High Frontier: Human Colonies in Space*. New York: William Morrow, 1977.
Describes the future high-orbital manufacturing facilities now in the planning stage, explaining how they will be placed in orbit, how they will operate, who will work in them, and how living conditions will be controlled and sustained.

Panati, Charles. *Breakthroughs: Astonishing Advances in Your Lifetime in Medicine, Science, and Technology*. Boston: Houghton Mifflin, 1980.
An optimistic exploration of the future. Discusses some of the scientific, medical, and technological advances predicted in the near future that will dramatically alter our lives and life styles.

Pierson, George W. *The Moving American*. New York: Alfred A. Knopf, 1973.
Argues that residential mobility has a neglected and deep significance for Americans.

Powers, Robert M. *The Coattails of God: The Ultimate Spaceflight—The Trip to the Stars*. New York: Warner Books, 1981.
Reviews the technological feats of the past and forecasts what will happen in space travel.

Rosen, Stephen. *Future Facts: A Forecast of the World as We Will Know It Before the End of the Century*. New York: Simon & Schuster, 1976.
An illustrated book covering such topics as medicine, energy, food, communication, recreation, and transportation.

Sheckley, Robert. *Futuropolis*. New York: A&W Visual Library, 1978.
Impossible cities of science fiction and fantasy.

Tod, Ian, and Wheeler, Michael. *Utopia*. New York: Harmony Books, 1978.
Explores the nature of a perfect society as visualized and prophesied by history's great utopian philosophers, architects, writers, painters, and poets.